THEORIES OF PERFORMANCE

THEORIES OF PERFORMANCE

Organizational and Service Improvement in the Public Domain

Colin Talbot

OXFORD

UNIVERSITY PRESS

OXFORD
UNIVERSITY PRESS

Great Clarendon Street, Oxford OX2 6DP

Oxford University Press is a department of the University of Oxford.
It furthers the University's objective of excellence in research, scholarship,
and education by publishing worldwide in

Oxford New York

Auckland Cape Town Dar es Salaam Hong Kong Karachi
Kuala Lumpur Madrid Melbourne Mexico City Nairobi
New Delhi Shanghai Taipei Toronto

With offices in

Argentina Austria Brazil Chile Czech Republic France Greece
Guatemala Hungary Italy Japan Poland Portugal Singapore
South Korea Switzerland Thailand Turkey Ukraine Vietnam

Oxford is a registered trade mark of Oxford University Press
in the UK and in certain other countries

Published in the United States
by Oxford University Press Inc., New York

© Colin Talbot 2010

British Library Cataloguing in Publication Data
Data available

Library of Congress Cataloging-in-Publication Data
Data available

Typeset by SPI Publisher Services, Pondicherry, India
Printed and bound in Great Britain by
MPG Books Group, Bodmin and King's Lynn
ISBN 978–0–19–957596–1 (hbk.)
      978–0–19–957595–4 (pbk.)

1 3 5 7 9 10 8 6 4 2

For Carole

⬚ ACKNOWLEDGEMENTS

This book would not have been possible without the generous support of the ESRC, who granted me a Fellowship (RES-153-27-0013), and Manchester Business School, who gave me a semester's sabbatical.

The book also, in part, represents a culmination on many years work in the field of performance in public services, as a researcher, teacher, consultant and advisor and the people who have contributed to the evolution of my ideas are far to numerous to mention them all. I mention only some who have had a particularly important impact – if I miss anyone out, my apologies. They are not all academics: Geert Bouckaert; Steve Harrison; Ralph Heintzman and Brian Marson; Christopher Hood; Peter John; John Kamensky; Jeremy Lonsdale; Larry Lynn; Nick Manning; Janine O'Flynn; Christopher Pollitt; Beryl Radin; Adam Sharples; Nick Sloan; Carole Talbot; Kieran Walshe; and Matthew Derbyshire, who was my editor at Oxford for most of the process of producing this book but has since moved on.

Unusually, I also want to acknowledge the cooperation and other help I have received from a number of organisations over the years, in particular: National Audit Office (UK); Interior Ministry (Japan); Treasury Board Secretariat (Canada); Treasury Select Committee (UK); Public Administration Select Committee (UK); GCHQ (UK); Careers Scotland (UK); British Council (UK); and the World Bank.

⬚ CONTENTS

⬜ LIST OF FIGURES

☐ LIST OF TABLES

1 Introduction – Why the Issue of Performance Will Not Go Away

Performance measurement and management of public services has been on the rise across many countries in recent years. It is widely perceived to have started around the late 1980s or early 1990s, but in fact discussions about various aspects of performance – not always using that label – go back far beyond that period. In 1916, for example, the US Congress established a "Bureau of Efficiency" to tackle waste in US federal government (Lee 2006). But it is also clear that there is currently a very real "performance movement" (Radin 2006a), and one which is likely to expand further as many advanced states face fiscal problems following the 2007–9 global financial and economic crisis. Demands will grow for government that "works better and costs less" (Gore and National Performance Review 1993) as the consequences of the financial and economic crisis for public finances develops. The performance of public agencies is thus both a perennial and a contemporary issue – just one of the many paradoxes surrounding the subject.

There are theoretical, empirical, and practical reasons why this subject will not go away, and while it may wax and wane, it is certain to always return to center stage in academic and policy circles from time to time for the same reasons.

The theoretical and empirical reasons are both simple and complex. In the early 1980s, writing about what was then called "organizational effectiveness" (OE) studies, a couple of experts in the field pointed out that all theoretical conceptualizations of organizations implicitly addressed the issue of which organizational forms were more or less effective (i.e., performed) (Cameron and Whetten 1983b). While they were writing about all organizations, this applies equally to public and private sectors. Moreover, in empirical research on organizations, "effectiveness" (or performance) was the ultimate dependent variable – in the end all studies were studies of what made organizations more or less effective. The really complex theoretical and empirical problems start to arise in defining and then measuring effectiveness or performance.

And finally there is a simple practical reason why interest in effectiveness or performance would not go away – all organizations, public and private, are there for a purpose (or purposes) and those with an interest in those purposes are always going to ask the question of how well are they doing. Moreover, this final reason also ensures that theoretical and empirical research interest in the effectiveness and performance of organizations will continue to excite scholars – or at least those who are engaged with practical concerns as well as theory. And those that are not so engaged with practical issues will probably still be interested in critiquing, if only in order to dismiss them, the outputs of those who are, so in reality most will continue to engage with the issues.

More than three decades later, scholars in a different field – public policy and administration – made a very similar point when discussing the latest set of indicators for comparing the performance of governments – the Bertelsmann Stiftung's "Sustainable Governance Indicators" (SGIs):

> As a measurement instrument, the [SGIs] rests upon a few implicit and explicit causal assumptions. One of the central causal assumptions of the SGI – and, indeed, of the disciplines of political science and public policy studies as a whole – is that quality of life . . . depends to a substantial, though not exclusive, degree on systematic political and administrative processes. . . . Without this foundational belief in causality, there would be little reason to study governmental and administrative systems.
>
> (Jann and Seyfried 2009)

Public organizations – by which I mean departments and ministries, agencies, units, programs, systems, etc. – sit at the intersection of the interest in organizational effectiveness and performance generically and interest in the performance of the public sphere as a whole. In a sense the performance or effectiveness of public organizations (broadly defined) is thus an ultimate dependent variable for *both* the generic study of organizations and the study of the public domain.

From this perspective, the study of performance of public organizations can be seen as embracing a vast literature on organization and on government dating back centuries, never mind a couple of decades. It would clearly be impractical to even attempt a review, much less any sort of synthesis, on such a broad array of research and practical experience. To a large extent this is not (or should not be) necessary, as many of the more contemporary strands within organizational and governmental studies have in any case already been created by "standing on the shoulders of giants" of the past, as Isaac Newton famously remarked about his own achievements in physics. Although this is not always the case, and past lessons have been forgotten, or the source of current thinking become obscured by the mists of time – as will be seen later in the book (e.g., Chapter 7).

So while one or two references may be made to older scholarship and practice, mostly this book will concentrate on fairly modern (in a historical sense) attempts to understand, and improve, the effectiveness and performance of public organizations, that is mostly from the latter half of the twentieth century up to the present. That is more than enough to deal with, and indeed still too much for any one scholar to fully comprehend.

Virtually every discipline and subdiscipline in social sciences, and a few others too, has had something to say about organizational and management theory and public administration, policy and management theory and thereby, by implication, about the performance or effectiveness of public organizations. Anthropology, economics, political science, social psychology, and sociology have all contributed to both organizational studies and public administration, as both are inherently multidisciplinary in relation to these fundamental social science disciplines. Other fields from the more physical and biological sciences have had something of interest to contribute – systems theories, complexity theories, ethology, psychology, evolutionary psychology – just to mention a few.

Moreover, all these fields and disciplines, as we will discuss later, have been riven by rather more foundational conflicts over ontology, epistemology, and methodology and interpenetrated by crosscutting "philosophy of science" disputes, or the "paradigm wars" as some have called them. They have also been engaged in various border disputes – for example, economics, in particular, has sought to "invade" the traditional territory of political science and public administration through public choice and related theories.

Moreover, the increase in the sheer volume of academic publishing has been matched by the increase in publications – mainly books – written by consultants or practitioners mainly for the latter. These advance a huge range of possible ways in which to improve the performance of businesses, as a brief glance at the business section in any airport bookstore would show. Strategic management, business process reengineering, total quality management, human resources management, value management, knowledge management, innovation, customer focus, balanced scorecards, and fifty-seven varieties of leadership have all been advanced as answers, usually THE answer, to improving performance. Many of these have, of course, also been copied into public sector practice.

Within more academic organization studies the paradigm war has been fought out with competing, fundamentally different, ontological, and epistemological perspectives (Burrell and Morgan 1994) or simply employing a wide variety of metaphors and analogies to frame approaches to understanding organizations (Morgan 1986). Each of the issues, approaches, and theoretical perspectives mentioned above has produced its own stream of literature, research and "how to" books – sometimes running into the thousands.

And that is just in general business, management, and organization studies without even starting to look at the field(s) of politics, public administration, and public management. And in each and every case the implicit or explicit dependent variable is effectiveness or performance.

Consilience Deficit Disorder

The material examined in these pages is inevitably selective, and the process of selection is a difficult one, to put it mildly. One answer – adopted by far too many scholars – is to keep your head down and concentrate on a fairly narrow field, and dig as deeply as possible into that. In the process, wider ontological, epistemology, and methodological issues are, as far as possible, sidelined. If challenged on this, many would claim that grand theory building is impossible, or at any rate unfashionable, and the best we can hope for is some micro or possibly midrange theories that connect a few dots.

Closely allied to this attitude is the view that pluralism and diversity in social science approaches is actually a good thing – there is nothing wrong with researchers having, implicitly or explicitly, totally incommensurable paradigms – as long as everyone has something "useful" to say. I have coined a term for this collective problem – Consilience Deficit Disorder (CDD).

The term "consilience" comes from the work of biologist E. O. Wilson, the originator of "sociobiology" and the highly controversial idea of "gene-culture" coevolution in the origins of modern humans. Wilson has argued that modern science, especially social science, is suffering from a general lack of "consilience" (Wilson 1998). By "consilience" he means that science has to be internally consistent, both within and between disciplines. This may seem obvious but there are those even in the so-called "hard" sciences who question such assumptions and argue that we live in a "dappled world" where theories only have very limited applicability and do not necessarily have to "join-up" with theories in other domains (e.g., Cartwright 1999), or that the various social science disciplines are, and should remain, quite distinct branches of knowledge (Steuer 2003).

Consilience as an alternative is both an attitude of mind, as well as a scientific proposition. For example, the fundamental problem in theoretical physics is the search for a "grand unified theory" (GUT) or "Theory of Everything" (TOE) that can bring together the insights of quantum mechanics and relativity theory, both of which have substantial empirical verification but as yet have not been "joined-up".

The idea that they can be unified into a single theory is both an attitude of mind as well as a hypothesis that cannot, as yet, be proved. The attitude of mind is not simply a belief, however, in the way that religion is a belief without any supporting evidence. It is rooted in sound scientific thinking.

The belief that a GUT or TOE is possible is an inductively derived one – over the last three or four centuries we have made enormous strides in understanding how the universe operates precisely by assuming there is some underlying causal consistency. Induction often gets a bad name, especially in some of the more esoteric branches of scientific philosophy, but the reality is that induction has often worked well in establishing the "first draft" of scientific ideas. On this basis it is reasonable to induce that we will make further progress toward GUT or TOE, as well as toward the rather grander synthesis or reconciliation of the physical and social sciences that Wilson advocates. Induction is of course fallible – all swans are not white – but in this case there is pretty good reason to think consilience might be correct. Moreover, the alternative, to assume that causal links and consistency between different branches of science is impossible, leads fairly rapidly into rather dismal nihilistic cul-de-sacs.

Wilson chose the word "consilience" to try to avoid the accusation of simple or crude determinism. To say that various levels of knowledge – physical, chemical, and biological, for example – have to be consilient is not to say that the evolution of human beings can be predicted from the nature of quantum mechanics. Rather, it is to assert the evolutionary explanation for the emergence of human beings has to be consistent with the underlying laws of physics, chemistry, and biology.

The social sciences in general have largely ignored or attempted to avoid this requirement for consilience. The study of management and organization – the disciplinary area that has probably had greatest influence on the study of performance – is especially guilty in this regard. Some experts in the field have repeatedly pointed out how management research largely fails to cumulate knowledge – data and theories; is beset by "the tyranny of the new" although often is just repeating the past theories and findings under new labels; is cursed by self-promoting "gurus," including academics; is prone to fashions and fads, and to succumbing to "halo" effects of "successful" organizations and individuals (Huczynski 1993; Micklethwait 1996, Shapiro 1996, Pfeffer and Sutton 2006; Rosenzweig 2007). These failings are largely due to the tendency to ignore the need for consilience. If there is no overriding imperative to try to make theories "joined-up," is it hardly surprising that little cumulative progress seems to be made?

There are some, sporadic, attempts to overcome this. For example one recent work that tried to take an overview of the development of management theory is a welcome, if as yet insufficient, contribution (Smith and Hitt 2005). This volume – subtitled "the process of theory development" – invited many well-known theorists, with significant contributions to management theory to their names, to reflect on the process of theory development. What is notable is that despite an apparent invitation to discuss philosophy of science issues, neither the contributors (bar one) nor the editors themselves appear to follow this up.

Throughout the volume most of the authors also reflect on the development of their own contributions within relatively narrow bounds and few, if any, attempt any consilience even within the broader field of organization and management theory, much less wider fields. The one author who does address the "philosophy of science" issue argues that management researchers exhibit a "strong desire for independence" from other management researchers and that "[c]umulative activity is further weakened by journals that encourage claims of independent discovery" (Huff 2005, p. 346). Interestingly, this author also goes on to argue that "normal research programs," in the sense proposed by Kuhn (1970), simply do not happen and the best we can expect is "islands of coherence," which is an excellent description of most of the other contributions to this volume. Rather than accepting this as simply a fact of (human) life, as Huff would have us do, the argument advanced here is that such "consilience deficits" need to be challenged.

Management being an inherently multidisciplinary area of study does not help – it is far too easy for scholars to engage in un-consilient "pick and mix" strategies, borrowing eclectically from multiple base disciplines and subdisciplines, and even the physical sciences, without any real effort at building consilient theories or usually any real check on the validity of their approaches. Paradoxically, even within management studies there has also been a tendency to diverge into narrower and narrower communities of interest studying strategy, marketing, finance, human resources, or other sub-fields that further reduces the prospects of consilience even between various aspects of management studies, never mind with wider disciplines.

Underlying this lack of consilience in social sciences generally lies a problem with a basic understanding of human nature, an issue from which social sciences has retreated from explicitly exploring since World War II (Barkow et al. 1995; Wilson 1998; Pinker 2002). This does not mean that social sciences have not implicitly adopted views about basic human nature – they mostly have, and both of the main ones held by most social scientists are deeply flawed.

The two dominant views of human nature in the social sciences have been the "rational utility maximizer" (RUM) of economics and the "blank slate" (BS) standard model shared across many social sciences. Economists would generally argue that their RUM assumptions have nothing to do with actual human nature and are merely an axiomatic assumption for theoretical purposes – a claim it is hard to accept. Other social scientists generally try to ignore the issue of human nature while simultaneously adopting a model of it – that humans are all, everywhere, born *tabula rasa*, blank slates, onto which societies, organizations, institutions, cultures, families, and autopoietic (self-generated) processes can write anything.

Both these approaches totally ignore what we know about human evolution, behavioral genetics, evolutionary psychology, gene-culture coevolution, ethology and the evolution of complex behavioral repertoires, human universals, etc. (Brown 1991; Barkow et al. 1995; Pinker 2002). Slowly, and mostly reluctantly, economics and social sciences are starting to realize that the findings of the more physical, so-called "hard," sciences can no longer be ignored. Behavioral economics (Thaler and Sunstein 2008), for example, incorporates findings from behavioral and cognitive science that run contrary to the basic tenets of neoclassical economics – but this is still a minority view in economics and has yet to feed through into a complete overhaul of the discipline.

What has all this to do with the performance of pubic agencies? It raises profound problems about how we view the (possible) foundations for any really robust theoretical understanding of the issues surrounding performance. It means that all attempts at theorizing organizational effectiveness or performance in the public domain ought to try, at least, to be consilient with other well-established, supported by evidence, theories and strive for integration and consistency of explanation.

Take as an example the assumption that all humans, every where and when regardless of other factors, act simply as RUM then this leads to some pretty clear conclusions. In a recent report for the UK National Audit Office the authors base their review of "sanctions and rewards" in the public sector explicitly on these assumptions of neoclassical economics and their conclusions, and the issues they address, such as problems of "gaming," flow from this approach (Deloitte 2008).

Yet we know that both parts of the RUM assumptions are wrong, or at least in need of substantial modification. Humans do not always act rationally, they may act on "bounded rationality" (Simon 1983) or "heuristics" (Gigerenzer 2000) or even apparently irrationally (Sutherland 1992; Ariely 2008). Nor do they always seek "utility maximization" but sometimes act with altruistic motives (Sober and Wilson 1998). So any theoretical construction based on RUM assumptions is not consilient – it does not seek to be consistent with other theory and evidence – and of course it is likely to lead to erroneous conclusions and hypotheses. To be consilient we would need models of both human decision-making processes (rationality) and of motivation that was consistent with the current evidence. These may well include elements of RUM-type behaviors, but it is pretty clear that they would not be just RUM-based. Only then could we really start to explore something like "sanctions and rewards" in a theoretically sound way.

To be fair, some thinkers do at least apply a sort of sub-consilient approach in the sense that they pick a theoretical stance and stick to it – that is their research agenda fits within a "research program" informed by a particular "paradigm," to use the fashionable terminology widely adopted from Kuhn's work on the history of science (Kuhn 1970).

There are plenty of examples of scholars[1] in the public performance field who have adopted a specific theoretical stance – for example, public choice theory, neo-institutionalism, or a social constructionist approach – and attempted to thoroughly explore it. However, as Kuhn was at pains to point out, paradigmatically bounded thinking is only of limited use and systematically screens out any data or theory that does not fit with the paradigm. Consilient thinking on the other hand is at pains to try and encompass disconcerting theories and data and seek to integrate them in a consistent, causally logical manner.

The other – and probably predominant – tendency in public management generally, and the study of performance in particular, has been to adopt a sort of theoretical, eclectic, "pick and mix" approach. That is to borrow bits and pieces of theory and mix them into an analysis. This tendency has been explicitly encouraged by social-constructionist approaches to social science that maintain that all theories are merely subjective and none can be objectively privileged over any other. In organization theory in particular this has taken the form of maintaining that there are multiple "frames" or metaphors that can be used to analyze organizations that are of equal value (Morgan 1996). In political science this has taken the form of so-called multi-theoretic approaches, first popularized in Allison's classic study of the Cuban missile crisis (Allison 1971). As there is no "reality" out there, except what we socially construct, and against which we can test any particular theory or hypothesis, there is no basis to judge between competing theories.

This has encouraged an attitude toward theory that is dubious at best – for example one pair of scholars in the field have adopted an explicitly social constructionist stance in one place, only to drop it without explanation and adopt what is implicitly a realist stance in another (see Chapter 3 for further discussion of these terms). Others have mixed together social constructionist arguments about performance data (it is all socially constructed and bears no relation to any reality) with rational utility maximization explanations of behavior (people "game" or otherwise cheat in their own self-interests) without any acknowledgment of the theoretical problems and contradictions involved in such a method.

A consilient approach would reject completely this approach to theorizing and especially its social constructionist justifications. It is worth quoting E. O. Wilson at length on this:

Outside our heads there is freestanding reality. Only madmen and a scattering of constructivist philosophers doubt its existence. Inside our heads is a reconstitution of

---

[1] In this section of the argument I am not going to "name names" for diplomatic reasons.

reality based on sensory input and the self-assembly of concepts. Input and self-assembly, rather than an independent entity in the brain - the "ghost in the machine" in the philosopher Gilbert Ryle's famous derogation - constitute the mind. The alignment of outer existence with its inner representation has been distorted by the idiosyncrasies of human evolution.... That is, natural selection built the brain to survive in the world and only incidentally to understand it at a depth greater than is needed to survive. *The proper task of scientists is to diagnose and correct the misalignment.* The effort to do so has only begun. No one should suppose that objective truth is impossible to attain, even when the most committed philosophers urge us to acknowledge that incapacity. In particular it is too early for scientists, the foot soldiers of epistemology, to yield ground so vital to their mission. (Wilson 1998 p. 66 – emphasis in original)

ENGAGING WITH THE PERFORMANCE QUESTION: REALISM AND REALITY

So the basic approach taken in this book is one of consilience – trying to integrate various theoretical strands into a coherent understanding of performance in the public domain – or at least the start of such an approach. It is also one based, broadly, on a realist philosophy of science position. Stated simply this accepts that there is, ontologically, a real world "out there" but that when trying to know this real world, especially the real world of human social organization, there are significant epistemological challenges to be met, because human social institutions and organizations are, partly, socially constructed (for further discussion of this see Chapter 2).

Engaging with the subject of public organizational and services performance has been, for the present author, something of an iterative process. It began well over a decade ago when I first began studying how UK civil service agencies perform, a key part of which was how they were being performance measured and performance managed (Talbot 1996a). In parallel I also looked at how such agencies were governed or "steered" and how real were the supposed processes of devolution of things like personnel policies (Talbot and Huish 1996; Talbot 1997). This eventually germinated into two major international comparative pieces of work on the international fashion for "agencification" in government and the performance component to such structural reforms, both conducted with Christopher Pollitt one funded by the Economic and Social Research Council (ESRC) (Pollitt et al. 2001, 2004) and one by the UK Department for International Development (Talbot and Caulfield 2002; but also see relevant chapters in Pollitt and Talbot 2004).

The work on performance also led to an interest in what are now sometimes called "multidimensional performance models" – especially the balanced scorecard (Talbot and Johnson 2005) and European "Excellence" model – both of which have been widely applied in the public sector. This even led to a rather ambitious attempt to create an "excellence" model specifically for the public sector (Talbot 1998, 1999). More recent work specifically on performance has addressed issues such as "public value" (Talbot 2008a, 2008b; Talbot and Wiggan 2009) partially supported by The Work Foundation and performance regimes (Talbot et al. 2005a, 2005b) supported by the National and Wales Audit Office's.

Alongside research work on performance, I have also spent a great deal of time (over more than a decade) working with, as an advisor or consultant, a wide variety of public organizations and individuals on issues of performance. I have worked with a diverse group of bodies on helping to develop and implement performance measurement systems including British Council, Careers Scotland, GCHQ, the Northern Ireland Office, a consortium of social services departments and various other local and national organizations in the United Kingdom.

I have also helped the National Audit Office with several studies of performance systems over the past decade (Comptroller and Auditor General 2001, 2005, 2006a, 2006b, 2006c, 2006d, 2007a, 2007b, 2008, 2009), including carrying out a small comparative study of how other governments manage performance measurement systems (Talbot et al. 2001).

I have advised the Public Administration Select Committee for their study "On Target" (Public Administration Select Committee 2003) and have given evidence to and/or advised the Treasury Select Committee on Public Service Agreements since their inception in 1998. Finally I have worked with several overseas governments and organizations including advising the Canadian Treasury Board during the development of their Management Accountability Framework; the Japanese Interior Ministry on their "Government Policy Evaluation Act"; and government officials in Australia, Bangladesh, Estonia, Hong Kong, India, Jamaica, Malta, Slovenia, Tanzania, and in the World Bank and Organization for Economic Cooperation and Development (OECD).

These various assignments and discussions are recounted here not for egotistical or credibility reasons, but to illustrate a point about "ways of knowing" in applied areas like public management. This mixture of research, consultancy, teaching, and advisory roles have given me enormous opportunities to see what performance measurement, management, and reporting looks like "from the inside" as well as from the more outside perspective of an academic researcher.

The knowledge gained from "insider" engagements is always, inevitably, impressionistic, fragmentary, and clearly not as systematically gathered nor scientifically designed as would be the case for traditional research. And sometimes there are of course confidentiality/disclosure issues. But what this active engagement with policy-making and practice does afford is a real "feel" for how issues are developed and played out that even the best-designed research rarely gives us. I have often found – especially when engaged as a consultant – that I get closer to the truth of what is actually going on within organizations than any amount of external research would generate. When going into an organization as a researcher one often gets only the "official story," whereas when entering as a paid consultant you often get nearer to the truth, because organizational actors want you to understand and help them.

In this sense, consultancy and advisory work helps to keep theorizing "grounded" in a very real sense. As long as this type of experience is an addition to, and not a substitute for, more serious research it can be a vital addition in an "applied" area like public management and performance.

All of the above work was essentially part of my "day job" as an academic, but alongside this I was also concerned about some major issues of human nature, motivation, and decision-making that, it seemed to me, lay behind many of the theoretical assumptions of those interested in public performance and were, in a sense, unavoidable (even if many of my colleagues do their best to avoid them). This resulted in the publication of a somewhat polemical book entitled *The Paradoxical Primate* which, as the name suggests, was an attempt to start to make some sense of our evolved contradictory human nature (Talbot 2005*b*). In particular this also emanated with a fascination with the "competing values" which seemed to pervade organizational life (Cameron et al. 2006), and politics and public administration as well.

All this culminated in the award of a Fellowship as part of the ESRC "Public Services Programme" (ESRC research grant RES-153–27–0013) to look specifically at "theories of performance." The task I set myself was to try to bring together into some sort of coherent theoretical framework what we know about performance in the public domain, including specifically the contributions from the fifty or so projects within the ESRC Programme. In this I was also supported by Manchester Business School who also gave me a sabbatical as part of this project.

This book is the principal output from this Fellowship and its structure and content represent the culmination of this work. The structure reflects the three main concerns that have animated the work:

- What do existing theories, in the very broadest sense, have to tell us about the nature of performance in the public domain? In particular, how does theory cope with the apparently conflicting values and interests surrounding and permeating the public domain?
- What is the specific institutional context of performance, including the roles of multiple stakeholders, in the public domain and how does this shape the performance of individual organizations?
- What are the main elements, factors, or dimensions of organizational, and specifically public organizational, performance?

The process of constructing answers to these questions has (very) broadly proceeded along the lines suggested by "realistic evaluation" (Pawson and Tilley 1997) which consists of a continual, iterative, interplay between provisional theoretical propositions and causal explanations on the one hand, and engagement with data and evidence on the other. This has been a fascinating experience in which, while some of my original ideas on things like performance regimes and paradoxical human behavior, for example, have not fundamentally changed, but have been substantially modified and I hope refined. Most importantly of all, it has led me toward proposing a possible way of theoretically integrating what until now had been a set of relatively separate ideas and conjectures. But I will leave that "punch line" until the final chapter of the book.

Shape of the Book

It is customary at this point to give a long and detailed outline of the book. Instead, a short outline is given here because the book is structured into parts and each of these has an introduction that lays out in more detail what it covers.

It is worth saying at the outset that the book mirrors reality by concentrating mostly on the performance of public organizations, as has the contemporary performance movement itself. Wider issues about governments, systems, policies, and programs are not ignored but they are not the principle focus of this book.

Part I tries to set up both some of the many problematic issues that have arisen during the current movement to performance measure and manage public sector activities (Chapter 2) and also to set out in very broad terms what "theory" may (or may not) have to say about the issue (Chapter 3).

Part II looks at the context within which public organizations have to operate. The first two chapters in this part deal with the "performance regime" that (attempts to) govern or steer the performance of public agencies. This regime consists of two parts: the institutions (in the old-fashioned sense of institution) that make up the performance regime – executive government, legislatures, courts, audit and inspection bodies, and others (Chapter 4); and how these various institutional actors may seek to intervene to shape the performance of public agencies. The public values that in turn shape the institutional structure and intervention strategies are also examined (Chapter 6).

Part III switches from these exogenous factors to the more endogenous questions of what, internally, drives organizational performance and how it can be measured. The history of theory, research on, and practice of generic (public and private) organizational performance is explored (Chapter 7) and then onto a more specific examination of theories, explicit and tacit, of what drives the performance of public organizations (Chapter 8).

Part IV starts a process of trying to tie together these various elements. Firstly, the impacts and reactions of public servants and their organizations to the drive for enhanced performance is examined – how have they reacted and how does this relate to the theoretical propositions about how they should have reacted (Chapter 9)? Secondly, the final chapter (Chapter 10) outlines a framework for understanding what shapes performance in the public sector: (*a*) performance regimes, (*b*) organizational performance models, and (*c*) public values. It tries to show how these three can be brought together into a more comprehensive way of knowing about performance, and suggest what gaps, holes, and concepts have to be further explored.

SHAPING PUBLIC PERFORMANCE

My preference was to leave the introduction at this, and allow the story to unfold more or less as it had for me in the process of researching and writing the book. The "punch line" would be left until the end, the final chapter, with the preceding chapters gradually revealing my conclusions. But several reviewers of the first draft of the manuscript strongly urged me to put something more about my conclusions "up front" so the reader had some idea where the story was going. Reluctantly, I have to agree they are probably right so here, grudgingly, is a brief overview of my conclusions. These are set out thematically, but related to where they appear most prominently in the structure of the book.

PROBLEMATICS OF PERFORMANCE (CHAPTERS 2 AND 9)

Chapter 2 of the book is mainly a synthesis of what issues have already been raised by others about the problematic issue regarding the measurement, reporting, and management of performance in the public domain. It provides a useful function in aggregating these issues and structuring them into a series of themes: units and levels of analysis problems; conceptual problems; technical problems; political and values problems. Although this summarizing is new, and there are a few novel points emerging from this analysis, the chapter itself does not say a great deal new but rather is a "stock take" of some of the arguments about performance from a more pragmatic than theoretical viewpoint.

The chapter does flag up some issues about theoretical assumptions – such as the rational utility maximization assumptions underpinning some of the critiques of performance policies that focus on issues like gaming. These issues are pursued further in Chapter 3 (theories and performance) but are also further analyzed in Chapter 9. Here the point is strongly made that such narrow behavioral assumptions cannot account for the diversity of responses to performance policies – for example, some individuals/organizations undoubtedly engage in gaming, but the evidence does not even support the idea that this is the majority response, and fails to explain the phenomenon of individuals/organizations that respond positively, and do not "game," when subject to exactly the same performance pressures as those that do indulge in "gaming."

THEORIES AND PERFORMANCE (CHAPTER 3 AND THROUGHOUT)

This chapter attempts, for the first time as far as I am aware, to take a very broad look at what various disciplinary and theoretical perspectives can, and do, bring to the study of performance of public agencies. I do not propose to rehash the analysis here, but to focus on a few key points.

The first is that of making explicit the "philosophy of science" position adopted in studying performance. While a few (especially economics influenced) researchers use fairly explicit "positivist" approaches, and a few at the other extreme adopt "constructionist" approaches, most sit somewhere in the middle adopting no explicit approach and pragmatically borrowing concepts and ideas from various ontological, epistemological, and methodological traditions – essentially they implicitly adopt some variety of a "realist" stance.

While some welcome this "pluralism" and "pragmatism," I argue strongly that it creates major barriers to cumulating theory and evidence about this (or any other) topic. I introduce the concept of "consilience" from the work of Wilson (1998) to support the argument for making theoretical and empirical investigations of performance more coherent and grounded in the wider body of social science knowledge. This includes adopting a more explicit "realist" stance and some more explicit theories of things like human motivation/values (see Chapters 6 and 9) at the individual level and resource-dependence theories at the organizational level, that enable more systematic cumulation of knowledge. The twin themes of "realism" and "consilience" resurface throughout the book.

PERFORMANCE REGIMES (CHAPTERS 4 AND 5)

Some of the work of conceptualizing the idea of "performance regimes" had been completed before this Fellowship and project began (Talbot et al.

Figure 1.1 Performance Regime Institutions

2005*a*, 2005*b*) but the Fellowship provided the opportunity to refine and extend these ideas. The institutional framework within which public organizations operate – what Moore has called the "authorising environment" (Moore 1995) – has been refined and the theoretical basis for assessing the impact and roles of performance regimes actors – derived from resource-dependence theory – has also been further developed (see Chapter 4 and (Talbot 2008*c*)) (Figure 1.1).

While the types of interventions carried out by performance regime actors had only been very briefly sketched in earlier work, this project has enabled the development of a much more systematic analysis, and analytical framework, for understanding these interventions (Chapter 5). Four broad intervention types are identified: (*a*) managerial-contractual; (*b*) capability-based; (*c*) systemic-competitive; (*d*) systemic-voice and choice. The analysis strongly suggests that further research is needed on both the different types of interventions but also how they interact with one another. While there has been some partial work on effectiveness (or otherwise) in some of these four categories – especially (*a*) and (*d*) – even in these cases there is insufficient evidence accumulated and synthesized to draw any real conclusions. In others – especially (*b*) – there is hardly any real research.

PERFORMANCE MODELS (ORGANIZATIONAL) (CHAPTERS 7 AND 8)

The two chapters dealing with organizational performance models present a major attempt to bring together and start to synthesize what we know about organizational performance. In particular, by revisiting the pre-history of performance in the organizational effectiveness movement (circa 1945–1980s) and the organizational culture and quality movement (circa early

Figure 1.2 Public Organization MPDM – Tentative Synthesis

1980s onward), current developments can be put into better perspective and previous lessons learnt. These earlier periods have been largely ignored in the literature on both private and public sector organizational performance.

The evolution of organizational performance "models," from unifactorial through multifactorial to multidimensional performance models (MDPMs) is particularly important. The plethora of, often strongly overlapping, private and public sector MDPMs becomes apparent as soon as these are brought together – a task that has been almost completely ignored in the literature until now. In Chapter 8, an initial attempt is made to identify what the common dimensions of performance might be in the public domain, based on an analysis of the MDPMs that have emerged over the previous couple of decades (or more; see Figure 1.2).

PUBLIC VALUE(S) (CHAPTER 6)

Although the issue of public values always formed a part scope of the project, it was originally seen as part of an MDPM – the competing values framework (CVF). The latter had emerged at the end of the organizational effectiveness movement and was seen by its originators as a way of integrating multiple models (Cameron and Whetten 1983a, 1983b).

However, it became apparent that the issue of values needed to be treated independently and that the CVF "model" was not really an MDPM at all. This insight emerged relatively late in the research process. The resulting chapter draws on a range of values-based or related theories – including CVF, cultural theory, relational models theory, and others – to start to construct a model of competing public values. The key insight of CVF – that competing values can be captured within a single framework – is combined specifically with the categories of relational models theory to create a new synthesis called "competing public values" (Figure 1.3).

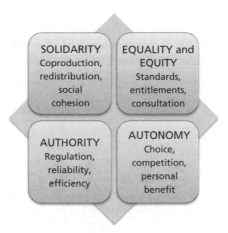

Figure 1.3 Competing Public Values?

The key contribution of Relational Models Theory here is that these competing values derive from evolved human social instincts and are therefore consilient with the emerging findings of fields like evolutionary psychology and behavioral economics, that focus on how people actually behave and how such behaviors might have evolved, rather than purely theoretical constructs like "rational utility maximization" that clearly, at best, only account for some human actions.

SHAPING PUBLIC PERFORMANCE (CHAPTER 10)

The final chapter attempts to bring together the three substantive themes of the book/research – the idea of competing human values and their impact on what the public and users value about collective (state) action; the idea of performance regimes within which public agencies have to operate; and the idea of multidimensional models of agency performance (see Figure 1.4).

This "map" of the conceptual issues confronting the problem of theorizing and analyzing of performance in the public domain is not meant to be a definitive or conclusive statement. Rather it is offered as a map of what the key issues are, and the start of filling in some of the more detailed terrain. There is still a great deal of work to be done on each of the three key issues, as well as on how they interact. The twin themes of "realism" and "consilience" have hopefully been shown to be both necessary and possible in the investigation of these issues.

Moreover, these problems are not just theoretical ones – they also correspond (as they should) to the key issues of policy and practice in achieving performance improvement in the public domain. How are we to understand,

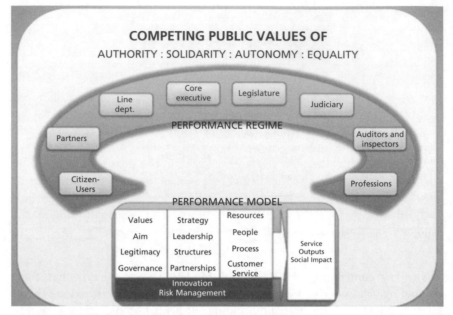

Figure 1.4 Shaping Public Performance – Bringing it All Together
Source: Talbot (2010).

and investigate, how the public values public-domain activities? How does, and should, the complex exogenous institutional framework and account-abilities of the public domain impact upon public agencies performance? What are the key endogenous dimensions of performance within public agencies?

This was an ambitious project and it certainly has not answered all the questions it has posed. But it has, I think, shown that a more integrative, coherent, consilient, and realism-based approach to developing the theory of public service performance is more possible than has hitherto been achieved.

AND FINALLY

Some of you may have read, or seen, or heard, about the supercomputer "Deep Thought" in Douglas Adam's science fiction multimedia[2] comedy "Hitchhikers' Guide to the Galaxy." "Deep Thought" was built to answer the fundamental questions of "Life, the Universe, and Everything" and after 7.5 million years came up with the answer: 42. But if 42 was the answer, what was the question again? Deep Thought could not say what the real Ultimate

---

[2] "Hitchhikers" has appeared as a radio series, TV series, films, computer games, and a "trilogy in four volumes" books.

Question was, but suggested he could help to design the computer that would come after him, "who's merest operating parameters he was not worthy to design," that could do the job.

So, I feel a bit like Deep Thought – although the analogy is not exact. It has not been 7.5 millions years, for one thing (although sometimes it has felt like it). No, what I have managed in this book is merely to outline what the question(s) are we ought to be asking and sketched some ideas about what sort of answers we should be looking for. Getting to "42" will take a lot more than one researcher or one book – if it is even possible.

In "Hitchhikers" the theory is suggested that it not possible to know both the Ultimate Question and the Ultimate Answer in the same Universe because they will cancel each other out, along with the Universe. This Universe would then be replaced by another even more bizarre and difficult to understand Universe – and some suspect that this has already happened.

PART I

PERFORMANCE AND THEORY

Introduction to Part I

The two chapters in this part of the book set up the issues surrounding performance in a broad-brush way. They are in essence the "practice" and "theory" chapters (in that order) and illustrate that even seemingly purely practical issues cannot escape theory, and theory cannot escape engagement with practice.

In the first chapter (Chapter 2) of this part, some of the problematic issues surrounding the "performance movement" are set out. The first of these concerns the issue of what is the objective of performance measurement – the unit of analysis problem. Key issues include defining the boundaries of the public sector; the complex nature of multilevel government; the separation of powers within "government"; the multifunctional nature of many public agencies; policies and programs that cut across multiple levels and public organizations; relationship that extend beyond simple hierarchy into govern- ance, systems, and networks. These units of analysis issue are all too often neglected in scholarship and thinking about public performance, sometimes creating elisions between categories that create more confusion than clarity.

This book makes a crucial distinction between public agencies as the primary unit of analysis to which it is addressed (see especially Chapters 7 and 8) and the public performance regime within which these agencies operate (see Chapters 4 and 5). This is not to say that performance measurement of whole systems, or governments, is not important – simply that it is easier and probably more useful to make a start in "clearing the theoretical ground" by concentrating mainly on individual public agencies as the primary unit of scrutiny.

The second set of problematic issues are those of conceptualizing what exactly is meant by the term "performance?" A sometimes bewildering set of terms have been used to describe what would appear to most reasonable people to be getting at the same basic concept – performance, achievement, results, organizational effectiveness, excellence, quality, outcomes, etc. Even when the same words are used, it is easily demonstrated that their definitions often vary. One crucial issue flagged up here is whether "performance" embraces both the "enablers" or "drivers" or organizational performance as well as the actual results, or not? These numerous conceptual confusions do not make the job of constructing serious and robust theories of performance any easier, yet they have to be addressed if any real progress is to be made.

The third set of problematic issues concern the technicalities of measuring performance (assuming operational definitions can be agreed), which include (a) the problem of indicators versus measures; (b) the effects on performance of measuring – does the weighed pig really not get any fatter? (c) the inevitability of error in reporting systems; (d) subjective versus objective measurement; (e) the problems of bounded rationality and composite indicators; (f) efficiency and productivity issues; (g) measuring outputs; (h) measuring and attributing outcomes; and (i) the thorny problem of nonlinear systems.

Finally, the chapter briefly sets up a later discussion (see especially Chapters 6 and 10) on politics, public value, and public values. Despite all these problematic issues, as argued strongly in Chapter 2, the issue of performance of public agencies and services is not likely to go away any time soon. So the choice not to abandon all hope, but to start to find ways to unpick some of these problems, and/or put them into a proper perspective.

Chapter 3 begins this process by asking what existing disciplines and theories can start to tell us about performance. It begins with a crucial discussion of basic issues about the nature of reality (ontology), how we can know this reality (epistemology), and the techniques for knowing (methodology). As already indicated in Chapter 1, the author is not a neutral observer in these debates but takes a particular stance – realism, or to use a rather old-fashioned Marxist term these days, materialism. Reality, including social realities and public agencies performance, is really real – although it does contain an important element of social construction.

The chapter proceeds with a quick "Cooks Tour" of disciplinary perspectives – anthropological, economics, political science, social psychology, and sociology. It notes some useful insights, but also concludes that the artificial barriers between disciplines, and the "paradigm" divisions both within and across them, severely limit the usefulness of any purely disciplinary approach. If anything, using the single issue of public organizational performance as a test, this chapter illustrates just how woefully inadequate modern social sciences disciplinary perspectives have become to tackling any real-world social issues.

The chapter then concludes with a discussion of some specific bodies of theory that are especially relevant to performance, including institutional theory, resource or resource-dependence theories, complexity, and finally evolutionary or ecological theories of organizations.

2 Problematics of Performance

Introduction

This chapter begins to unpack some of the problematic issues associated with studying, measuring, and using performance analysis and data in the public domain. As the chapter progresses, readers might be tempted to wonder "why bother – it's clearly all too difficult." Patience is in order, however, because although there are indeed many problematic issues these are no greater than similar issues experienced in some other areas of social activity – for example, measuring the economy – where technically workable and generally accepted solutions, or at least approximations, have emerged. Performance may be slightly more problematic, but the formalized study of, and attempts at measurement of public sector and services performance are at a relatively early stage. Complete "answers" may never be possible or prove unacceptable, but we are in the early stages of finding out – despite the problems and issues identified here.

Several sets of problematic issues will be examined in turn:

- The "unit of analysis" problem – what entity is being measured or analyzed? How easy is it to draw precise boundaries in the public domain?

- Conceptual problems – what is meant by "performance?" What is included and excluded? What is meant by concepts like "outputs" and "outcomes" and are they agreed, operable, definitions?

- Technical problems – what are the problems associated with measuring the various aspects of performance?

- Political and values problems – pluralistic values and politics and resulting fuzzy objectives raise issues about what to measure? And "rational utility maximization" by managers, staff, users, and citizens' undermine performance systems in practice.

In the final, concluding part, examples from parallel areas of social enquiry – especially economics – will be used to illustrate some of the possible solutions, or at least approximations, which might work for performance reporting.

Many of the themes and issues introduced here will be further developed later in the book – for example the issues of: models of organizational performance; of multiple stakeholders – the performance regime – demanding multiple "performances;" of "competing values" in the public domain etc., will be a theme that resurfaces throughout.

Units and Levels of Analysis Problems

When we speak about performance of public entities – governments, organizations, systems, policies – what exactly do we mean? What is included and what excluded? How do we delineate both between public and nonpublic domains and within the public domain between different entities? Indeed, is it even possible to make clear distinctions, given the amorphous nature of many public domain systems?

A great deal of the scholarly literature on public sector performance simply neglects, ignores, or fudges these issues and thereby creates possible confusion. For a useful summary of the problematic nature of these issues however see Rolland and Rones' paper (2009) which was presented as part of a major EU-sponsored initiative trying to map public organizations across the EU.

BOUNDARIES OF THE PUBLIC DOMAIN

The first problematic issue is the boundary of what is "public" and what is not – and to what extent nonpublic domain entities may have to be included in analyses of performance. This issue has been compounded in recent years as several governments have shifted to and given emphasis on "outcomes."

At the risk of jumping ahead (later in this chapter we discuss the conceptual issues more fully) we need to introduce a very simple conceptual schema at this point. A cautionary note first – the terms used here are fairly widely, but not universally, agreed (HM Treasury 2001) and the schema is extremely simplified.

In this simple model (Figure 2.1) "inputs" are generally defined as resources consumed in producing public sector outputs, which are in turn defined as actual goods or more usually services provided. Outcomes are the actual

Figure 2.1 Simple Performance Model for Public Domain

changes to health, wealth, happiness, and other desired social results that are attributed, at least in part, to the delivered outputs. It should be noted that this model highlights one of the key characteristics separating the public and private domains and their organizations. "Outcomes" are the primary concern (or should be) for public domain activities, whereas for private sector organizations they are at most a voluntary "add-on" – as in the corporate "social responsibility" movement. This is discussed further below and in subsequent chapters (Figure 2.1).

The point is that – for the public domain – a focus on "outcomes" means that inevitably the boundaries of performance are pushed beyond the boundaries of individual public agencies. This is best illustrated by way of an example – for example, a hip-replacement operation supplied by a public sector health organization. The desired outcome(s) are that the patients can walk better, without pain, and live a relatively normal life as a result of having their hip joint replaced by an artificial one.

But of course simply replacing the hip joint does not guarantee such an outcome. Other public agents may be involved – for example physiotherapy services. The patients themselves are involved in "coproducing" the outcome in that they have to actively participate in their rehabilitation. Their family and friends may also need to be involved. Voluntary, private, or public dieticians may also help by helping the patient to loose weight accumulated during the period of incapacity. The patient may use a private gym to get exercise. And so on. The overall result therefore depends not just on the public agency providing the hip operation but by other public, private, and voluntary agencies and agents – pushing the notion of "performance" well beyond simply the public domain.

The boundaries of the public domain itself are also notoriously difficult to define. Take the example of UK universities – which for official statistics purposes are counted as "private sector" whereas they are generally considered by the public and policy-makers as part of the public sector. One scholar has even argued that all organizations are to some extent "public" to the degree they are sanctioned by the state (Bozeman 1987).

These fuzzy boundaries therefore raise substantial issues about analysis of performance in the public domain. Later in the chapter these issues will be teased out a little more in a discussion of "attribution" issues.

MULTILEVEL GOVERNMENT

Except in the very smallest states, government is usually a multilevel affair (OECD-PUMA 1997). In federal systems there are usually federal, state, and local levels of government for example. Even in unitary states there are usually at least two levels – central and local.

This multilevel nature of government complicates analysis of performance because many areas of public activity take place at several levels of government simultaneously. Even where activities take place only at a lower level – for example provision of schooling in England – decisions taken at another level of government may impact on these activities lower down. Decisions taken in Whitehall over funding, or regulation of the curriculum, or exams and award structures, for example will impact upon local education authorities and schools performance in ways that are not always obvious. Several crises off performance failures in the UK central government in recent years have revolved around just such multilayered issues – for example, crises in the Prison Service, Passports Agency, and Rural Payments Agency all revolved around issues of which decisions at which level of government were responsible for the performance crisis. For the example of the Prisons Service, see Talbot (1996c).

Nor are these influences always easily identifiable simply by formal definitions of the different layers of governments' legal and constitutional duties and relationships. One of the benefits of the revival of institutional analysis in politics and government in recent years is that we are increasingly aware of the complex nature of the real – formal and informal – relationships between these different levels of government.

So it is important to be aware of these complex relationships when studying the performance of any specific unit of government. A unit of local government, for example, may be more or less constrained and "steered" in what it does by higher levels of government that is bound to have some effect on its performance. Treating the local government unit as if it was a "closed system" – without these external constraints and influences – could easily distort analysis of performance considerably.

This becomes especially important where the performance of similar entities is compared across the same level. All English local governments, for example, are in roughly the same position with regard to the influence of central government and can be, and have been, compared horizontally with the assumption that differences are not attributable to differential central government influences. Whereas in the United States local governments in different states are not necessarily in the same relationship to their state governments and therefore less easily directly comparable, at least not without taking into account the differences in state-level influence on performance.

SEPARATION OF POWERS

A further complicating factor in government is what the Americans call the "separation of powers" – that is the distinct roles of different "branches" of a single level of government. In the United States' case this is usually taken to be the separate roles of the Presidency, or executive branch; the Congress, or legislative branch; and the Courts, or judicial branch. All of these branches can – and often do – seek to steer the performance of federal agencies and organizations.

Just to take two examples: in 1916 the US Congress established the Bureau of Efficiency to try to drive up the efficiency of US federal agencies (Lee 2006). Nearly eight decades later members of Congress again attempted to assert influence over federal agencies performance by formulating the first drafts of what later became the Government Performance and Results Act (1993).

So important is the issue of institutional configurations and their possible influence over performance of public agencies that two whole chapters (Chapters 4 and 5) of this book are devoted to the notion of a "performance regime" (Talbot et al. 2005; Talbot 2008c) within which such agencies operate. As with multilevel government, if separate but similar agencies work within the same performance regime, when comparing their performances these external influences can be largely discounted – but in many cases they cannot. And when looking at the overall performance of all such agencies these influences can be important, especially as they tend to change and evolve over time (see Chapters 4 and 5). Some scholars have already begun to identify the problematic nature, and implications of, the "separation of powers" for the performance movement in the United States (Radin 1998; 2000; 2006b) and in the United Kingdom (Johnson and Talbot 2007b; 2008) but such analyses have so far been few in number.

MULTI-ACTIVITY GOVERNMENT

A third set of complicating factors about the nature of government comes from the fact that most governments – which for performance purposes are often counted as single entities themselves – are very multi-activity based. National governments are usually more multifaceted than state or local governments – if for no other reason than they usually reserve defense and foreign relations areas to themselves.

So, when the Audit Commission in England set out to carry the "Comprehensive Performance Assessments" (CPA) of all English local authorities they had to aggregate the performance of a whole range of different services from waste collection and disposal through road repairs, environmental health regulation, and economic regeneration policies to social services provision and much more. Similarly the Government Performance Project (GPP) and Federal Performance Project (FPP) in the United States, which had similar aims to England's CPA but was carried out by academics and a nongovernment organization, also had to take into account a wide range of services (Ingraham et al. 2003).

Even some individual public agencies encompass a surprisingly wide range of activities. The Department of Homeland Security in the United States, formed after 9/11 from the merger under a single department of a wide range of security, policing, and emergency activities, is perhaps an extreme example but makes the point. Everything from emergency response (Federal Emergency Management Agency – FEMA), through coastguards to intelligence agencies come under this mammoth department (Kettl 2003).

This creates problematic issues about measuring performance because if an organizational perspective is taken somehow the performance of all these separate streams of activity have to be aggregated into a single performance assessment – where performance in different activities may vary wildly. Thus, within UK civil service agencies the number of "key" performance indicators varied between one (The Royal Mint) and thirty plus (Customs and Excise), and these were supposedly "focused" agencies (Talbot 2004a). Similarly disaggregating performance by activity area requires sophisticated "activity-based costing" and performance measurement that often do not exist within single public agencies that have historically structured their finances around functions rather than activities.

POLICIES AND PROGRAMS

One of the ways in which the activities of governments is often discussed (and financed) is around specific policies or programs of activity aimed at a specific single or small set of problems. Such policies and programs most often do not fit neatly into organizational boundaries – often involving different public agencies at the same levels of government and multiple levels of government as well (not to mention sometimes nongovernment actors).

Traditionally the "performance" of such policies and programs has been measured not by the tools and techniques of the performance measurement movement but rather by a separate, parallel but closely related approach – evaluation. Evaluation studies have developed a policy and academic community all of its own, with its own journals, conferences, and most importantly tools and methods (which are themselves the subject of heated debate within this community) (Guba and Lincoln 1989). To some extent this evaluation movement has predated – at least in the United States, many European countries, and the developing world – the performance movement.

Whereas "activity-based" performance measurement (mentioned above) tends to be concentrated within organizational boundaries, policy and program evaluation almost always spans these boundaries. Evaluation has rarely been integrated with the performance movement in either theory or practice (Blalock 1999) even though most Organization for Economic Cooperation and Development (OECD) countries, for example, claim to be doing both (Curristine 2007).

The shift in emphasis toward "outcomes" in performance reporting and analysis – discussed above – ought to bring evaluation studies and performance analysis closer together as this is also the usual objective of evaluations. However, the signs of this – in both theory and practice – remain weak. The analysis of the performance of programs and policies – arguably something that ought to be a key component – therefore remains largely outside the compass of the performance movement, something that is highly problematic.

A small anecdote might illustrate this. I was involved with a new Scottish national agency – Careers Scotland – helping their management to put in place a performance management system for the new organization. During the course of this work we discovered that the Scottish Executive (government) has also commissioned a three-year evaluation of the new agency. Upon discussing this with the consultants carrying out the evaluation, it became apparent that there was a substantial overlap – probably in the region of 80–90% – in the date they wanted to collect for evaluation purposes and we wanted to collect for performance measurement. The main discrepancy lay in areas of qualitative assessment, which they included more of. I approached the management of Careers Scotland, the Scottish Executive, and the evaluation consultants to suggest merging the two projects – to no avail. The barriers among the managers, policy-makers, and the researchers between "evaluation" and "performance" perspectives were just too great to overcome. Both projects proceeded in splendid isolation from one another.

GOVERNANCE, SYSTEMS, AND NETWORKS

We have already alluded in the discussion of the boundaries of the public domain, and also in the discussion of the structures of government, to the fact the boundaries of what the object of any analysis of "performance" applies to is often complex and sometimes fuzzy in nature and therefore hard to define precisely.

In recent years there has been a considerable growth in scholarship around the twin notions of "governance" – most usually defined as the processes of interaction between government and society at large – and "networks" – both networks of policy formation and of implementation. (Indeed at least one scholar has tried to assert that "governance" is "networks" (Rhodes 1997)).

These governance and networks perspectives raise substantial issues about the measurement of performance in what some have called the "hollow state" (Weller et al. 1997*a*). This analysis suggests that power is being leached away from core executives by several processes – transfer upward to supranational bodies (e.g., in the UK case the European Union) and transfers sideways and downward through devolution, decentralization, agencification, the growth of networked governance, and privatizations. The result is a weakened core executive – to so-called hollow state.

Analysis of the practical problems for performance associated with this phenomena in five US federal bodies showed that a very complex set of variables and relationships was involved (Frederickson and Frederickson 2006). Similar analysis in the United Kingdom pointed substantial difficulties in "cascading" down and aggregating up performance analysis and management (Comptroller and Auditor General 2001). (This is an issue that will be more fully discussed in Chapter 5.)

PUBLIC ORGANIZATIONS

Finally, in terms of levels and units of analysis, we come to the thorny problem of what is a public organization – where do its boundaries lie? Government, or governance, is a complex, multilevel web of relationships, structures, and institutions (in both the historical sense parliaments and courts, as well as the modern sense of rules of the game), etc. So while terms like "school," "hospital," or "agency" can sound deceptively simple, the degree of external penetration of seemingly obvious public sector agencies' boundaries can make these issues sometimes more difficult than would first appear.

This is clearly important as most of the former "organizational effectiveness" movement (1945 to early 1980s), the quality and cultural management movement (early 1980s onward), and the current performance movement (early 1990s onward) has focused on *organizations*, in both the public and private sectors (see Chapters 7 and 8). The boundaries of private organizations are usually treated as relatively unproblematic, although this is in fact questionable as the main form of modern private sector organization – the limited liability joint stock corporation – has far more porous boundaries and is also shaped by external forces (Bozeman 1987; Micklethwait and Wooldridge 2005). It is however widely accepted that the boundaries of public agencies are far more difficult to define, and that they are often in any case engaged in "delivery chains" for publicly desired outcomes that are complex (see above). Defining what constitutes the unit of analysis when considering performance is thus crucial.

A concrete example of where this can arise is the crisis in the England and Wales prison service in the early 1990s. HM Prison Service was by then an "executive agency" within the Home Office (interior ministry), with its own Director General, (CEO), "Framework Document" (constitution), budget, reporting procedure, etc. Without going into too many details, following a couple of high profile prison escapes by maximum security prisoners the Director General (Derek Lewis) was dismissed. Huge controversy followed over whether the problems were really his responsibility or those of the Home Secretary (the Minister responsible) – in other words where the performance failure lay – inside the organization or between it and its political masters? (Talbot 1996b; Lewis 1997). This boundary issue was compounded for many when after his dismissal Lewis sued for, and got, compensation – including all his performance bonuses on the grounds he had fulfilled the performance targets set by the Home Secretary.

Conceptual Problems

We have made a start on considering the thorny problem of what exactly is "performing" when performance analysis is carried out – what government or organization or system or network or policy is being analyzed? But what is meant by the term "performance" itself – what constitutes "performance" – is it just "results" or "outcomes" as some policy-makers seem to suggest, or is it more than that?

Here we begin to enter a conceptual minefield in which seemingly simple and unproblematic concepts soon begin to dissolve in a miasma of qualifiers and fuzzy definitions and complexity mushrooms.

CATEGORIES: INPUTS, OUTPUTS, OUTCOMES

Let us begin with some definitions of basic concepts. Two examples have been chosen from the many available – the first is from an official source – a set of definitions jointly agreed by five public bodies in the United Kingdom centrally involved in performance policies and reporting (HM Treasury, the Cabinet Office, national Audit Office, Audit Commission, and Office of National Statistics). The second is from the United States and is by an independent scholar who has been highly influential in the development of the performance movement for over three decades. These two examples are chosen not because they are especially problematic, but because they are all too representative of the general semantic and conceptual lack of clarity and consensus in the field – which in turn can have significant practical consequences.

Inputs

The resources that contribute to the production and delivery of an output. Inputs commonly include things such as labour, physical resources, and IT systems for example.   (HM Treasury 2001)

Resources (i.e. expenditures or employee time) used to produce outputs and outcomes   (Hatry 1999)

Outputs

Outputs are the goods and services produced by the organization. Outputs are delivered to an external party (usually to the public either individually or collectively) and comprise the majority of day-to-day interaction between people and government. Outputs include things such as issuing licenses, investigations, assessing applications for benefits and providing policy advice.   (HM Treasury 2001)

Products and services delivered. Output refers to the completed products of internal activities: the amount of work done within the organization or by its contractors (such as number of miles of road repaired or number of calls answered).   (Hatry 1999)

Outcomes

Outcomes are the impacts on, or consequences for, the community, of the activities of the Government. Outcomes reflect the intended results from government actions and provide the rationale for government interventions. Improving the health status of the population is an example of an outcome. A distinction is sometimes made between intermediate outcomes and end outcomes. Intermediate outcomes are the more short term, easily measurable outcomes which result from an activity, where as final outcomes are the longer term outcomes which may be harder to capture.

(HM Treasury 2001)

An event, occurrence, or condition that is outside the activity or program itself and that is of direct importance to customers and the public generally. An outcome indicator is a measure of the amount and/or frequency of such occurrences. Service quality is also included under this category.   (Hatry 1999)

It would be possible to devote a whole chapter just to discussing the nuances and differences between (and even within) these two sets of definitions. Let us just focus on a few.

While HM Treasury et al. (we will use HMT as an abbreviation) specify that "inputs" are related to outputs, Hatry relates them to both outputs and outcomes. There are several conceptual problems here.

First, neither definition accounts for the issue of resources that are consumed but are not attributable to outputs (and/or outcomes) – that is, resources that are simply wasted, producing nothing. Such "waste" may be perfectly legitimate – for example having been consumed by an R&D effort that eventually went nowhere. Or it may be simply waste in the more pejorative sense. Either way, the conceptual definition of "inputs" surely has to in some way account for all inputs to a system, not just those that can be directly linked to outputs (or outcomes).

Second, the difference between the first definition – linking inputs to only outputs – and the second – linking to both outputs and outcomes – is substantial. Linking inputs to outputs is difficult enough – both conceptually and in practice, but adding the category of outcomes would be much more complex and therefore problematic (see also discussion of outcomes below).

The two definitions of "outputs" are more conceptually consistent – except that Hatry's definition includes internally problematic elements. The "amount of work done" and "number of calls answered" sound like activities that do not necessarily constitute "products and services delivered." Both could constitute non- or even counter productive activities and would require further clarification before really being considered as "outputs." In most conceptual frameworks (including Hatry's own and HMT's) such activities are more often included in a separate, intermediate, "processes" or "activities" category between "inputs" and "outputs."

The conceptualizations of outcomes again contain important differences. Hatry's contains an implied subjective element – "of direct importance to customers and the public" – that is absent from HMT's definition. Hatry also includes "service quality" in outcomes whereas if it refers to the quality of the outputs, which are defined by Hatry as "goods and services," then it should really come under "outputs" not "outcomes."

This leads to a further interesting point to note – inputs, outputs, and outcomes can be analyzed in terms of both quantity – units of output for example – and in terms of quality – the relative quality of those units of output. Similarly "user" or "customer" or "public" satisfaction could apply to all three – satisfaction with levels of resources applied, with outputs or services delivered, and with the resulting outcomes.

So each of our three basic concepts – inputs, outputs, and outcomes – can also be broken down into three components: quantity, quality, and satisfaction. This means we already have nine potential dimensions of performance, and there are many more potentially available.

Note that in the HMT definition of outcomes a distinction is introduced between intermediate and end outcomes. Actually in these two frameworks several further concepts are introduced, including:

- **Intermediate outcomes** – already mentioned in the HMT definition of "outcomes" but also mentioned separately by Hatry although defined differently.

- **Efficiency** – mentioned by both – refers to the relationship (ratio) between inputs and outputs, but defined slightly differently.
- **Economy** – HMT only – refers to reducing the costs of inputs.
- **Effectiveness** – HMT only – the extent to which outputs achieve desired outcomes.
- **Cost-effectiveness (or value for money)** – HMT only – relationship (ratio) between inputs or resources utilized and outcomes achieved.
- **Process** – Hatry only – workload or activities within an agency not yet completed.

This is by no means an exhaustive list of the definitions offered in these two sets of statements about the conceptual bases of performance measurement in the public domain. As already indicated, these are not exceptional in the degree of difference in the detailed definitions of what, at first sight, appear to be relatively straightforward concepts.

Some of this confusion and imprecision is undoubtedly due to the developing nature of the field – the HMT et al. publication speaks to a conscious effort on the part of at least some actors to try to clarify, and gain consensus around, a stipulative set of concepts and categories. But there are also issues as to what extent clarity is actually possible? These are essentially attempts to place categorical boundaries around activities that are in reality far more contiguous and fuzzy.

These conceptual issues are further complicated by linking them to the "levels and units of analysis" problems discussed above. This is best illustrated by example: take the personnel training or human resource development function within a public agency as an exemplar of this problem. Applying the simple conceptual framework (Figure 2.1) then the "outputs" for the HRD function are better-trained staff and the outcomes are that they perform their work better. But both these outputs and outcomes are merely part of the inputs and/or internal processes of the agency as a whole – they are not agency outputs or outcomes in any sense. This is an issue that can generate vast amounts of confusion when these conceptual frameworks are applied in practice.

Does any of this matter or is it just traditional academic "angels on a pinhead" nitpicking? It matters a great deal because unless the conceptual framework is clear and agreed by all the potential users of performance information a great deal of confusion can arise. For researchers it is critical if serious research analyzing performance trends and comparisons are to be undertaken. For policy-makers, public managers, users, and citizens it is vital that they are not "comparing apples and oranges." As we will see in the section dealing with the more technical measurement problems, establishing a sound conceptual framework is a prerequisite for any robust measurement implementation.

MULTIPLICATION OF CONCEPTS AND MEASURES

As well as some of the precision issues discussed here it is worth noting at this point the multiplication of concepts that is the consequence of the complexity of the system under consideration. In the simple model of public performance it is already possible to multiply three initial concepts to nine by subdividing each by the concepts of quantity, quality, and satisfaction. Inserting a fourth category – which is commonly done – covering internal processes or activities between "inputs" and "outputs," which can also be subdivided, increases the number of categories of performance to twelve. Adding the concepts of "efficiency" (input – output ratios) and "effectiveness" or "value for money" or "cost-effectiveness" (input – outcome ratios) add still more.

It should also be noted that these conceptual additions interact – thus disaggregating inputs, outputs, and outcomes into quantity, quality, and satisfaction impacts on how efficiency is measured. Recent work in the United Kingdom by first the Atkinson commission and then the Office of National Statistics (ONS) have tried to estimate the productivity of the UK National Health Service (NHS) (Lee 2008). Productivity is of course not quite the same as efficiency (as conceptualized above), but very similar in concept (see later in this chapter discussion of technical issues for the differences between the two). The ONS estimates for NHS productivity vary by 0.5% depending on whether the quality rather than just the quantity of outputs are measured. This may not seem like a big issue, but on a budget currently (2009) of around £100 billion, this is the equivalent of a half-billion-pound difference – a not inconsiderable difference in purely financial terms. Of course a change in the quality of, say, outputs can also have huge practical implications – using an inferior quality hip-replacement joint can lead to dire consequences for patients even while quantity of output is maintained – and has done.

The practical implication of multiplying concepts within the overall framework of public service performance is that the amount of measurement required for both research and practical reasons also tends to increase. This is further compounded by the complications of units and levels of analysis and can lead to an almost exponential explosion of possible, and sometimes actual, attempts to measure performance in a multiplicity of ways (Pollitt et al. 2010)

RESULTS AND CAPACITY

Before leaving the topic of conceptual problems one further difficulty needs to be introduced, which will be fully explored in Chapters 7 and 8 on organizational and public organizational performance. In the simple model of performance (Figure 2.1) what happens inside the organization, system, or program between "inputs" and "outputs" is sometimes treated as a "black box" and only actual "results" – that is, outputs and outcomes – are deemed as important. This has found its way into phrases such as "output" or "outcome-based government," for example. It is what is delivered that matters, not how it is delivered.

Such an approach has been increasingly challenged in both the public and private sectors. In the private sector the growth of performance reporting approaches, most famously characterized by things like the "balanced score-card" (Kaplan and Norton 1992) or the European Foundation for Quality's "Excellence" model, have emphasized the analysis of both "results" and internal "capacities."

In the public sector both of these models, and some "homegrown" ones, have adopted similar all-embracing approaches – for example the "Comprehensive Performance Assessment" (CPA) of English local government includes both "results" and "capacity" (and even prospective future capacity) in the analysis and ranking of local authorities' performance. The European Union's "common assessment framework" (CAF) for public services adopts a similar approach.

This raises an important conceptual problem – are internal "capabilities" or "capacities" legitimately included in the concept of "performance" or not? This is certainly not a new issue – it was, for example, already being discussed in the "organizational effectiveness" literature of the 1960s and 1970s, (e.g., Price 1968). We will return to it – but for now it is worth noting as a major conceptual and practical question, which we will explore further in Chapters 7 and 8.

Technical Problems

The problems encountered in the performance movement do not just relate to what to analyze (unit of analysis) and what conceptual framework to employ, but extend to technical difficulties in the actual measurement of these various units and aspects of performance.

MEASUREMENT PRACTICALITIES – INDICATORS AND/OR MEASURES?

The first and most obvious point is that it is virtually impossible to fully measure any aspect of performance – that is to count absolutely everything that happens. There is both a practical and a theoretical component to this problem.

The practical one is that the cost of trying to count every possible aspect of performance would be prohibitive and probably impractical. Because of the possible/probable escalating categories of performance discussed above, the amount of data that would need to be captured would be vast. As a small example, during an exercise to establish what was already being measured and what might be added in Careers Scotland – the agency mentioned above – the team established some 600 + possible areas of measurement for what was a relatively small agency.

The theoretical problems are even trickier. They relate to problems like "measurement effects," inevitable imprecision in measurement systems, and the problems associated with highly complex systems.

This is why in much of the performance research and practice the idea of "performance indicators" (PIs) has become popular. The idea is that PIs are – as the name suggests – indicators of performance rather than direct measures of absolute performance. PIs usually rest on a sampling approach or on a selective, or proxy, approach. Sampling usually involves using measurement of a small, statistically significant, subset of actual activities in the desired category to estimate the actual level of overall activity. A selective approach, on the other hand, usually uses one dimension or metric which does not capture complete activities (as sampling does) but which is thought to be a reliable indicator of the complete activity.

Unfortunately, these distinctions between "measures" and "indicators" are often observed more in theory/policy than in implementation and the distinction is difficult to maintain in practice. In the case of our two experts discussed above (HMT and Hatry) one uses the measurement/indicator distinction as discussed here (HMT) while the other defines PIs as "a specific numerical measurement of each aspect of performance...under consideration" which is quite different.

Alongside these major, practical, and theoretical limitations there are a set of other technical problems. We will run through just some of these here.

MEASUREMENT EFFECTS

The act of measurement itself frequently changes what is being measured, so that what is actually recorded is not the performance of "x" but the performance of "x" when it is being measured. Take the example of the speedometer of a car. It does measure the actual speed of the car, but that speed is the result of the "natural" speed minus the tiny amount of friction involved in measurement process. In physical systems it is sometimes possible to measure without significantly interfering with the system itself, through purely noninvasive observational techniques, but in systems involving human actors who know that the activities they are involved in are being measured, this is impossible.

Humans, as is well established in research, react to being observed and change their behavior, making it impossible to measure except by what are today regarded as unethical hidden observational techniques. Indeed, the famous positive "Hawthorne effects" – established in human work-performance experiments in the 1930s – are in part a measurement effect (and not the only possible one). Of course, dysfunctional reactions to measurement are also possible and there is plenty of evidence of examples of gaming, threshold effects, ratchet effects, etc. (for more detail see Chapter 9). These positive and negative effects are obviously an issue for the objective of any performance measurement policies designed to improve performance, but they are also technical questions for performance measurement itself.

There is an additional measurement effect in public agencies that results from performance assessment. Any measurement requires the agency itself to take action and utilize resources – in data collection if nothing else. This of course would not be happening if the agency/activity were not being measured. The consumption of resources in the process of measurement therefore affects the performance of the system being measured, by transferring resources from something else into the measurement process. And of course it is possible that two similar systems may use more or less efficient ways of measuring. This creates paradoxical possibility that one agency "A" may actually be performing on its core role better than another agency "B," but that the effects of a more expensive performance measurement system used by "A" make it appear the other way round. (Of course, it is possible to argue that the use of the more expensive system means "A" is "really" performing less well than "B" but that way lies madness).

THE INEVITABILITY OF ERROR

Measurement effects are only one source of error in any measurement system. There are plenty of others in public agencies and services where most of what is being counted has to be, as a first step, recorded by humans. To be sure, there are some types of information which can now be initially recorded "mechanically" – for example, "time to answer" on telephone systems or "time to process" for computer-based systems. Although, even in this latter case, if the first inputting into the system is done by humans there is scope for possible error (e.g., if the operative has to assign a date of input rather than one being automatically generated).

For most public sector activities – which by staffing and resources volume are mainly "human services" (i.e., education, health, social services, etc.) – the initial input of data into any performance system is human and therefore prone to error.

Human error then is a major source of performance data error. There are many possible causes for human error. The most benign are obviously just straightforward errors – mistyping a date, or data point, for example. These may also include mis-categorizations – ticking the wrong box or misunderstanding the categories. At the other extreme is the deliberate falsification of entries to distort results in a desired direction.

A great deal is often asserted about the supposed proneness of performance data systems to the latter type of deliberate distortion or error – much less is known about the extent and scale of the problem. Those hostile to measurement often produce a stream of exemplars – but these are usually characterized by being small-scale, anecdotal, or at worst apocryphal. They usually tell us very little, other than to "confirm" the positive or negative preconceptions of the authors and readers. The most authoritative, large-scale studies with good access to data have been carried out by audit and inspection bodies and while these have exposed many problems, even in the worst cases the levels of gaming and errors exposed has rarely exceeded 10%, and this usually in the early stages of a measurement system (see Chapter 9 for more details).

SUBJECTIVE VERSUS OBJECTIVE MEASURES?

An issue that constantly recurs in the performance literature is the distinction between so-called "subjective" and "objective" data. We leave aside for a moment those constructionists who believe all performance data is subjective – more on them in Chapter 3. For most analysts the distinction between subjective and objective is usually posed by issue such as public perceptions and fear of crime versus the actual levels of crime and risk of being a victim. Thus, typically in survey data elderly people are more fearful of street crime when actually young people are much more likely to be victims, or the case where popular perceptions are that burglaries are rising in an area when all available evidence suggest they are actually falling. Both of these scenarios have been widely reported in different countries, but for a discussion see (Skogan 1986; Marshall et al. 2007)

A simple error that occurs in much practitioner, and far too much academic literature, on performance is to designate survey data of public or user opinion as "subjective" data. This is of course nonsense. Such survey data – provided of course it has been reliably and validly collected and analyzed – is objective data about people's subjective perceptions. "People" really do think that, for example, they are at greater risk of burglary than they were previously – that is an objective fact. That their subjective views (objectively recorded) differ from other objective data (police reports, crime surveys, etc.) is also a fact – and a highly interesting one.

There are only three possible explanations for such discrepancies: the so-called "objective" data is wrong, the objectively collected views are in fact misplaced, or both are partially wrong.

That the "objective" data is wrong is not at all impossible. Collection of crime statistics is a notoriously difficult area because not all actual crime is reported to the police – in the United Kingdom, for example, the discrepancy between the volume and trajectory of crime rates as recorded by the police (from crime reported to them) and the British Crime Survey (a long-running household survey) is legendary and the subject of many political games.

That people's perceptions of crime levels may be wrong is also possible. Many criminologists have been looking at whether, for example, the wide-spread TV and other media reporting of crime affects public perceptions and the answer is generally that it probably does. One well-known phenomenon is when a single very high-profile and shocking crime sparks a fashion for reporting many similar types of crime, creating the impression that this type of crime is on the increase (e.g., knife or gun crime).

The third option – that both the reported crime and perceived crime levels are to some extent inaccurate is probably more likely than that one or the other is completely correct. In any case, the fact that people perceive crime in a particular way is itself an objective fact and an important one. Crime-fighters (police and other criminal justice agencies) have come to realize that part of their mission is not simply to reduce crime but it is also to reduce the fear of crime and enhance citizens' sense of personal security.

What the frequent discrepancy between data about crime and the fear of crime tell us – and them – is that reducing one does not automatically lead to a decrease in the other. And conversely, some crimes may actually be on the rise (e.g., identity theft) about which the public is relatively unaware or unconcerned. It is increasingly being recognized by managers and policy-makers across a range of public services that managing both objective outputs and outcomes and perceptions of the outputs and outcomes are significant. From a technical, performance measurement point of view this of course makes the task far more complex.

BOUNDED RATIONALITY AND COMPOSITE INDICATORS

As already discussed in this chapter the number of possible dimensions and attributes of performance can – and does – increase the amount of measure-ment demanded. One effect of such increases can often be "information overload" as it becomes increasingly difficult for public policy-makers, man-agers, users, and the public to make sense of the mountains of data generated. In English local government, for example, roughly the Audit Commission published 200 pieces of performance data every year for over 200 local authorities – that is, 40,000 pieces of information. (Actually, even more was collected and published by other audit and inspection bodies and the local governments themselves.) In Japan, the Government Policy Evaluation Act (2002) has led to the annual publication of around 10,000 evaluation and performance reports – each containing multiple pieces of information.[1] In the United States, alongside the federal governments' Government Performance and Results Act (GPRA) and Program Assessment Rating Tool (PART), every one of the fifty states also now has a performance reporting system in place (Moynihan 2008).

This veritable avalanche of formalized performance reporting brings with it significant problems of information processing for anyone wanting to use the data. As Herbert Simon famously noted, humans are limited in our ability to process information and use what he called "bounded rationality" – that is we accept limits on both the volume of information and how rationally we process it, often using heuristic "rules of thumb" (Simon 1996; Gigerenzer 2000). In an originally somewhat whimsical article which has since achieved seminal status, the social psychologist George Miller proposed "The Magical Number Seven, Plus or Minus Two" as a natural limit to our capacity for processing information (Miller 1956).

In performance information systems this has led to a tendency to try to organize and simplify performance data into hierarchical sets of aggregated data or "composite" indicators. This movement has been particularly noticeable in composite indicators "which compare and rank country performance in areas such as industrial competitiveness, sustainable development, globalization and innovation" – so much so that this quote is from the introduction to a joint OECD – European Commission handbook on the subject (OECD and European Commission 2008). Perhaps the most well-known set of such indicators are the World Bank's "Worldwide Governance Indicators" (WGI), which compare 212 countries on a wide range of measures and aggregate these to a single "score" ranging from a possible "high" of + 3.00 and "low" of − 3.00. The data is derived from thirty-three different sources and thirty organizations, with a total 310 individual bits of data about each country (Kaufmann et al. 2007).

In the UK composite indicators and composite "star ratings" (drawn from the hotel star ratings systems) other methods have been used to rank and compare schools, hospitals, police forces, etc.

The advantages are said to be summarizing complex, multidimensional realities for policy makers; ease of interpretation; ease of tracking over

---

[1] Information from study visit to Japan by author. For more detail see: www.soumu.go.jp/main_sosiki/hyouka/seisaku_n/pes/events.html

time; and ease of comparisons. The disadvantages are said to be possible misinterpretation; simplistic conclusions; may be misused (especially if insufficiently transparent); aggregations may be manipulated (OECD and European Commission 2008).

The most common methods used in such aggregation are usually indexation (e.g., converting raw data into common scales of 0–100), aggregating (i.e., adding together several indexed data), and weighting (i.e., assigning a weight to individual indexes during the aggregation process).

Aggregate indicators are not without their critics, to put it mildly (Pollitt 2009a). Criticisms range from the ways in which the data is constructed – indeed some critics deny the "real" existence of public sector performance as an independent phenomena and adopt a purely social constructionist approach (e.g., Moynihan 2008; van Dooren and Van de Walle 2008). This will be discussed in the next chapter. Other criticisms tend to focus more on the difficulties inherent in producing and aggregating large data sets like the WGI or league tables in the UK NHS in any reliable and scientific way (Jacobs et al. 2006; Jacobs and Goddard 2007; McLean et al. 2007; Pollitt 2009a).

Another set of criticisms relate to the purposes, usage, and probable effects of such aggregate performance measures – especially unwanted effects like gaming (i.e., playing the system), "threshold effects" (i.e., hitting the target and then stopping), etc. (e.g., Bevan and Hood 2006a; Bevan and Hood 2006b; Van de Walle and Roberts 2008; Pollitt 2009a). Crucial here is the actual evidence on any such effects – how widespread are they? How significant in their impact? Are they stable over time or do they increase or decrease? Are there patterns as to where and why they occur and are there mitigating factors? Chapter 9 will review some of the actual evidence, which tends to show that some of the somewhat deterministic claims for these effects – they will happen everywhere – are overblown. There is, however, also evidence of significance (though usually not in a majority of cases or with major consequences).

It is a pity that some of this thinking about these issues is so almost "ideological" in its antipathy to performance measurement that the need for evidence to support assertion is dispensed with or treated in cavalier ways. For example Van de Walle and Roberts (2008) list a whole series of possible difficulties and dysfunctions in the effects of performance information without providing any empirical evidence that these things actually happen, or to what extent. Their arguments could be correct, but evidence would be useful. Another tack has been to establish criteria of perfection for performance measurement systems that are so exacting that any system will surely fail (e.g., McLean et al. 2007). Neither of these approaches is, by itself, helpful and the second is positively harmful in its unrealistic approach.

EFFICIENCY AND PRODUCTIVITY AND LOCAL VERSUS SYSTEMS EFFECTS

Another technical problem that arises in the study of performance is the difference between productivity and efficiency. We already noted earlier in the chapter that estimates by the ONS showed a steady and consistent decline in NHS productivity from 2001 to 2005 of about 2% per annum (Figure 2.2).

These figures relate to productivity adjusted by quality of outputs. The unadjusted figures – which go up to 2006 – also show productivity falling by a total of 10% and annual average of 2.5%. In an overlapping time period (2004–7) the British Government was claiming that the NHS had made efficiency savings of over £7 billion (or around 7% of total spending).

Could the trend decline in productivity, which was steadily falling, have suddenly reversed so dramatically? If productivity paralleled efficiency – as it would be reasonable to assume it should – this would mean a quite staggering reverse from a 2–2.5% a year drop to a 2.5% a year increase. This would be the equivalent of not £7 billion of savings, as the government claims, but of more like double that amount – £14–15 billion – from the previous trend. This seems highly unlikely, and indeed the year for which the figures directly overlap (2004–5) shows a big discrepancy. While the government claims efficiency savings of £1,031 billion or 1.5% for 2005, productivity fell by 2.2%

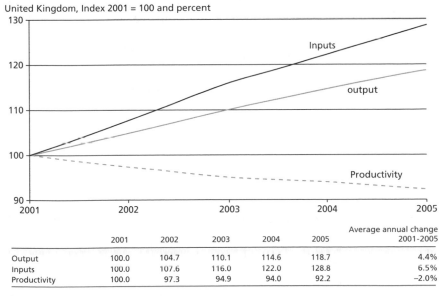

	2001	2002	2003	2004	2005	Average annual change 2001-2005
Output	100.0	104.7	110.1	114.6	118.7	4.4%
Inputs	100.0	107.6	116.0	122.0	128.8	6.5%
Productivity	100.0	97.3	94.9	94.0	92.2	–2.0%

Figure 2.2 Health Care Productivity
Source: (Lee 2008).

or the equivalent of £1.5 billion – a difference of almost 4% or the equivalent of £2.5 billion.

There are technical reasons that could mean that both these sets of data are in a sense "correct," which in part prompted ONS to try to furnish an explanation in a paper setting out the similarities and differences in the way HMT and ONS measure efficiency (HMT) and productivity (ONS) (Simkins 2008). In this paper, ONS stressed that measuring efficiency and productivity served essentially the same goal: measuring the performance of public services (Figure 2.3).

The first major point is that productivity and efficiency do not use the same metrics – productivity is measured in "volume" – that is, actual things – while efficiency is measured in monetary terms. While this is true, it is also hard to see how this can reconcile the size of the recorded discrepancy between efficiency savings and productivity decline.

The second major difference is that productivity measures do not include reductions in the costs of inputs, because they measure in volumes. So one whole stream of activity in the UK Governments' efficiency drive – economy measures or reducing the costs of inputs, is excluded from the ONS productivity measures. This could account for part of the discrepancy – for the only year for which we have overlapping figures for health (2004–5) the Department of Health (DoH) claim was that £0.33 billion efficiency savings had been made from procurement savings (economy) – which would account for only 13% of the difference between the efficiency and productivity figures of £2.5 billion. So while this difference in the way efficiency and productivity is calculated is significant, it can only resolve a relatively small proportion of the discrepancy in the results.

	Trends	2005 £bn	2005 percentage	2005 procurement
ONS Productivity	–6% to 7.5% 2003–05	–1.5	–2.2	n/a
HMT Efficiency	+7% 2004–07	+1.03	+1.5	£333m
Totals/Difference		£2.5bn	3.7%	

Figure 2.3 Differences in ONS and HMT Figures for Productivity/Efficiency of the NHS
Sources: Calculated from Secretary of State for Health (2005), HM Treasury (2008), and Lee (2008).

The third explanation – which ONS hint at but do not fully explore – is the difference between the "units of analysis" used in efficiency and productivity measurement. The focus of the ONS work on productivity is the whole health "system." Where they use measurement of specific activities, it is merely to get indicators for use in calculating overall productivity (Simkins 2008).

Efficiency interventions, and measurements, are however focused at a much lower level – they tend to focus on measuring specific activities, projects, programs, or units. This raises a major technical and practical problem. It is quite possible to achieve "real" efficiency improvements in one part of the system that generates overall efficiency losses. This problem was highlighted in a Parliamentary report which pointed out that efficiency gains in health from earlier patient discharges after in-hospital treatments were counted as a major efficiency gain (Committee of Public Accounts 2007). However, the measurement failed to take into account the resulting rise in readmissions to hospital for complications, which offset most, if not all, of the efficiencies gained through early discharge. This is an example of a localized efficiency saving leading to an overall systems efficiency loss.

It would be wrong to attribute the around £7 billion discrepancy for the NHS, which is the remaining amount once measurement differences are eliminated, entirely to this localized-gain and systems-loss phenomena without further research, but it is clearly possible that it does account for a substantial part of the difference. The implications for policy and practice in performance and efficiency management are substantial – it suggests a much more holistic, and whole systems, approach is needed when approaching efficiency drives than is traditionally the case. The technical implications are also large – it poses substantial issues about how to draw systems boundaries – or what the unit of analysis should be – and what to include and exclude in any attempt at performance, efficiency, or productivity measurement.

MEASURING OUTPUTS

The HMT–ONS efficiency and productivity debate in the United Kingdom is part of a much larger discussion about the problematic issues of measuring the outputs of public services and activities. It arises in this debate because efficiency or productivity measurements are both about the ration of inputs to outputs. The measurement of inputs is (relatively) unproblematic, although even here there can be problems as we have seen. But the measurement of outputs is proving much more problematic.

In 2003, the ONS asked Tony Atkinson to conduct a review of measurement of government output for National Accounts. This UK initiative was not the only one in this field, but it does seem to be the most developed. Australia,

Italy, the Netherlands, and New Zealand have been undertaking similar exercises, with Finland, Germany, and Norway following. Interestingly, although the United States has extensive experimental experience of measuring public sector productivity it has not incorporated any of this into its national accounts (Atkinson 2003).

The problem the Atkinson Review were tackling was that traditionally in both the UN's *Systems of National Accounts* and other standards, the measurement of public sector outputs is imputed from selected inputs – so input and output ratios remain relatively constant – that is, there can be no real measure of productivity growth in the public sector. This so-called output–input rule is obviously misleading and Review was charged with developing a more direct way of measuring outputs, and hence productivity changed. This work has since transferred to the ONS, and as their reports illustrate there is a large technical and resources commitment required to address these issues.[2]

OUTCOMES AND ATTRIBUTION PROBLEMS

Another major technical problem is the so-called "attribution problem." This often surfaces in the assertion that "outcomes are difficult to measure." There is a semantic ambiguity in this assertion – if by "outcomes" is meant the outcomes that have been directly caused by the outputs of public agencies, it is of course correct. If, however, by "outcomes" is meant simply changes to the circumstances of the target group – for example, in their health, wealth, or happiness – then the assertion is wrong. Measuring such changes for some (many?) aspects of public activity is relatively easy and has been the mainstay of much socio-economic statistical activity in advanced countries for decades – measuring the economy, health, crime rates, etc. What is very difficult is reliably and validly attributing changes in these metrics to public agency activities. There are simply so many external, confounding, variables that mess up the picture.

The task is not entirely impossible however. Firstly, where there are multiple, similar, agencies at work, then comparisons between their outcomes are possible and – if they are all working in similar environments or the variation in their environments can be controlled for statistically – the variations in outcomes can possibly be attributed to variations in outputs.

The problem is further compounded however where outcomes are not easily observable – for example where an agencies' objective is "national security" or "better relationships with other countries," typical objectives

---

[2] See www.ons.gov.uk/about-statistics/ukcemga for numerous reports on this work.

for security or diplomatic agencies. In these cases neither actual changes to the desired states, nor the contribution of public action is easily measurable (Wilson 1989). Some such agencies have recently begun to try and benchmark their services, but progress has been slow and problematic.

NONLINEAR SYSTEMS AND COMPLEXITY

One complication which does produce very problematic performance measurement issues is the degree to which systems on the public sector are "nonlinear" – that is instead of a linear relationship between, say, inputs and outcomes there may exist circumstances where there is no linear relationship but instead the type of recursive feedback loops studied by chaos and complexity theorists can cause either exponential increases or decreases in results – the so-called butterfly effect – because of small initial differences in conditions (Byrne 1998; Haynes 2003). Such effects, if unrecognized, could easily lead to "false positives" – for example, attributing substantial improvements in outcome results, large-scale changes to inputs when actually some minor changes to processes are responsible. Full consideration of these issues is beyond the scope of this book, but complexity science clearly raises important issues that have to be eventually integrated into our understanding of public performance. Some further discussion appears toward the end of the next chapter.

Problems of Politics, Values, and Objectives

The final area of problems to raise, but only briefly as these will be dealt with much more extensively in subsequent chapters, are the thorny issues of politics, values, and (often conflicting or conflicted) public sector objectives. Where public agencies have multiple, fuzzy, or conflicting goals – which is often the case – deciding what to measure becomes a major problem. This problem highlights the contention that performance measurement in the public sector is not merely a technical question but inevitably raises questions of values and political choices (Moore 1995; Bozeman 2007; Talbot 2008b). Moreover, public value and public values like equity, democracy, participation, citizenship, democracy, etc. are both difficult to agree upon and also difficult to measure.

These issues will be explored in the following chapters – especially in Chapter 6, but also in Chapters 4, 5, 8, 9, and 10.

Conclusions

This chapter may have seemed excessively negative in so far as it has tried to point to as many of the objections, problems, lacunae, and difficulties associated with the modern performance movement in public services as possible and it has probably not captured them all.

Some of the problematic issues here appear technically solvable. Some seem tractable to a combination of technical and political solutions and others are amenable to theoretical solutions, although these latter are probably the most challenging.

Some of the definitional issues discussed early in the chapter are technically solvable in the sense that a consensus could be reached among academics, policy-makers, and practitioners about the definitions of many terms and concepts without too much difficulty. Many such terms and concepts are not necessarily theory or value-laden and what prevents consensus is not disputes over theoretical issues or values, but mainly practical issues. Similar problematic definitional issues have been largely managed and resolved in areas like economics, finance, and accounting – although there are of course still disputes and those who would maintain that even relatively non-contentious terms and concepts are really value or theory laden.

Many of these issues are not merely tractable through purely technical means however. Where there have been relatively settled definitions these have usually come about through a long process of both technical improvement and consensus building that embraces not just expert opinion but also policy-makers and others, although curiously these processes have largely been analyzed by critics rather than supporters (e.g., Eberstadt 1995; Porter 1995; Desrosieres 1998). (Nevertheless, even some critics of the overall trend to quantification in economic, social, and other areas have now come to recognize its value (Oakley 2000).) Setting aside these critiques for the moment, it is not impossible to envisage a long-term politico-technical process whereby the measuring of, for example, the outputs of public services might not obtain the same sort of relative consensus that surrounds the measurement of the financial resources that go into producing them, or some of their outcomes in economic and social statistics.

The theoretical challenges facing performance measurement are rather large. As will be seen in Chapter 7, the study of organizational performance (private and public) fairly early hit a major theoretical roadblock in trying to define the "organizational effectiveness" construct and many concluded that is was not objectively definable, and therefore not possible to measure. This is hugely compounded by the lack of theoretical consensus, and indeed consilience, that were alluded to in the Introduction (Chapter 1) and are explored more fully in Chapter 3. While there have been some attempts to reconcile conflicting approaches to performance – in both the private and public sectors – they do not yet appear to have convincingly overcome these problems. Exploring how that might be achieved is in many ways the subject of the remainder of this book.

3 Theories and Performance

In a book about "theories of performance" it may seem odd to have a specific chapter about "theories and performance." Is that not what the whole book is about? Well, yes and no. While issues of theory appear throughout the book this chapter is specifically about Theory with a capital "T," or at least what most people think of as "Theory." Theory has become an extremely elastic term that can apply to everything from grand theory about the nature of the universe (e.g., relativity) or human social organization (e.g., Marx's class-conflict theory of history) down to fairly micro-level "theories" about physical or social phenomena. This chapter looks more at the former than the latter, although there is some micro-theorizing too.

So from this grand Theory perspective, the chapter looks at so-called disciplinary perspectives – exploring what have become jokingly known as the "ologies" in British (and western?) popular culture – anthropology, economics, political science, social psychology, and sociology – have to say, or might say, about performance. It also looks at some specific theories that have been highly influential in recent years in social sciences.

But first, it considers some fairly fundamental – even foundational – issues that have been the subject of fierce controversy across the social sciences – what do we mean by "science" in this context?

Most social scientists, whatever their discipline, receive at least some exposure to issues in what has become know as the "philosophy of science" by the time they get their doctorate. Yet it is fair to say that this exposure results in precious little adoption of any explicit "way of knowing" in the writings of many social scientists, and this applies doubly so to the more applied fields like management, public administration, and public management.

To be fair, there are some parts of relevant disciplines where skirmishes in the so-called paradigm wars have been waged, in some cases for decades. In organization theory (Burrell and Morgan 1979) and evaluation studies (Guba and Lincoln 1989; Guba 1990; Lincoln and Guba 1998) they have been rife, although even here not all pervasive. But in much of the management literature they have been largely absent, as they have in public administration and public management. In some of the broader "disciplines" they have however become endemic – especially in political science, sociology, and economics.

Why is this important? In studying performance anyone explicitly or implicitly adopts a stance on important ontological, epistemological, and methodological issues that have riven various parts of the social sciences for years. They ought to be impossible to avoid, yet most writers on performance have successfully done so – at least as far as adopting any explicit stance is concerned.

The chapter will examine several possible and actual theoretical approaches to performance, starting with some of the possible "philosophy of science" issues and progressing toward more concrete, applied, theories, with a detour through so-called disciplinary perspectives (e.g., anthropology, economics, political science, etc.).

Before we start it is however worth pausing to consider what is meant by "social sciences," a term we have used up to now as if it were unproblematic. There are however several issues with the term as generally used. The first is that what is really meant by "social sciences" is actually "human social sciences" – in other words how humans form and behave in social groups (Wilson 1975). There are of course several other species on Earth that engage in elaborate social organizations, but these are generally excluded from what we call "social sciences" – indeed some social scientists take great exception to any suggestion that studies of animal or insect social behavior might have any relevance whatsoever for human social organization (Wilson 1998).

Why might this be important? There are two ways in which studies of nonhuman species forms of social organization might be helpful in understanding the performance of human social organizations. The first is where such studies might shed light on the evolutionary origins of human forms of organization. This approach generates heated opposition from many traditional social scientists who hold to what has been called the "standard social science model" or SSCM (Barkow et al. 1995) or more pithily the "blank slate" approach (Pinker 2002). From this "blank slate" viewpoint humans are radically different from, and represent an evolutionary break with, predecessor species; and studies of their social behavior can tell us nothing about our behavior – which is entirely shaped – or socially constructed – by environmental and experiential factors (nurture) and has no basis in our evolutionary heritage (nature). As we will see later in this chapter when we discuss neoclassical economics perspectives and social constructionist approaches, this evolutionary perspective is important because it confounds important aspects of both approaches.

The second way in which nonhuman studies of social organization might be important is by comparison. Understanding different ways of organizing, based on different assumptions and mechanisms, may help to highlight what is important or not in human social and economic organization (e.g., Pentland 2008). This approach does not require the acceptance of any necessary evolutionary connection between human and nonhuman social organization, but it is generally rejected by many social scientists along with the previous, evolutionary, perspective also on the grounds of human uniqueness. To be fair, in some economics-based explanations of things like cooperative behavior, animal, and even machine/computational correlates have been used (Axelrod 1990; 1997) but these are the exception to the SSCM rule.

This seeming diversion into evolutionary explanations is important because, as we will see, many approaches to the performance of humans, collectively and individually, are rooted in conceptions of human nature – whether the "rational utility maximizer" of economics or the "blank slate" of social constructionism. Thus discussions of what it means to be "human" – what are our motivations, decision mechanisms, etc. – are inescapable, we would contend, in discussing how and why human organizations, including public ones, perform.

Ways of Knowing: Positivism, Constructionism, and Realism

We turn now to some basic, philosophy of science, issues about how performance can be theorized. These issues are rarely discussed in literature specifically on performance, and there is insufficient space here to do justice to the full range of the "science wars" that have raged in the past few decades over these more general issues.

Arguably, for most of the twentieth century science generally, and social science, were dominated by what is generally known as "positivism" as the approach to ontology, epistemology, and methods. It is probably worth pausing just to explain these terms.

Ontology refers to the nature of reality – for example, does reality, and (some) of the categories we ascribe to it, exist independently of our observation and classification of it? So, for example, does a public organization have a "real" performance that is "out there," independent of any cognition or perspective on it, or is it merely a "construct" dependent on the observer?

Epistemology refers to how we can know about that reality – that is, even if there is a "real" reality really out there, how does it get represented in human cognition and science? Can we only know reality subjectively, that is filtered through our own experiences and preconceptions, or can it be known "objectively" or "scientifically"? So, for a public organization – even if we accept that it does have a real, actual, level of "performance" how can we know what that is without subjective factors interfering with our understanding?

Finally, methods refer to the technical issues of how we attempt to observe phenomena (although "method" is also sometimes confusingly (mis)used as "methodology" to refer to the whole bundle of ontology, epistemology, and methods). So, for example, the sort of technical problems encountered in measuring the performance of public systems, programs, policies, and organizations discussed in the previous chapter fall into this category.

The three great strands in thinking about these issues are the already mentioned (a) positivism and its antithesis (b) constructionism (also referred to as relativism) and the relatively "new kid on the block" as the approach is called, and (c) "realism" (or critical realism), which seeks to transcend, but draws upon the best of, both positivism and constructionism.

The positivist tradition – which has probably been dominant in much of the analysis of performance – is roughly characterized as follows, using public organizations as an example. Public organizations do have real, actual, levels of performance that exist independently of any observation. As public organizations are complex systems, the best way to "know" about this performance is to disaggregate individual elements and study them, and the relations between them, through carefully defined constructs, operationalized into specific measures, against which data are collected and analyzed through well-designed statistical analysis. The emphasis is heavily on reductionist and quantitative methods. Much of the early "organizational effectiveness" literature of the 1960s and 1970s was very much of this nature (see Chapter 7) and it continues to be influential.

The constructionist tradition is a reaction to the perceived problems of positivism in general, and in relation to human systems in particular. Constructionists argue that humans are incapable of understanding "reality" other than subjectively and that "science" is merely a set of culturally specific assumptions that can have no claims in truth or accuracy, because all observation and categorizations are inevitably subjective. Purist constructionists go so far as to claim that "reality" does not exist independently of observation. Less fundamentalist exponents accept that there are real material things going on "out there" but that our understanding of them is inherently subjective and socially constructed.

Thus for public organizations for social constructionists there is no "real" performance to be studied, merely different sets of actors, understandings, and constructions of performance, all of which are equally valid to the extent that none can claim any privileged correspondence to any independently "real" performance. The emphasis in study is therefore qualitative and interpretive – the focus is on understanding what various groups and individuals think about performance and how it is "socially constructed" by them.

Social constructionism (or constructionism, deconstruction, relativism, postmodernism, and a variety of other labels which amount to largely the same thing) has been a strongly emergent trend in social sciences and has gained some purchase in the field of public policy and public management (e.g., Rein and Schon 1992; Fischer and Forester 1993; Hollinger 1994; Fox and Miller 1995; Hummel 2007; Miller and Fox 2007).

As we will see later (Chapter 4) public sector services and organizations are particularly subject to multiple views, stakeholders, and controversy about what they should be achieving and, as a consequence, how best to measure whether or not they are achieving often fuzzy or confused objectives (see also Chapter 1). It is easy in this context to apply to notions of social constructionism to the idea of performance – that is, to conclude that there is no such thing as "real" performance, only multiple, equally valid, perceptions of performance. Thus two scholars of performance use a phrase attributed to Albert Einstein: "reality is merely an illusion, albeit a persistent one" in their introduction to a symposium on performance measurement (van Dooren and Van de Walle 2008). They go on to juxtapose a "Popperian tradition that assumes an objective truth independent of the knowing subject" versus "the Kuhnian tradition [that] assumes that truth in science is a socially constructed paradigm."

The Einstein quote is widely attributed to him, but never sourced and no reading of his work could possibly turn him into a social constructionist. However, this use of a physical science "authority" is typical of social constructionist writing and one that was soundly exposed as superficial and unfounded in a famous hoax article published in *Social Text* (Sokal and Bricmont 1998).[1] Nor is Thomas Kuhn a social constructionist in the sense used by van Dooren and Van de Walle. In his classic work Kuhn asserts that while the historian of science may be tempted to think that "when paradigms change, the world itself changes with them," this is not the case. He goes on to say that "of course, nothing of quite that sort does occur...outside the laboratory everyday affairs usually continue as before" (Kuhn 1970, p. 111). For Kuhn reality existed independently of our knowledge of it, only our understanding changed with a "paradigm shift"[2] and only in that sense is science "socially constructed." In other words his was an investigation of epistemology, not ontology and therefore closer in spirit to the realist tradition than that of social constructionism.

---

[1] "In 1996, an article entitled 'Transgressing the Boundaries: Toward a Transformative Hermeneutics of Quantum Gravity' was published in the cultural studies journal *Social Text*. Packed with recherché quotations from 'postmodern' literary theorists and sociologists of science, and bristling with imposing theorems of mathematical physics, the article addressed the cultural and political implications of the theory of quantum gravity. Later, to the embarrassment of the editors, the author revealed that the essay was a hoax, interweaving absurd pronouncements from eminent intellectuals about mathematics and physics with laudatory – but fatuous – prose" (Sokal and Bricmont 1998, quoted from book introduction).

[2] Incidentally Kuhn himself later regretted the use of the term "paradigm" which he thought had taken on a "quasi-mystical" character (Kuhn 1977).

The realist tradition broadly attempts to straddle these irreconcilable positions. Ontologically it accepts that there is indeed a real reality "out there," independent of our observation of it. To that extent it agrees with positivist assumptions. However, in relation especially to human organizations, it also sees that there are major epistemological problems in understanding how we can "know" this reality that are not resolved by the reductionist and quantitative methods of positivism. Indeed these methods can sometimes be positively misleading – especially when examining very complex human systems that in reality cannot be disaggregated without losing crucial data and relationships. Realists generally advocate "mixed methods" as a solution – using multiple quantitative and qualitative approaches to try to get closer to an understanding of these complex phenomena.

A classic example of this clash of views is explored by Ann Oakley, a feminist social scientist, in her book *Experiments in Knowing* (Oakley 2000). She recounts how for years she railed against "masculine" positivist approaches and advocated more "feminized," subjective, constructionist, qualitative, social science approaches to studying women's oppression. However, she gradually realized that she (and others) frequently, if unwittingly, relied on "positivist" social science when citing statistics about discrimination against women and other forms of oppression in order to justify the research agendas and policies she and they advocated. Her book is an attempt to reconcile these contradictions and to recognize that actually both approaches have something to offer in understanding human institutions.

A particular subset of these disputes is the issue of what E. O. Wilson (1998) has called "consilience" – that is, the underlying unity of science – versus those who see no necessary links between different "islands" of knowledge (Cartwright 1999). In the latter view, for example, the link between conceptions of human nature and the dynamics of organizations would probably be denied. Thus, economists who make what they consider simplifying axiomatic assumptions about "rational utility maximization" by individuals would deny that there is any necessary connection between these assumptions and actual human beings, human psychology, etc. These latter positions have been reinforced by the institutional divisions within the social sciences between the various "disciplines" (which will be considered in the next section), although lately there has been some growth of "interdisciplinary" social science that at least seeks to bring differing explanations into contact with one another.

Wilson and others (including the present author) would contend that it is not only possible but also necessary to construct explanations and theories that are consistent with other aspects of science, including other social sciences. Thus, for example, it is not possible for economists to reasonably assert that all humans, everywhere, act as "rational utility maximizers" when other social sciences provide ample evidence of nonrational or altruistic behavior. That is, not to underestimate the problems associated with such "consilient" social science, but it is to say that it cannot be sensibly ignored either. Even in economics this has become the case, with the recent emergence, for example, of what is called "behavioral economics" (Thaler and Sunstein 2008) that explores some of the nonrational ways in which humans make economic and other decisions.

How does all this impact on research into and theorizing about public sector performance? Relatively few in the field adopt an explicit philosophy of science stance; a rather *laissez-faire* attitude toward this subject usually prevails (as was argued in Chapter 1, and see Pollitt 2010). Nevertheless, the "philosophy of science" of some experts in the field has been explicitly spelt out – most notably by those adopting a social constructionist position (e.g., Fox and Miller 1995; Herman and Renz 1997; Miller and Fox 2007; Van de Walle and Roberts 2008; van Dooren and Van de Walle 2008). At the other end of the spectrum, most researchers using more positivist methods tend to simply take their stance for granted without (usually) stating it explicitly (e.g., Lynn et al. 2001; O'Toole 2003; Boyne et al. 2006; Boyne and Chen 2007). In the middle lies a great swathe of researchers who by implication seem to adopt a realist stance, rarely explicitly, or at any rate they certainly do not appear to adopt a strong or consistent positivist or social constructionist approach (but sometimes borrow from both).

An example of where this impacts on performance theory and research is a fairly recent exchange in the journal *Administration and Society* where one writer, from a "weak" social constructionist position (Luton 2007), launched an assault on the problematic nature (in his view) of the relationship between objective reality and our possibility of "knowing" what it is. Luton takes an agnostic position on whether objective reality exists or not (hence a "weak" position) but draws heavily on social constructionist arguments, especially Fox and Miller (1995; Miller and Fox 2007). In particular he cites Miller and Fox (2007, p. 37) arguing that

the proposition that performance can be reduced to variables that can be measured, and that outcomes, results, effects and even nonevents can be attributed to programs and policies, amounts to a fanciful faith in what social science methodology can accomplish.

In response to Luton's attack on "empiricism" (by which he clearly means positivism and probably realism too) some well-known empiricists responded with a vigorous defense of empirical approaches, while recognizing the problematic nature of construct development, operationalization of these constructs, developing robust methods, and careful analysis of data (Meier and O'Toole 2007; Lynn et al. 2008). (A rejoinder from Luton seems to move his position even further into the social constructionist camp (Luton 2008).)

Ways of Knowing: Disciplinary Perspectives

Many of the issues discussed in the previous section cut across traditional academic disciplines in the social sciences – it is possible to find advocates of all three of the (simplified) philosophical positions in every branch of human social sciences. This in itself raises serious questions about what is meant by "disciplines" as discrete modes of enquiry into human behavior, because one of the two main planks of the defense for disciplinary boundaries is that each discipline has a distinctive set of theories and methods that are incommensurable with the other disciplines. The other defense is that each studies a distinctive aspect of human behavior, which is also increasingly – and probably always was – untrue. We will examine what each discipline focuses on generally, as well as their predominant theoretical and methodological assumptions, and how this might apply to performance of public services and organizations.

There is an important caveat however, because what follows is based upon the dominant or conventional view of what each discipline constitutes while we should recognize that probably as much variation and controversy now exists within each discipline as there does between them (Easton and Schelling 1991).

For the sake of simplicity we take the five basic disciplines in social sciences as being anthropology, economics, political science, social psychology, and sociology (based on Steuer 2003). As Steuer points out, there are several "contributing disciplines" and several "sub" or "combinations" of disciplines, but these five will suffice for our purposes here.

ANTHROPOLOGY

Anthropology began life as the study of "man" – that is, the human species, as distinct from zoology that looked at the rest of the animal world. It was interested in the evolutionary origins of humans as a species and what our ancestors looked and behaved like. It had a strong interest in "primitive" societies as these were seen as further back on the evolutionary "ladder" that led to modern civilizations.

A continuing, related, branch of knowledge to this early anthropology is modern ethology – the study of animal behavior and especially its comparison with human behavior.

However, mainstream modern anthropology – heavily influenced by thinkers like Franz Boas, Ruth Benedict, and Margaret Mead – firmly rejected this evolutionary perspective and posited instead a radical break between humans and animals, and focused instead on detailed studies on all sorts of societies with human variation and diversity as the core belief. This cultural social anthropology focused on human cultures and their apparently infinite variety and infinite malleability. Its methods were the small, immersive, case studies in which anthropologists went into the "field" and observed in minute detail how other (still usually "less-developed") societies worked.

Their methods were (are) more about description than explanation. The emphasis is on getting "inside" societies or more often small communities (including organizational communities) to try to understand the rituals, symbols, myths, stories, cultural artifacts, mores, and language of these specific groups. All such groups are generally considered to be unique – and here mainstream anthropology is heavily influenced by the "blank slate" view of human nature and relativist, social constructionist, views. They strongly deny that there are any "human universals" or regularities in human behavior, which is entirely shaped by the diverse (and diverging) human cultures (Brown 1991).

Anthropological approaches have long been deployed in the study of organizations, but they became especially fashionable in the 1980s and the 1990s with the "cultural turn" in organizational studies and especially more popular writing about quality and culture in organizations and how this relates to excellence (see Chapter 7). If organizational cultures are seen as key determinants of success, then trying to get "inside" such cultures using anthropological approaches – detailed, qualitative, ethnographic, case studies – would seem an obvious approach.

The perceived success of Japanese companies, and their very different cultures, were a particular focus, and stimulus, to this focus on culture and again here to some extent anthropological approaches were useful in trying to get "inside" this apparently different culture at both the country (Pascale and Athos 1981) and company levels (Like 2004). These studies of Japanese organizations also owed much to the earlier pioneering work of leading anthropologist Ruth Benedict and her classic study of Japanese culture, *The Chrysanthemum and the Sword: Patterns of Japanese Culture* (Benedict 2006 [1946]).

Many of the most well-known "organizational culture" studies of this period drew on anthropological techniques (Peters and Waterman 1982; Deal and Kennedy 1988; Collins and Porras 1994; Hickson and Pugh 1995; Collins 2001). However it would be wrong to say these sorts of studies were "anthropological"; rather they merely drew upon anthropological research techniques without adopting the underlying philosophical assumptions about the impossibility of deriving "law like" regularities from these detailed and qualitative comparisons. On the contrary, the whole purpose of these studies was to try and form universal conclusions about what works in developing organizational excellence – that is, improving the performance of organizations.

There have been many other studies in the general organizational literature that focus on culture, such as the huge comparative studies by Hofstede (2003) and others (Hampden-Turner and Trompenaars 1993) – for a summary see Morgan (1986, chapter 5).

Some modern anthropologists – contrary to the mainstream – have sought to establish patterns and regularities in human societies and understand "human universals" (Brown 1991). Notable here is the work of Alan Page Fiske and the "relational models" theory which we will examine further in Chapters 6 and 9 (Fiske 1991; Haslam 2004). This links to the question of public values that is considered further in Chapter 6. Public values help to shape what is considered "good" or "bad" performance in public organizations and are thus essential to the understanding of such performance, and approaches derived from anthropology – including relational models theory and cultural theory (see Chapter 6) – address these issues.

ECONOMICS

Economics, probably more than the other disciplines discussed here, has always been concerned with the "performance," broadly defined, of public as well as private institutions and has consciously sought to contribute to knowledge of the public domain. Adam Smith defined political economy (as it was known then) as being about both private wealth and the "wealth of nations" and supplying "the state or commonwealth with a revenue sufficient for the public service" (Smith 2003 [1776]).

Classical economics or "political economy" in the eighteenth and nineteenth centuries was primarily concerned with searching for theories of value – perhaps most famously expressed in Marx's attempt to create a "labor theory of value." These explorations concentrated on what went into forming and creating "value" and "wealth" – was it labor, physical resources, rent, etc.? Classical political economists like Marx, Smith, Hume, Mill, and Rocardo were closer to practicing a unitary social science than modern disciplinary "economics," insofar as they did not make the modern distinctions between politics, economics, sociology, and anthropology but contained elements of all these disciplines in their thinking. They were as interested in class as they were in cash, in institutions as much as in individuals.

Starting in the mid-nineteenth century and coming to full fruition in the early part of the twentieth century, "neoclassical" economics moved away from these concerns and methodological approaches and developed a strong focus on individuals (and firms and households treated as if they were individuals) – what has been called "methodological individualism." It also shifted from concerns with value to concern for "utility" or later "preferences" of individuals and how satisfactions of these are maximized.

Finally, it adopted strong assumptions about rationality. Hence we get to the oft-used phrase at the heart of modern economics: the "rational utility maximizer."

During the twentieth century this neoclassical economics also began to be applied to the public domain, with the growth of "public choice" economics – which "rational utility maximization" by individuals to the behavior of citizens (as voters, taxpayers, and consumers of public services), politicians, bureaucrats, etc. (Lane 1987; McLean 1987).

Other economic ideas – such as transaction costs and institutional economics – combined with public choice have been widely regarded as fundamental to the "New Public Management" (NPM) reform movement of the past three decades (Pollitt 1990; Hood 1991) and specifically to the introduction of "performance measurement and management" into the public sector (Pollitt and Bouckaert 2000; OECD 2005).

Modern neoclassical economics has not been without its critics. The main challenges come to the fundamental axioms underpinning this approach that have been disputed both theoretically and empirically (indeed the critics would also argue that the neoclassicists have more often then not failed to link theory and evidence).

The first attack is on the issue of rationality. The first challenge is that of limited human capacity for information processing, and limited access to the necessary information, means that the best that can be achieved is "satisficing" through "bounded rationality" rather than optimization through pure rationality (Simon 1983). Building upon Simon's insights about "bounded rationality," more recent scholars have developed the idea of "heuristics" or "rules of thumb" that humans seem to adopt in problem solving (Gigerenzer 2000).

An even more fundamental challenge is to suggest that (some) human decisions are not necessarily based on rationality at all – whether pure, bounded, or heuristic – but have their origins in other decision mechanisms entirely. Behavioral economics, which has recently come to prominence, starts from the empirical observation that real humans in real choice situations seem to often use mechanisms that are seemingly irrational (Ariely 2008; Thaler and Sunstein 2008). Irrational does not necessarily imply inconsistent, as the title of Ariley's book – *Predictably Irrational* – suggests. Rather the sources of "irrational" regularities in decisions can be traced to various psychological, social psychological, and emotional mechanisms.

The final challenge to neoclassical economic assumptions to be noted here concerns human motivation. Evolutionary theorists have posited the idea that human social organization can lead, through kin and group selection processes, to the emergence of genuine inherited altruistic behavioral traits that confound the "utility maximization" part of the rational utility maximizer axioms (Sober and Wilson 1998).

As already indicated, economic ideas are widely believed to have contributed implicitly or explicitly to the trend toward performance measurement, reporting, and management in the public sector. The widely held view is that if the right "incentive" structures between "principals" (the government) and "agents" (public service organizations and workers) can be put in place, and agents performance against these incentives properly measured, substantial improvements can be obtained.

Interestingly, many of the critics of "targetry" and performance policies utilize similar economic ideas to try to show how this may produce dysfunctional or counterproductive results. Assuming that the "agents" are rational utility maximizers, these critics seek to demonstrate how they will "game" the system, and even cheat, to gain the maximum reward for the minimum effort.

The empirical evidence about how organizations and individuals respond to performance measurement and management is rather more inconsistent than either the supporters of critics would usually admit, as we will examine in Chapter 9. Some of this inconsistency can best be explained not by the axioms of neoclassical economics and public choice, but by some of the critiques outlined briefly above.

Before leaving the subject of the economics discipline as applied to public services performance it is important to note one other major problematic issue – that of measuring outputs (and outcomes) – as already discussed in Chapter 2. The difficulty of measuring accurately the quantity and quality of public services output, poses serious problems for economic analysis. This has long been an issue in welfare economics and its offshoot cost–benefit analysis but has now also become a problematic issue for the performance movement.

POLITICAL SCIENCE

Perhaps the oldest of the social science disciplines, insofar as the study of politics has been around for at least 2,500 years and probably as long as states and governments have existed. The discipline goes under numerous labels that sometimes represent a slightly different focus and sometimes a different philosophical approach. These include politics, government, political theory, political philosophy, political behavior, as well as various subdisciplines like public affairs, public administration, policy analysis, international relations, etc.

Political science (the umbrella term that we will use here) is generally accepted as the study of power in and around the government. By power is usually meant the ability to coerce or cajole compliance from citizens of a specific community or to mobilize support for specific collective action decisions. But while the focus has usually been on "government" and the "state," political ideas have been expanded to include politics within organizations, society, communities, civic organizations, and even personal life in the feminist slogan "the personal is political." Political science and especially political theory is also interested in how various political positions and forces coalesce into ideologies like socialism, communism, liberalism, conservatism, and fascism.

As with the other social sciences, political science has experienced its share of the "paradigm" wars. In recent years, and especially in the United States, economic ideas have gained ground in political science and "rational actor" models have been widely applied to studies of legislatures, bureaucracies, voting patterns, parties, interest groups, and much more. These have been strongly resisted by some who advocate more pluralistic models of enquiry (Self 1993; Stretton and Orchard 1994). But approaches have included, alongside rational or public choice and pluralism, elite theories, Marxism, neo-pluralism, feminist theories, "green" theories, post-structuralism, governance, neo-institutionalism, etc. (Dunleavy and O'Leary 1987; Hay et al. 2006).

Historically, politics (rather like sociology – see below) was very concerned with structures – indeed the term "institution" in early political studies referred to the main pillars of the modern state such as executive government, the bureaucracy, the legislature, the courts, political parties, etc. (Finer 1946). European political science has remained influenced by this more traditional approach and by the influence of legal and constitutional studies. This traditional institutional approach is important to understanding the institutional context of performance policies as explored in Chapter 4 on performance regimes. Ideas about types of power, such as resource-dependence theory, are also important in understanding the types of performance interventions used that can be deployed by governments (Chapter 5).

Political theory and political philosophy, which overlap to a great degree, have both explored the normative and conceptual bases of various political systems including concepts like liberty, equality, fraternity, authority, and legitimacy. These have also, historically, been linked to debates about human nature – as, for example, in the conflict between Hobbes and Rousseau's conceptions of humans as either basically destructive or noble – and how humans can and do respond to various forms of social and governmental structures. These basic debates still take place around ideas like rational-actor/public choice, which assume a model of human nature – rational utility maximizers – that has large implications for human action. Assumptions about human nature clearly relate to explorations of performance – individual, organizational, and policy – in the public domain (see especially Chapter 10).

It is interesting how little of the study of the "performance movement" has actually been informed by the wider study of political institutions (Radin 2006*b*) in contrast to the influence of rational actor/public choice approaches, for example. While there are exceptions, where performance policies have been placed in their politico-institutional context (Pollitt and Bouckaert 2004) mostly these issues have been ignored (again, see Chapter 4 for further exploration of this issue).

SOCIAL PSYCHOLOGY

Social psychology – at least as a formal discipline – is probably the newest kid on the block among the five disciplines considered here, only becoming a recognized subject in the 1930s. An offshoot of psychology and sociology, it continues to bear the imprint of both. As the name suggests, social psychology is interested in the psychology of interpersonal relations in a variety of social settings, including communities, work organizations, and other groups. While some social psychology has been marked by methodological individualism similar to economics – especially but not entirely the laboratory-experimental tradition that flourished from the 1930s through until the 1960s – others have focused more on the group or social setting as the unit of analysis.

At the more individualistic end of this spectrum lie works like that of Festinger on "cognitive dissonance" – why individuals seek to minimize or avoid ambiguous or contradictory data and settings by simply refusing to recognize some cognitive inputs. In a similar vein, Kelley's work on "attribution theory" considers how humans make inferences about why things around them happen the way they do. And perhaps the most famous set of social psychology experiments, Milgram sought to establish to what extent, and why, humans demonstrate "obedience to authority" even when acting in such a way violates their own espoused standards (Milgram 1997).

Milgram's experiments also highlight another feature of social psychology – an ongoing interest in actual social problems. Milgram's work was a direct result of concern with trying to understand why so many German (and other) people went along with the Nazi atrocities during World War II. Similarly, the most well-known work of another founding figure in social psychology – Kurt Lewin – arose from concern with community and interracial tensions in the United States following the disruptive effects of World War II on US communities. Lewin's work on change – through "action research" that led to key concepts in organizational/social settings like freezing unfreezing in; force-field analysis; and action research itself; all sprang from the engagement orientation characteristic of much social psychology, especially in the post-World War II period.

Industrial or organizational psychology – sometimes referred to as I/O psychology (Latham 2007) – has also contributed to issues relevant to performance over a very long period, from the 1960s up to the present. I/O psychology stands on the cusp between individual and group, organizational and social psychology although a great deal of it has tended to focus on the individual as the unit of analysis – especially in the area of goals and motivation theory (Locke et al. 1981; Latham 2007). While this literature seems to demonstrate clear positive links between goals and performance at the individual level (Locke et al. 1981), one of the principle researchers in the field cautions that "it is one thing to build models of individual motivation that will increase team effectiveness; it is another to anthropomorphize groups, organizations, and nation states for the sake of economy in theory building" (Latham 2007, p. 258). However, this particular leading authority and the I/O field generally shows little interest in actually building theories at the "group, organization, or national" levels or of examining how different levels of analysis might interact.

Other direct offshoots of social psychology applied to organizational settings include work on small-group dynamics; human factors in organizations and the "human relations" school of organizational analysis; and especially organizational development (OD) which flourished in the period between the 1960s and 1980s, but continues to be a significant feature of organizational studies and action, although more often going under the title of change management these days. All of these approaches were very much focused on what was then called "organizational effectiveness" (OE) (Burke 1987, p. 132). This whole field of OD and associated organizationally focused studies, although exclusively drawn from social psychological perspectives, is a critical part of the research agenda to try to understand what makes some organizations perform better than others, at the macro-organizational, meso-group, and micro-individual levels.

Before leaving social psychology it is worth noting that another field of study is closely related, that of how humans and other animals have evolved social relations between them – fields of study such as ethology, sociobiology, and evolutionary psychology. We will return to this at the end of this chapter and in Chapters 9 and 10.

SOCIOLOGY

In many definitions sociology is said to be the "scientific study of society," but conflicts within the discipline mean some would call into question the "scientific" part of this statement (anti-positivists) while others would even question the use of the term "society" as reification and/or a socially constructed notion. There is, to borrow a phrase, "no such thing as society."

As a relatively "new kid on the block" – the term was coined by Comte in 1843 but only became widely used in the twentieth century – sociology is variously seen as in essence either an unruly derivative of the other social science disciplines or, alternatively, the "queen of social sciences" because it (allegedly) synthesizes and stands above the other, narrower disciplines.

Most sociologists would agree that the "founders"[3] of their discipline were Marx, Durkheim, and Weber – but even this is problematic as these three authors had very different approaches to the study of society. One possible area of commonality is that they all focused on social structures – classes, institutions, and organizations. This interest in social structures continues and has clear affinity with some anthropological studies. But whereas early anthropology tended to focus on the "primitive" societies early sociology was most interested in processes like industrialization, the creation of the capitalist system, the emergence of large-scale bureaucracy, and the attendant changes to social structures and functions.

Within this concern for structures also lies the problematic issue of "agency" – how far are individuals shaped by, rather than shaping of, social structures and how do we account for change? Since Marx's famous remark that "man makes history, but not in circumstances of his own making" (Marx 2009 [1852]) this has been an ongoing debate among sociologists with the most famous attempt at theorizing this being Gidden's notion of "structuration." These debates clearly have implications for how individuals (or organizations) might shape, or be shaped by, performance policies and regimes (see Chapters 4, 5, and 9).

Sociology has proved the most accommodating social science "home" for social-constructionist, ontological, and epistemological views that were prefigured in the symbolic-interactionism of Talcott-Parsons. Indeed social-constructionist ideas are in large part a reaction to concerns of earlier sociologists with "objective" structures in society (Berger and Luckmann 1975).

Sociological approaches have been influential in the study of organizations and in one highly prominent work Burrell and Morgan (1979) attempted to organize the highly diverse schools of thought in sociology into a matrix which made some sense of these different approaches to organizations

They suggest two dimensions of contending views: the first is between a focus on change, how it occurs and why it happens versus a focus on stability and regulation (control) within societies and organizations. The second

---

[3] Although it is questionable whether any of these three would actually call themselves "sociologists."

dimension is that between the "subjective," by which they mean something close to social constructionism, versus the "objective," by which they mean positivist or realist ideas about social institutions and structures.

The resulting matrix produces four contrasting sociological "paradigms" (their word) or "meta-theoretical" stances:

- Subjective change: It produces "radical humanism," which critiques the ideological "status quo" and analyses "false consciousness" in the hopes of producing radical change.

- Subjective regulation: It produces what they call the "interpretive" paradigm that shares many of the concerns of radical humanism, but its focus is on what produces stability and control in societies rather than what produces change.

- Objective change: It forms the "radical structuralist" paradigm that focuses on social structures as "real," in a realist or positivist sense, but is interesting on dynamic forces, tensions, and change within these structures – what produces upheavals, revolutions, and revolts?

- Objective regulation: "Functionalism" (or as it has also been called "structural functionalism") is perhaps the oldest paradigm in sociology with its concern for structures and regulation – what is it that keeps societies organized, stable, and functional?

This clearly is only one possible way of categorizing the highly different approaches within sociology (and other social sciences) toward "organizing." As we will discuss further in Chapters 7, 8, and 10, there are other candidate theories (e.g., cultural theory, competing values, and relational models) that make similar attempts to produce meta-theoretical frameworks that integrate several "paradigms" within a single framework.

However, it is useful in raising an issue of what each of these different paradigmatic perspectives would have to say about "performance" in the public domain. Clearly, each would approach the issue very differently – for example, "functionalist" approaches would see performance policies as primarily a positive instrument of control and regulation of objectively existing organizations; whereas "radical humanist" would view performance measurement as either an instrument of oppression to be critiqued and exposed or, perhaps, if used by the "oppressed" themselves, a weapon of liberation, self-control, and autonomy. This approach from organizational sociology relates very strongly from some of the problematic issues about organizational performance discussed later in the book.

Before leaving the discipline of sociology it is worth also noting another of its offshoots that has had something to say about performance: social policy. The development of a social policy tradition – especially since the massive growth welfare state provisions in many countries after World

War II – has produced a problem-focused subdiscipline that seeks to understand "what works" in producing social, educational, health, and other changes in society. Borrowing heavily from other disciplines (e.g., welfare economics and cost–benefit analysis of economics) social policy has contributed to trying to understand policy options and implementation. Evaluation studies, especially, have been largely based in social policy areas (although not exclusively).

As with its parent discipline, however, social policy is riven by many of the same paradigmatic conflicts and while some have welcomed and used performance measurement policies, many have rejected them as forms of oppressive "managerialism."

Some Specific Theories and Performance

In this section some specific theories with direct relevance to performance are considered. Obviously, these are highly selective because, as previously discussed, performance in various guises is so ubiquitous across a whole range of social science disciplines and branches it would be impossible to cover all possible contributions. The ones that have been selected here appear because they have had significant purchase on debates about organizational performance in general and/or public organizations in particular. They are also ones that have cut across traditional disciplinary boundaries and in some cases have had significant influence in all, or most, of the five disciplines discussed above. They have also often dissected themselves by the sort of different paradigm perspectives discussed at the start of the chapter.

INSTITUTIONAL THEORY

Institutionalism originated historically in the study of the gray area between organizations and rules of behavior – so colloquially "institutions" referred to political things like parliaments, monarchies, political parties, and social institutions like marriage, money, etc. Old-fashioned institutionalism very much focused on the aforementioned political structure – often as comparative studies of different countries' institutional arrangements – for example, presidential versus parliamentary systems (Finer 1946). More modern approaches focus more on the "rules" end of this spectrum (Scott 2008).

If one wanted to appreciate the breadth of institutional theorizing in the social sciences, then a look at three recent collections of perspectives on institutionalism would soon show the vast amount of effort that is going to its development (Rhodes et al. 2006; Greenwood et al. 2008; Pierre et al. 2008). Unfortunately these collections also demonstrate that "institutionalism" as a concept has become so broad, and used in so many different ways, that without some substantial change it seems a very problematic concept. This is compounded by the fact that institutionalism has taken strong root in several very different disciplinary soils, particularly in organizational sociology (Greenwood et al. 2008) and in political science (Rhodes et al. 2006; Pierre et al. 2008), with relatively little connection between the approaches.

Institutionalism also exists within economics, but ironically economic rational choice approaches to institutionalism have had much more impact in political science (Shepsle 2006) and to a lesser extent organizational sociology (Roberts 2008) than within economics. For a prehistory of economic institutionalism see Hodgson (2004).

Moreover, there are, both within and across the disciplinary perspectives, many competing forms of institutionalism: normative (March and Olsen 1989; Peters 1999), historical (Sanders 2006), constructionist (Hay 2006), rational choice (Shepsle 2006), network (Ansell 2006), traditional or empirical (Rhodes 2006), institutional realism (Grafstein 1992), etc.

Peters (2008) makes an effort to reconcile at least some of the differences between four of these (just from within the political science discipline): normative, rational choice, historical, and empirical. He argues that there are at least some shared elements:

- A belief that structures (however defined) are an important element in explaining human behavior
- That structures persist over time, even when individuals change
- That structures cause greater regularity in human behavior than would otherwise be the case
- That "positive feedback" between individuals and the institutions they inhabit over time reinforce institutions and patterned behavior

However, there remain very important conflicts between the four versions of institutional theory. Normative institutionalism sees individual's preferences as entirely shaped by institutions, whereas rational choice see preferences as exogenous to institutions (note that this is the same point, in a very different language, as that made in Chapter 1 about the conflict between "blank slate" versus "rational utility maximization" versions of human nature). Peters goes on to argue, citing Allison (1971), that these and other conflicts between different institutional theories can best be treated as multi-theoretic perspectives on the same "problem" and that each tells us something useful and each has "blind spots." Again, as discussed in Chapter 1, this is the type of multi-theoretic argument that leaves us with incompatible, partial, theories that cannot be brought together. And, again as argued in Chapter 1, this is because at least one of the theories (rational choice) is deeply flawed and incomplete as a model of both human decision-making and of motivation – something which Peters is reluctant to address, preferring to adopt the much less satisfactory solution of simply accepting the irreconcilable nature of the two competing versions of institutionalism.

Institutional theory (or rather theories) can relate to the issue of performance in public agencies in several ways. First, and most obviously, the issue of institutions in the historic sense (governments, parliaments, courts, etc.) can constitute an important context within which public agencies operate – their "performance regime" (see Chapters 4 and 5). Second, institutional approaches in the sense of "rules of the game" can be important as a perspective in understanding how performance policies of governments and others might seek to change these rules – see the discussions on systemic performance interventions in Chapter 5 as examples of this. Thirdly, various approaches to change within organizations aimed at improving performance can also be seen as attempts at changing the "rules of the game" – see the discussions on organizational performance models and approaches in Chapters 7 and 8.

RESOURCE-DEPENDENCE AND RESOURCE-BASED THEORIES

An area of organizational research and theorizing that has particular relevance to performance is the emergence of resource-dependence and resource-based theories. Confusingly, despite the similar titles these two streams of research are not linked.

Resource-dependence theory was outlined in a seminal book by Pfeffer and Salancik first published in 1978 (Pfeffer and Salancik 2003 [1978]). This approach focused on the idea that organizations were successful to the extent that they could gather resources from their external environment – indeed their book's main title was *The External Control of Organizations*. This overall approach was clearly heavily influenced by general, or open, systems theory. It has interesting things to say about competing demands on organizations from various external stakeholders, demands that are made in exchange for the supply of resources. Hence the focus on the term "resource dependence," although they also talk about resource exchange.

Resource dependence, or exchange, has special relevance to the public sector for several reasons. As discussed later in the book – public agencies always exist within an external "performance regime" (see Chapter 4) or "authorizing environment" (Moore 1995), are subject to externally imposed "mandates" (Bryson 1995), and most usually rely for their key resource – funding – on external providers – governments. The resource-dependence approach was further developed by Rhodes (1986, 1988) in his analysis of the intergovernmental relationships between British central and local government, which explicitly uses a resource-dependence perspective. Hood (1983) (Hood and Margetts 2007) also uses resource dependence in his studies of the "tools of government" (which Rhodes also drew upon).

Resource-based theories of the firm concentrate much more on the internal capabilities, capacities, and resources of the organization (Barney and Clark 2007). The theory emerged from concerns over what it was that made firms – that is, hierarchically structured forms of organization – preferable to markets as a way of organizing economic activities. Why, and how, might hierarchic firms be more efficient forms of organization and why are some firms more competitive than others? In their modern form these theories emerged in the early 1980s but were linked to much earlier theorizing about things such as transaction costs, rent-seeking, organizational competences, etc. Strangely, despite the obvious affinity of the resource-dependence and resource-based approaches there has been little engagement between the two approaches – so the recent summary "state-of-the-art" analysis of resource-based theory cited above (Barney and Clark 2007) does not even mention the resource-dependence approach or Pfeffer and Salancik's seminal book. This can in part be attributed to the differing focus of the two approaches – one external and systems based and the other internally focused – but this is hardly an adequate excuse for the lack of integration.

Both resource-dependence and resource-based theories have the obvious advantage that they focus on real assets that exist "out there" and are not merely social constructs. Although some of the internal capabilities explored in resource-based theories do focus on "intangible assets" such as intellectual property, complex tacit knowledge, and internal social relations in the firm, these are all regarded as ontologically "real," if not always easy to comprehend and thus philosophically these approaches fall within the broad positivist-realist camp.

Both approaches are useful in thinking about public organizations – as will be seen in later chapters including those on "performance regimes" (Chapters 4 and 5) and on organizational performance (Chapters 7 and 8).

COMPLEXITY THEORY

Complexity theory, complex adaptive systems (CAS), or complex evolutionary systems – the new scientific discipline that studies complex systems goes by a variety of names. It is itself a very complex field, with many complexity theorists adopting radically different ontological and epistemological approaches. At one extreme, some see complexity as supporting a social constructionist approach to social sciences (Stacey et al. 2000; Streatfield 2001).

Other complexity writers remain firmly within more traditional scientific positivist, or perhaps realist, paradigms. While accepting that complex systems exhibit properties – particularly nonlinearity and emergent properties – that resist analysis using reductionist approaches they nevertheless see complex systems as "real" and although causally complex not immune to analysis (Kiel 1994; Byrne 1998; Axelrod and Cohen 1999; Rihani 2002; Haynes 2003).

There is an important point to note here also about predictability. Complex systems are not readily predictable, because even minute variations in starting conditions can cause large, nonlinear, variations in outcomes. Some argue that this somehow "proves" that traditional scientific approaches are inadequate because they always take the form of "if X then Y" predictions. This is a simple misunderstanding, because science does not demand that all systems of causality be predictable, merely that they be explicable in terms of causality. Evolutionary theory is the most obvious example of this – the outcomes of evolution can be explained causally but they cannot be predicted. This does not make evolutionary theory unscientific.

In transferring complexity theory to the study of organizations and management, many writers often adopt one or other of these general approaches. Many writers also often justify the need for, or even attribute the rise of, complexity theory to the increasing complexity of society and of organizational life.

The current author is more sympathetic to complexity theory being seen not as an alternative to traditional science but as complementary. Broadly speaking, mechanistic science (Newton), relativistic science (Einstein), quantum mechanics, and complexity science are four aspects of the scientific exploration of our universe. While complexity science exhibits features that are not immediately or obviously compatible with, say, Newtonian mechanics it does not replace such science – that is, a fallacy perpetrated by many popularizing writers of scientific ideas in general, and complexity in particular. Using a superficial understanding of the idea of "paradigm shifts" in science, they confuse Newtonian science and a Newtonian worldview. More sober scientists understand that mechanics, relativity, quantum mechanics, and complexity while not (yet) integrated are not in principle irreconcilable.

Nor is complexity theory an outgrowth of the growing complexification of society and organizations. While it undoubtedly has utility in analyzing and understanding increasingly complex social and organizational systems the whole point of complexity theory is that it attempts to develop a unifying framework for analysis of any complex adaptive system – from ant colonies to modern human organizations. This of course encompasses all forms of human organization, from hunter-gatherer societies to a modern networked IT company. Thus those who argue that complexity theory is a result of complexification of our social world rather miss the point.

Complexity theory, being a new and innovative field, is still in a process of formation and many interpretations exist. This is not the place for a full rehearsal of the full panoply of complexity theories. Axelrod and Cohen (1997), however, offer the following useful succinct definition:

Agents, of a variety of types, use their strategies, in patterned interaction, with each other and with artefacts. Performance measures on the resulting events drive the selection of agents and/or strategies through processes of error-prone copying and recombination, thus changing the frequencies of types within the system.

The link to performance here is obvious – it is the crucial factor in determining what agents and/or strategies are "selected," or to put it another way, are more successful or better performers than other agents/strategies. It also links rather neatly to the next section, which looks at evolutionary approaches to organizational performance.

EVOLUTIONARY AND ECOLOGICAL PERSPECTIVES ON ORGANIZATIONS

Applying ideas from evolutionary science to organizations has become increasingly popular in recent years. One particular strand of this thinking poses a major challenge to much of the research on organizational performance – private and public – that will be discussed later (Chapters 7 and 8). This has been most famously explicated in the book *The Halo Effect* (Rosenzweig 2007) which argues that most studies of successful organizations get the relationship between cause and effect wrong. Many famous studies of organizational performance and the factors that influence it are based on a methodology which goes something like this: (*a*) identify a group of successful companies/organizations; (*b*) see what they have in common in terms of internal factors like strategy, leadership, human resources policies, culture etc. (or even what is different between them and a control group of less successful companies); (*c*) conclude that the commonalities are what brings about enhanced performance. Examples include many of the most famous studies of organizational success (Peters and Waterman 1982; Collins and Porras 1994; Collins 2001).

But, Rosenzweig and others point out that these factors may actually have nothing to do with success. There may be other – often extrinsic, environmental, factors – that made the "successful" organizations what they are, and the common features may have little or nothing to do with their success. The organizations' success, if that is what it is, may be due to simple luck in selecting a strategy that happens to fit with a rapidly changing, and inherently unpredictable, environment. As a consequence, it may be that what is seen as "good" – such as good leadership qualities in senior managers – may only appear good because the organization is doing well. There are numerous examples where specific factors – for example, strong leadership – have been used to explain success on the way up and then also attributed as a cause of failure on the way down (Raynor 2007).

This school of thought also appears in the strategy literature in what Mintzberg and colleagues call the "environmental school" of strategy, which emphasizes on environmental pressures, ecological niches, and organizational life cycles and extinctions (Mintzberg et al. 1998).

If success were a largely random factor based on luck, as this approach in its strongest form suggests, then analysis of endogenous factors within organizations to ascertain why one performs better than another is a fruitless activity. Fortunately the real situation appears to be somewhat less random – or rather it contains elements of both randomness and predictability (or at any rate discoverable causality – for the difference see the previous section on "complexity").

Concluding Comments

This has been something of a *Cook's Tour* of theories that might be applied to understanding the performance of public organizations and services. It has been deliberately broad to show the possibilities, and limitations, of existing theories. But being so broad-brush obviously leaves the above analysis open to accusations of superficiality, which is to some degree inevitable given the limitations of space. Yet is it not reasonable to ask such broad-brush questions about what social sciences generally and specific theories might contribute to understanding this or other issues? The present author would argue it is not only possible but also a necessary precondition for making any real progress toward creating robust and consilient theories of performance in the public domain. It is not possible to "stand on the shoulders of giants" unless we are clear which giants and why we should stand on their particular shoulders rather than any others'. The rest of the book will try to draw on this analysis to try to show that progress toward more integrated, consilient, and relevant theories of performance is indeed possible.

PART II

GOVERNANCE AND PERFORMANCE

Introduction to Part II

The next three chapters address, in different ways, the "publicness" of public organizations. The first two address the institutional context within which public agencies operate, and the third addresses the public values that affect them.

Chapter 4 examines the institutional structures surrounding public agencies – the surprisingly long list of groups of actors who can (but not always do) seek to shape the performance of public agencies in different ways. Most narratives of performance in the public domain have assumed a rather narrow chain of what the economists would call principal–agent relations. This usually goes something like: the voters elect a government, which in turn instructs public agencies how to perform. Within government, there is some sort of "cascade" of "instructions to deliver" – to use a phrase from one former senior British government official (Barber 2007) – that trickle down through the hierarchy of public organizations to the "frontline."

This simplistic, linear, and hierarchic "model" of relationships ignores crucial facts about the public domain. We leave aside for a moment some of the problematic issues of multi-level governance discussed in Chapter 2, and concentrate just on a single tier of government at the national level. Even without the complications of different tiers of government, it is obvious that there is no single "principal" in central government – all governments to some extent operate what the Americans have called the "separation of powers" and thus there are always multiple principals with more or less tools of government at their disposal. Chapter 4 tries to analyze what these different principals are, what powers they might have, using a theoretical heuristic drawn from resource-dependence theory (see Chapter 2).

The opening sections of the chapter review the evidence and theory that points toward the conclusion that public agencies operate in a complex performance regime, drawing on work from various areas like accountability, organizational theory, regulation inside government, etc. The later sections develop a specific heuristic approach based on grouping together specific types of institutions (in the old-fashioned institutionalist sense – see Chapter 2) and draw on resource-dependence theory to decide which institutions ought to be included, and excluded from a framework for analyzing the key institutional actors and their interactions.

One issue that is drawn out is that it is not just the role and powers of institutional actors in any specific performance regime, but how these interact – the dynamics of the system. To illustrate concretely the relationship between, say, the US Congress and presidency and the UK Parliament and prime ministership in relation to the performance steering of public agencies is qualitatively different – even though both represent relationships between the executive and legislative branches of government. Moreover, it is important to recognize that these relationships evolve over time, and that some actors may openly seek to change them – as, for example, when UK executive government decides to delegate to a third party (the Audit Commission) responsibility for drawing up a set of performance measures to be imposed on all local governments.

Chapter 5 turns to the issue of the ways in which elements of the performance regime – principally, but not exclusively, the executive arm of government – attempt to shape or steer the performance of public systems and organizations. This is an almost entirely new area of exploration – that of explicitly seeing government and other actors interventions as ways of trying to shape or steer the performance of the public sector, systems, and organizations. While this has been implied in various areas of research and theory (e.g., Moore's "authorizing environment" or Bryson's "mandates"), this has usually been seen only from a (single) agency perspective rather than seeing it as a policy of government and others.

One way of examining what various institutions can do (but not always do) to shape performance is to apply something like Hood's "tools of government" (which in turn is drawn from resource-dependence theory; Hood 1983; Hood and Margetts 2007). Which of these "tools" are available to different actors such as executive government, legislatures, courts, auditors, inspectors, etc.?

Another useful analytic framework comes from the UK government, and this divides interventions not by institutions but by type of intervention. These are classified as managerial-contractual interventions (that seek to directly impose performance steers through targets etc.); capability interventions (that seek to steer and improve performance through enhancing and shaping the internal capabilities of public agencies); systemic-competitive interventions (that seek to reshape the context of agencies and steer their performance by creating quasi-markets or other competitive mechanisms between public organizations); and finally systemic voice and choice (that seek to empower users of services in order to steer and improve performance).

Chapter 6 turns to the issue of public value and public values. While this issue has lurked in the background of much of the performance movement it has all too rarely come to the fore, much less been integrated into theories of performance. Perhaps the only obvious attempt to address this has been Moore's work on public value (Moore 1995), but this has been detached from the wider work on public values (e.g., Bozeman 2007). In parallel to these discussions in the public domain, there has been a surge of interest in notions of value – including shareholder and stakeholder value – in the private sector.

The chapter examines all of these developments and starts the process of trying to make some sense out of public values and hence how notions of the public value of public agencies activities might be shaped. Drawing on a range of theories about differential human motivation, as opposed to one-dimensional models like rational utility maximization, a sketch is provided of how apparently contradictory public values might be analyzed within a single framework. This is highly speculative at this stage, but the analysis is also highly suggestive of ways in which a range of different theories might be made consilient and the study of public values brought within a manageable framework. This discussion is picked up further in Chapter 10, where the approach is further developed.

4 Performance Regimes: Institutions[1]

Introduction

This chapter begins the exploration of the idea of the "performance regime" within which public organizations operate – a term which is gaining increasing usage in the performance literature (Talbot et al. 2005a; Moynihan 2008; Walshe et al. 2010a). The term "performance regime" is used to convey a combination of

1. the *institutional context* of performance steering – who has formal rights and other instruments with which to "steer" public organizations and programs, for example, as between the executive and legislative branches of government (Talbot et al. 2005a). The institutional context may be simple and very much a vertical chain of "principal–agent"-type relationships or it may be much more polycentric with multiple principals. This may also include initiatives aimed at reshaping the institutional context – for example, delegating performance measurement to a third party inspectorate or audit body.

2. the nature of actual *performance interventions* – what actions do these various institutional actors actually take, individually and collectively, to try to influence the performance of public organizations and programs – through performance contracts, imposed targets, comparative "league tables," and other levers. This of course includes the possibility of not taking action – where, for example, a legislature might choose to ignore potential opportunities for intervention which executive mandated performance reporting provides it with (Johnson and Talbot 2007b).

The chapter will focus primarily on the "within government" institutional context, especially the institutional actors. Non-state actors are included only to the extent that they have state-sanctioned authority or power to intervene – for example, user-bodies that have statutory rights to be consulted (e.g., in the United Kingdom the former Community Health Councils) or professional

---

[1] This chapter is an amended and expanded version of an article that first appeared in Talbot (2008c).

bodies that issue "licenses to practice" (such as the medical professional bodies) and can thus attempt to steer the performance of public agencies. This is done here for purely analytical purposes, and is not to deny that such external actors might have means of attempting to steer agencies performance in (their) desired directions.

The issue of the actual performance interventions carried out by the institutional actors we identify here will be dealt with in Chapter 5, which explores the tools and resources available to performance regime actors and how they are deployed in practice much more fully.

The purpose here is to establish a workable, heuristic, analytical framework with which to examine current, changing, and comparative institutional contexts for performance: in other words, who are the key actors in any performance regime? The answer is rather broader than most current analyses would suggest.

The approach adopted lies broadly within the tradition of historical institutionalism – that is, an approach which sees history, institutions, and the interaction between institutional actors as important (Finer 1946; Rhodes 1997; Scharpf 1997; Peters 1999; Pierson 2004). However, the approach is focused more specifically on what might be called "realist institutionalism" (adapted from Grafstein 1992), which sees "institutions" – in the historical-institutional sense of things like parliaments, courts, executives, etc. – as for theoretical and practical purposes as "real," that is, existing independently of any observer.

In the first part of the chapter, the various sources of questions, queries, and problematic issues are identified in a selection of theoretical and research literature. The analysis was stimulated by ongoing encounters with the operation of performance regimes that clearly did not match the dominant "principal–agent" logic, which was (rhetorically) supposed to be dominating policy in this area (see, e.g., Bartlett 1991; Harden 1992; Jordan 1992; Propper 1992; Harrison 1993; Pollitt 1993; Greer 1994; Boston et al. 1996; Walsh et al. 1997; Lidbury and Petrie 1999; OECD-PUMA 1999; Fortin and Van Hassel 2000).

Five sources of problematic issues are identified and analyzed.

Firstly, the theoretical performance literature has produced a range of (mainly empirical) examples of the complexities of institutional and policy contexts for public services' performance which clearly go beyond simplistic "principal–agent" models.

Secondly, some empirical explorations of actual performance practices have exposed some of the complexities of the context in which public agencies operate.

Thirdly, and independently of discussions about performance, the accountability literature has also developed a number of theoretical and empirical approaches that emphasize the complex character of accountabilities for public services. These "multi-centric" approaches clearly have implications for performance – an organization that has multi-centric accountabilities is likely to be affected in the specific area of performance measurement and reporting as well as in its wider accountabilities.

Fourthly, the literature on audit and regulation within government has highlighted one particular set of institutional actors (regulators, auditors, and inspectors) who could clearly have an impact on performance.

Fifthly, the organizational theory literature has long recognized the existence of external stakeholders that may influence or try to shape the direction of any organization.

In the second main section of the chapter, Toward an Institutional Framework (p. 91) these approaches are synthesized and expanded to produce a framework of, or "organizing perspective" on, the possible key actors in the institutional context of performance of public services. This "performance regimes" framework, it is suggested, can be used to analyze changing "performance governance" contexts over time and between jurisdictions and sectors.

Issues in Shaping the Performance of Public Services

In this section, the focus is the research and theory on performance, and then more specifically various empirical examples of the sort of problematic issues which the performance regimes framework is designed to address.

PERFORMANCE WITHIN GOVERNMENT: RESEARCH AND THEORY

Much of the research that has developed on performance within public services has tended to concentrate on developing *organizational models of performance*. This has been done either empirically and inductively (e.g., Carter et al. 1992) or more normatively (Downs and Larkey 1986; Denhardt 1993; Moore 1995; Holzer and Callahan 1998). An example of large-scale, but deductively driven, research projects are the empirical studies conducted under the titles "Government Performance Project" and "Federal Performance Project" in the United States. These amassed a very large volume of data and analyses of the management elements that make for good performance, against a predefined model. The model itself makes little reference to the context, and specifically the "within government" context, within which public agencies operate (Ingraham et al. 2003).

There are some exceptions to this rule. An article by Boschken (1994), drawing on the work of organizational theorists, emphasizes the "multiple constituencies" for public agency performance, although these are of a very general character and not specifically "within government," the area which concerns us in this chapter. A large survey of performance practices across the UK public sector found that public managers rated legislation, modernizing government, and "best value" initiatives as the main drivers for change but they also included audits and inspections, national league tables, and even peer-performance reviews as significant factors (Creelman and Harvey 2004). It is notable here that there are at least five groups of actors, external to respondent's organization but all within government: government itself, parliament (legislation), audit, inspection, and peers.

Some work has placed an emphasis on complex levers controlling performance *within* individual organizations (e.g., Simons 1995; Bovens 1998; Behn 2001; Norman 2003). However, little of this work has focused on the complexity of institutional environments within the public sector within which individual public units or agencies function. This is disappointing because we believe there is a direct link between the internal complexities within organizations and the complexity of their external, within government, context.

There is a growing body of work on the *performance of government institutions* themselves (the executive branch, civil service, legislature, judiciary, etc.). One of the most fascinating is the attempt to develop measures for the performance of these institutions by the Brookings Institute in the United States (see Davidson 2003). Especially since the World Bank's turn to "institutionalism," symbolized in their 1997 *World Development Report* (World Bank 1997), there have been several similar developments for measuring the performance of developing countries' institutions. But this movement has tended to take either a macro, "whole of government" approach or has focused on individual institution's performance (McMahon and Sinclair 2002; Davidson 2003), and has largely left aside the interaction between governmental bodies and service delivery units and agencies.

Principal–agent models and performance contracting represent the main exception to the single organization focus. There is a large literature examining this application of new institutional economics and rational choice ideas to public services that supposedly forms a core part of the so-called new public management. For example, there are many studies of the introduction of "vertical" contracting between parent ministries and agencies (Pollitt and Talbot 2004; Talbot 2004a; Pollitt et al. 2005) or between purchasers/funders and providers/agents (Harden 1992; Boston et al. 1996; Walsh et al. 1997; OECD-PUMA 1999; Fortin and Van Hassel 2000). Some of this work also embraces "horizontal" contracts – that is, contracts, quasi-contracts or service delivery agreements between partner organizations. Most of this literature assumes a fairly simple principal–agent relationship and makes little allowance for what is referred to as the "multiple principals" problem in economics and which has also applied to government (Tirole 1994). While such ideas have been explored by economists, they have had little or no impact on public management literature generally and the performance literature in particular.

So, very few studies of performance in the public sector have focused on, or even addressed, the issue of the governmental *institutional context* within which performance occurs in the public sector. To the extent that external environments are considered, generally everything outside the individual organizations is considered as a relatively undifferentiated set of "external factors" or "stakeholders." No priority is given specifically to relationships mainly within Government. Some of the literature does address the issue of who performance information is for (see, e.g., Epstein cited in Halachmi and Bouckaert 1996), but the listing of "audiences" is usually fairly vague and general with no attempt at systematic analysis (something which is done in the strategic management/stakeholder literature – see below).

An important partial exception to the almost total focus on within organizations is an edited volume by Heinrich and Lynn (2000), which focuses on more network and "governance"-based approaches to service delivery. However, the focus on "governance" (as opposed to government) in their approach means a neglect of the multiple institutional actors *within government* – as is evidenced in the "reduced form" model of governance suggested in the opening essay (Lynn et al. 2000 pp. 14–17). Their model is as follows: O = function of (E, C, T, S, M), where: O = outputs/outcomes; E = environmental factors; C = client characteristics; T = treatments; S = structures; and M = managerial roles and functions.

They concede that this is merely a framework and that "a complex causal structure, however, almost certainly underlies these relationships in the true model: interdependencies undoubtedly exist among (and within) E, C, T, S, O and M." They also note that in some contexts the effect of a specific variable may be zero (which echoes a point made above, and below, that the elements in our performance regimes model are not always present or influential). Their model however, in focusing on the performance of *governance*, only partially includes the "within *government*" institutional factors that concern us. There is no explicit discussion of this issue, nor any way of analyzing these "within government" actors and pressures.

It is in the private sector orientated performance literature that the idea of stakeholders has been most developed. For example, Neely et al. (2002) offer a stakeholder model which includes: investors (shareholders, bankers, and other capital providers), regulators, pressure groups, labor unions, employees, communities, suppliers, alliance partners, customers, and intermediaries (e.g., sales agents) (Neely et al. 2002). These authors are clearly drawing on the generic literature on strategic management, and especially the subset which deals with "stakeholders," which has had a great deal to say about complex and multicentric influences over the direction of performance for organizations (e.g., see Mintzberg 1994; Scholes and Johnson 2000; Pfeffer and Salancik 2003 [1978]).

The relatively small literature on strategic management in the public sector has tended to likewise emphasize multiple stakeholders (Bryson 1995; Joyce 2000; Johnson and Scholes 2001). Bryson's work in particular has a strong focus on both "mandates" imposed on individual public organizations by superior public bodies as well as considering other stakeholders (Bryson 1995). Similarly Scholes offers methods for analyzing stakeholders of public organizations (Scholes and Johnson 2000). Work on how strategy is developed in public "subsectors" – for example, health and education – has also highlighted some issues about complex institutional environments (Pettigrew and Ferlie 1992; Ferlie et al. 1996; Pollitt et al. 1998). But little of this seems to have impacted on the public sector performance literature.

PERFORMANCE WITHIN GOVERNMENT: EMPIRICAL EXAMPLES

We turn now to some more empirical examples of where the complexities of performance within government begin to emerge.

Some studies have touched upon these issues of institutional complexity within government in relation to performance – for example, studies of the US Government Performance and Results Act (Radin 1998; Long and Franklin 2004) and of UK Public Service Agreements (Treasury Committee 2002; James 2004).

A study of UK civil service executive agencies in the mid-1990s revealed that rather than a simple "principal–agent" quasi-contractual relationship between each agency and its parent Ministry, what had actually emerged was a complex web of institutional actors who could legitimately influence the performance of the new civil service bodies (Talbot 1996*a*). This illuminated the nature of the influence exerted by central ministries (HM Treasury and Cabinet Office), line (parent) ministries, and the various units located within them both. Other researchers have identified further dysfunctional elements arising from such complexities surrounding UK agencies (e.g., Hyndman and Anderson 1998; Hyndman 2002).

Similar work on agency creation or reform programs and performance internationally has revealed similarly complex sets of relationships between agencies and their parent ministries, central ministries, and various regulatory and inspection bodies (Pollitt and Talbot 2004; Pollitt et al. 2005). In particular, the complexities of the regulatory framework and institutions within the US federal government and Canada have been identified (Graham and Roberts 2004) but this whole area remains generally under-researched and under-theorized.

Finally, the whole field of "performance audit" (generally, but not always, carried out by supreme audit bodies) has surfaced as an area of research. Two international comparative studies (OECD-PUMA 1996; Pollitt et al. 1999) of the specific role of "performance audit" and audit institutions in a range of developed countries, highlight the fact that beside government itself (whether parent ministry/department or central ministries/departments) audit bodies can have a significant impact on "performance" steers to service delivery agencies.

ACCOUNTABILITY AND THE COMPLEXITY OF INSTITUTIONAL ACTORS

A parallel field of study, but most often unconnected to performance, has been the accountability of public organizations and institutions. This is clearly not the place to carry out a full review of this field but there are several contributions which highlight the theme of complexity of institutional actors.

A study of five UK public services (Day and Klein 1987) focused on the complexity of accountability arrangements and the growth of extra mechanisms such as the Parliamentary Commissioner, Health Service Commissioners, the Commission for Local Administration, and the Police Complaints Board, all established in the early 1970s. They also cite the expansion of financial audit, especially the creation of the Audit Commission in 1982, the roles of Royal Commissions and other independent inquiries, and finally of professional bodies and associations. They saw all this as a growth of a range of accountability bodies based on "technical expertise." In a telling passage they note that direct accountability to elected officials rarely functioned as envisaged – in the case they examine of elected members of local education committees, who complained of their inability to hold the education service to account despite being themselves held to account for it (p. 240).

A more contemporary study of accountability in one ministry (the UK Home Office) similarly highlights the complexities (Flinders 2001). Flinders draws on earlier work which emphasized "multi-centric" accountability by which is meant accountability "... to different authorities, for different purposes, to different degrees and in terms of different, though mutually complimentary standards" (Spiro 1969, p. 96).

He also synthesizes more contemporary work from a number of authors (Lawton and Rose 1991; Oliver 1991; Stone 1995; Pyper 1996) to produce a "circuit of accountable government" diagram that incorporates, among other elements, the executive, parliament, audit bodies, judicial review, journalism, and pressure groups as the key actors (p. 20–3). He presents this in both a "paragon" or ideal form (p. 22) and then as an actual form (p. 23) highlighting those actors which do, and do not, exert influence in practice.

Table 4.1 Forms of Accountability

(Pyper 1996)	(Stone 1995)	(Oliver 1991)	(Lawton and Rose 1991)	(Flinders 2001)	(Hood et al. 2004)
Parliamentary	Parliamentary	Political	Political	Parliamentary	Legislature
					Agents of Legislatures
					Quasi-independent grievance handlers
					Quasi-independent overseers
Legal/quasi-legal	Judicial	Legal	Legal	Judicial	Judicial
	Managerialism	Administrative	Managerial	Managerial	Internal Overseers
Charterism and consumerism	Market	Public/consumer	Consumer/client		Private overseers (e.g., credit rating agencies)
Popular	Network relations		Professional		International overseers
					Public overseers of both public and private bodies

Note: First four columns are taken from Flinders (2001, p. 20).

His own model reduces some of this complexity to only three forms of accountability (parliamentary, judicial, and managerial). A more recent attempt at categorizing accountancy "agents" is also provided by Hood and colleagues (2004). We have combined all these categorizations in Table 4.1.

The various institutional actors identified in this analysis provide a useful starting point for constructing a heuristic framework for analyzing these actors, as we shall see later.

Behn offers a novel approach to accountability for public organizations – applying the idea of 360-degree appraisal (developed for individuals) to accountability at the organizational level (Behn 2001, chapter 11). He claims that we already have what he calls "360 degree harassment" of public organizations by various "clients, peers, partners, collaborators, customers, and suppliers" as well as "auditors, inspectors general and special prosecutors" or what he calls "designated accountability holders" (DAHs) (p. 199). By arguing for 360-degree accountability, Behn is specifically suggesting that the "feedback" associated with the 360-degree notion ought to go both ways – for example, not just from legislatures to agencies but from agencies to legislatures (e.g., when the latter "assign vague and contradictory missions to agencies" – p. 200).

In a study of the Challenger (space shuttle) tragedy, two US scholars develop an institutional perspective on what went wrong (Romzek and Dubnick 1987). They identify four different types of accountability: bureaucratic (superior/subordinate), legal (lawmaker/executor, principal/agent), professional (layperson/expert), and political (constituent/representative). They argue that these systems of accountability are substitutable and that they frequently shift over time – an agency may be held accountable in one way at one period but changes in the institutional environment may trigger a rapid shift to a completely different form of accountability, which then becomes dominant. In the case of the Challenger disaster they suggest that NASA operated under political and bureaucratic forms of accountability, which served to suppress the professional accountability system that might have prevented the disaster. A highly symbolic quotation is when a manager was asked to "take off his engineering hat and put on his management hat" (p. 234). Romzek and Dubnick argue that the subsequent investigations failed to identify this failure and a new legal/bureaucratic accountability regime was just as likely to fail as its political/bureaucratic predecessor.

O'Neill's BBC Reith Lectures on the subject of "trust" (O'Neill 2002 pp. 45–8) make a rather similar point about one form of accountability being displaced by another – in this case she suggests that professional accountability is being replaced by legislative, regulatory, and command forms of accountability in the UK public services.

What these examples from the accountability literature tell us is highly relevant to the framework we are developing: first, there are "multi-centric" forms, actors, and institutions involved in accountability (and they provide a long list of who these might be); second, they emphasize that it is possible to build maps or frameworks of who the key "designated accountability holders" (Behn 2001) might be; and third, they tell us that different accountability actors and forms may vary in influence across time, jurisdiction, and sectors.

REGULATION INSIDE GOVERNMENT

In 1997, Power, writing mainly about the United Kingdom (but also the United States), was able to conclude that we were experiencing the advent of "the audit society" (Power 1997). Others have bracketed the rise of audit, inspection, and regulation under the general title of "regulation inside government" (Hood et al. 1999). This has become the object of a number of research efforts over recent years.

Regulation inside the government means that one public organization shapes the activities of another (excluding judicial actors), the overseer is at arm's length from the organization being overseen, and the overseer has some kind of mandate to scrutinize the behavior of the "regulatee" and seek to change it (Hood et al. 1999, p. 9). These include audit, inspection, and regulatory functions, which may be combined in one body or organized separately.

Hood and colleagues identified a national-level growth in audit, inspection, and regulatory bodies within government between 1976 and 1995 of 22% (from 110 to 135) and a real terms doubling or trebling of expenditure on them and a 90% growth in staffing, at a time when overall public sector employment was shrinking (Hood et al. 1999, pp. 26–33). They also concluded these were a very diverse set of actors and they "found that all parts of the public sector faced multiple, not single, regulators, and that those multiple regulators tended to work independently and with little awareness of the activities of their counterparts" (ibid., p. 34). "Multi-centric" indeed.

These various forms of "regulation" (which encompasses audit, inspection, and regulation) effectively "steer" toward specific forms of performance in public service organizations. These may include conformance to internal process standards and to service delivery standards, and even in some cases what types of performance measures should be used – for example, the report of the UK National Audit Office (NAO) recommending reform of perform-ance targets and systems for the UK Benefits Agency (Comptroller and Auditor General 1998).

In 1966, Normanton was able to conclude that in the United Kingdom "there is less public accountability than in France, the United States or Federal Germany; and not merely slightly less but very considerably so" (Normanton 1966, p. 410). This highlights the dynamic nature of the role of audit – the trajectory from below-average public audit in the 1960s to probably above average in the 1990s shows a fairly dramatic shift. Such a shift also clearly has impacts on other forms of accountability and more specifically on the per-formance "steers" which are given to public service delivery organizations.

ORGANIZATIONAL THEORY AND PUBLIC ADMINISTRATION

Organization theory developed a strong interest in the environmental factors impacting on the internal regimes of organizations in the mid-1960s. Almost two decades of such analysis is summarized and synthesized in Mintzberg's *Power In and Around Organizations* (1983a) which stresses the role of what he calls the "external coalition" that steers the organization.

One specific approach which had a large impact on public administration was what is called a "resource dependence" approach to interorganizational relations and networks which has most often been attributed to the seminal *The External Control of Organizations* (Pfeffner and Salancik 2003 [1978]) but this has also been termed "resource exchange" (Cook 1977). This approach has morphed from general interorganizational relations through the study of central–local relations in government (Rhodes 1986; Rhodes 1988) to study of the "core executive" and particularly relations between various actors within the core state (Smith 1999, see especially the diagram on p. 6). This approach has, in general terms, potential to help to explain some of the complications of "performance regimes." There are other approaches which are also useful, for example, the "bureaucratic politics" writers who also stress inter- and intra-organizational power struggles. This is summarized nicely by Gray and Jenkins as "first, the acknowledgment of public administration's organizational basis and, secondly, the recognition of the importance of internal or administrative politics within this organizational system" (Gray and Jenkins 1985, p. 17).

Toward an Institutional Framework for Analyzing Performance Regimes

Performance regimes are defined as a combination of the institutional context within which public agencies work, and the institutional actors that can seek to steer or shape their performance together with the actual ways in which these actors exercise their powers (or do not). Types of interventions will be discussed in Chapter 5, but here the analysis of the institutional context is further elaborated.

The idea and necessity of a performance regime framework is strongly supported by the analysis above. Firstly, that the institutional context of performance is far more complicated than the simplistic "principal–agent" theories, which have tended to dominate thinking about what public sector performance would allow.[2] Secondly, rather than somewhat nebulous ideas about stakeholders and networks, it is possible to identify groups of functionally similar actors within the institutional environment of public service delivery. Thirdly, these institutional actors (or groups of actors) exist in a complex web of interactions. Fourthly, while these are suggested as universally possible elements in a "performance regime," it is clear that the importance of each element can be either of marginal or of great importance. This can vary over jurisdictions, between sectors, and over time. Finally, there are several levels and ways in which each element can exert influence which range from formal powers to various informal mechanisms.

It is of course the case that the institutional environment of individual public organizations is much wider than those institutions that have legitimate and formal rights to "steer" performance, but it is the latter which we are initially interested in mapping. By institutions, in this context, we employ a limited definition focusing on those public formal institutions involved in the "control of mobilisation of resources for the implementation of various goals and the articulation and setting up of certain goals for the collectivity" (Goodin 1996, p. 22).

---

[2] We should stress that some economists have moved beyond simplistic principal–agent models, and even the latter have something to offer. It is rather the simplistic interpretation of principal–agent models found in policy prescriptions which is being criticized.

The set of institutions which are included in the framework are (with UK examples in brackets):

- central ministries (HM Treasury, Cabinet Office)
- line ministries (e.g., Home Office, Department of Health, etc.)
- legislature(s) (e.g., Parliament, Welsh Assembly, and Scottish Parliament)
- audit, inspection, and regulatory agencies (e.g., Audit Commission, NAO, NICE [National Institute for Clinical Excellence], HM Inspectorates', OFSTED [Office for Standards in Education], Committee on Standards in Public Life, etc.)
- judicial and quasi-judicial bodies (e.g., judicial reviews, public inquiries, etc.)
- professional associations[3] (e.g., Royal [medical] colleges, etc.)
- users and formally constituted user bodies[3] (e.g., community health councils)
- other public agencies as partner organizations (e.g., police and CPS)
- agencies themselves (which may be subunits of a larger body, freestanding agencies, or any other organizational form)

The justification for this list derives mainly from the analysis above, but it is worth making a few points of clarification and support for the inclusions (and exclusions) from this framework. While we draw heavily on UK examples, we include other jurisdictions and suggest that the framework does apply to them as well. Before starting it is worth remembering this approach is suggested as a heuristic framework for analysis and not a theory or framework in itself.

We begin with the **central ministries or departments** – what is often called the "core executive" (Weller et al. 1997*b*; Smith 1999). This includes Prime Ministers' or Presidents' Offices, Cabinet Offices, Treasury, Finance, and Personnel Ministries. Clearly, they (may) have a crucial role in determining an overall policy approach to performance throughout the public sector as well as (potentially) setting targets for the core executive itself (Talbot 2000; James 2004). They can also indirectly affect service delivery units through line ministries – for example, in the United Kingdom since 1998 Public Service Agreements between the Treasury and line ministries effectively set targets for many agencies as well as the line ministries themselves. In other jurisdictions this category could include central commissions (such as the Public Service Commission in Canada) or common service agencies (such as the General Services Agency in the United States).

---

[3] To the extent that they have state-sanctioned powers to affect performance of agencies – for example, through "licenses to practice" or formal consultation rights.

Line ministries are those directly in charge of specific policy and delivery areas. There is of course a long history of tensions between central ministries and line ministries over spending and policy issues (Heclo and Wildavsky 1981; Thain and Wright 1996; Deakin and Parry 2000). There is no reason to expect that such tensions would not also arise in relation to performance targets, and early evidence from the United Kingdom certainly suggests this is indeed an issue (Talbot 2000; Comptroller and Auditor General 2001; James 2004). There are also of course issues about line ministries in turn setting targets for their agencies and other funded bodies (Comptroller and Auditor General 1998, 2000; Hyndman 2002; Pollitt and Talbot 2004; Pollitt et al. 2005).

The case for including legislatures is largely self-evident – although it is of course recognized that in different jurisdictions they may play substantially different roles in relation to performance. For example, in the United Kingdom, as compared to say the role of Congress under the GPRA legislation in the United States, the Parliament has had (until recently) little role in the overall performance regime. Whereas Congressional committees have to authorize performance reports and plans, in the United Kingdom this is not done and even scrutiny of performance by Select Committees is very patchy (although recently some have started more systematic engagement – see Home Affairs Select Committee 2005). Also, while Westminster plays little role, the newly devolved bodies in Wales and Scotland seem to be playing a more active part.

The inclusion of audit, inspection, and regulatory bodies is also fairly obvious, especially from the "regulation inside government" literature already examined above, and needs no further justification at this point. By setting standards or making specific recommendations these bodies can effectively impose performance measures or targets (see, e.g., the NAO's recommendations for the Benefits Agency – Comptroller and Auditor General 1998). In the case of the Audit Commission, for example, these powers can even extend to setting specific performance measures for whole classes of organizations (local government) (Campbell-Smith 2008).

Judicial and quasi-judicial bodies is perhaps somewhat less obvious. There has been a general rise in what some call "judicial activism" in a number of countries, especially the "public interest" or common law states (Lewis and Birkinshaw 1993; Hertogh and Halliday 2004). The rechsstaat model states have always had a well-developed public administration law tradition (Pollitt and Bouckaert 2004). Recent analysis of this phenomenon in the United Kingdom suggests it is real, but sometimes exaggerated (Flinders 2001; Syrett 2004). Moreover, a detailed study of the impact of judicial review and homelessness policies has shown the problematic nature of compliance (Halliday 2003).

Alongside judicial review there has also been a growth in the use of public inquiries – sometimes judicial and established statutes governing inquiries, as in the Scott Inquiry into arms sales to Iraq, or sometimes under Crown prerogative powers and not headed by a judge, as in the case of the recent Bichard Inquiry into the Soham murders. The (potential) impact of such inquiries can be gauged from the list of recommendations of the latter inquiry: these covered new IT systems, vetting procedures, training, codes of conduct, registration schemes, etc., and involved several government departments as well as police, social services, and other agencies. The inquiry into the Challenger disaster in the United States was of similar scope (Romzek and Dubnick 1987). In the United Kingdom there has also been the long list of inquiries into child abuse in residential homes (Corby et al. 2001) and elsewhere. All of these have the potential to shape and steer the performance priorities of public services by setting standards of "best practice" or criticizing poor process or substantive performance.

Professional institutes – especially those which exercise "gatekeeping" roles which grant practitioners licenses to practice – clearly have an impact on organizational practices by setting standards for professional practice as in Mintzberg's "professional bureaucracy" model (Mintzberg 1983*b*). For example, recently the UK midwives professional body prohibited members from collecting data from patients about their nationality and citizenship status, which the National Health Service requested them to do for monitoring "health tourism" purposes. This was a clear clash between line ministry and the professional organizations' "performance" requirements for individual midwives, which the professional association seems to have won.

Users (and, to a lesser extent, users' organizations) are widely cited in the literature as important factors in performance design (customer service). However, there are several mechanisms whereby users can have a more active role: if they have choice of provider (and especially if resources are attached to that choice through things like voucher systems or even direct payment); if their user organizations have formal representational powers (e.g., former community health councils in England's rights to be consulted about changes to health service priorities in their areas). These might include indirect influence through other institutional actors – for example, through individual complaints to audit, inspection, regulatory, or professional bodies; or through seeking judicial review; or complaints to a parliamentary ombudsman, etc.

Partners (through contracting or quasi-contracting) are a relatively new (at least in terms of study) category but clearly a class of actors which can affect performance (Walsh et al. 1997; OECD-PUMA 1999; Fortin and Van Hassel 2000; Pollitt and Talbot 2004). Where agencies are forced to establish contractual or quasi-contractual arrangements in purchaser–provider public sector quasi-markets (e.g., between NHS acute and primary care trusts), such contracts will usually themselves embed performance-steering criteria that are relevant to performance regimes. The contracting component is not necessarily restricted to partner organizations – there are often also "vertical" contracts – but this category is about horizontal contracts or quasi-contracts between partners that provide them with leverage over performance of agencies (sometimes called "service-level agreements").

Each of the above may (but not in all cases will) have formal rights to "steer" the performance of public services by either setting standards measures or targets or by demanding an account of performance.

Each can also have indirect influences – so, for example, in the United Kingdom recently, through Public Service Agreements the Treasury can influence line ministries that in turn impose performance imperatives on service delivery organizations. Similarly a legislature might, in principle, be able to instruct an inspection agency to monitor a specific type of performance – for example, the Public Accounts Committee in the House of Commons might ask the NAO to monitor or investigate specific aspects of performance. Users may seek a judicial review, and so on.

These actors have been mapped into a graphical model (Figure 4.1) as a possible generic model of the institutional environment of service delivery units for performance influences. The institutional actors include a range of purely governmental bodies as well as some formally independent actors who (may) have legally sanctioned powers or rights such as users or professional associations. At the moment we have little organized knowledge of even the formal extent of these rights and their exercise and interplay.

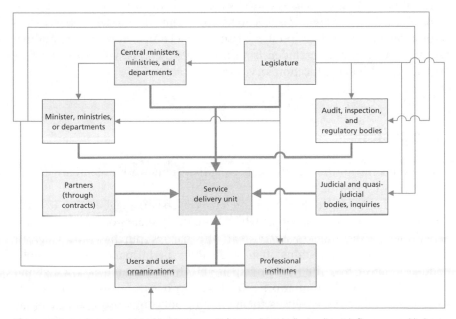

Figure 4.1 Performance Regimes Framework (Heavy lines indicate direct influence, and lighter lines indirect influence, on service delivery unit's performance)

Alongside formal powers there are likely to be strong informal influences and practices that shape the total context within which the performance of service delivery units are "steered." This is what the notion of "performance regime" is meant to convey – the entire ensemble of formal and informal institutional influences that direct or steer the expected performance of public sector service delivery units. ("Regime" is thus used in the more usual political studies sense of the constellation of institutional actors and their formal and informal cooperation and competition. This is somewhat different from the sense of "regimes" developed in urban "regime theory," which tends to focus on non-state actors and only informal relationships (Davies 2001).)

Excluded from analysis are those institutions which are not specific to public services but are involved in generic regulation-type activities – for example, bodies such as (in the United Kingdom) the Health and Safety Executive, Equal Opportunities Commission, or similar bodies that impose performance requirements generically across all employing organizations (although these can sometimes have effects on performance regimes). We will remain sensitive to the possibility that either specific interventions (e.g., a Commission for Racial Equality investigation into prisons) or even generic influences may apply differentially to different agencies.

Some generic influences from those institutions which do feature in our list – for example, requirements from HM Treasury or audit bodies for general accounting standards changes which apply to the whole public sector – will affect all service organizations. In terms of using the model these elements would only be important in inter-jurisdictional comparisons or longitudinal studies, but could be excluded from intra-jurisdictional comparisons (e.g., between health and education services in the same country).

Conclusions

Why is this institutional performance regimes framework potentially useful? What does it allow us to do?

First, what evidence does exist (see analysis above) suggests that it is the totality of a performance regime which potentially shapes or steers performance for specific services rather than the narrow purchaser–provider or principal–agent assumptions often made about performance drivers. Public bodies in effect have multiple principals and this is still under-explored and under-theorized. The framework provides a way of carrying out such explorations. It would be especially useful in carrying out comparisons, for example, between jurisdictions, between sectors, and over time to highlight differences and dynamics.

Second, there is ample scope for tensions between influences from different institutional actors. Both consonant and conflicting influences may coexist for a single service provider – with some types of performance being reinforced by several institutions and others highly contested. The literature on "resource dependence" provides useful examples of coalition building and the dynamics of networks inside government (Smith 1999) and how conflicting interests can be reconciled.

Third, the levers of power that are used by individual performance regime actors may also vary. Writers on power in and around organizations and "resource dependence" suggest several different, but very similar, sets of power levers (Hood 1983; Mintzberg 1983a; Rhodes 1988; Smith 1999; Pfeffer and Salancik 2003 [1978]; Hood and Margetts 2007), which could be used to examine the ways in which actual power is exercised – for example, the informational, authority, financial, and organizational levers mentioned by Smith (1999) based on Hood (1983). This is a substantial issue and will be explored further in Chapter 5.

Fourth, institutional influences are not always consistent over time. Individual actors may have changing preoccupations and priorities that may result in changing emphases in what they see as "good" performance by service delivery units they have some authority over (e.g., Audit Commission indicators for local government shifted from being largely input- and process-driven to being more output-focused over time). The constellation of institutional actors surrounding a specific agency can also change, with new bodies being created and rules and powers varied over time – for example, the changing role of the UK OFSTED or the creation of the UK NICE.

Fifth, it could allow an analysis of the influence of each institutional actor – for example, what emphasis do they place on different aspects of performance (e.g., process, outputs, outcomes, efficiency, equity, etc.)? To this end it would also be possible to develop a classificatory system for weighting the emphasis of specific performance "steers."

Sixth, although the framework itself leaves the "service delivery unit" as a "black box" (Ingraham et al. 2003), it would permit the analysis of the interactions between different performance regimes and different contents of the black box. These contents can be examined from two perspectives: the type of agency and managerial strategies.

It is possible to hypothesize that different "configurations" within service delivery agencies might interact very differently to the same performance regime. Thus, for example, using Mintzberg's typology (1983b), a "machine bureaucracy," "professional bureaucracy," or "adhocracy" might interact very differently with the same performance regime – for example, one dominated by simplified "principal–agent" contracting between a parent ministry and an agency. Wilson's typology (1989) of public agencies, which focuses on the observables of an agency outputs and/or outcomes to provide a classification (production, procedural, craft, and coping organizations), also provides a possible way of examining agency type performance regime interactions.

The framework would also allow for examination of policy and managerial strategies in relation to de facto performance regimes. It would be possible to hypothesize, for example, several policy or managerial reactions. The first we might call "ignore it" – where the problem simply goes unrecognized and unaddressed (all too often the case). The second might be "simplify it" – the drive for simple principal–agent contracts would be a good example. The third might be "coordinate it" – here there are examples such as the "Comprehensive Performance Assessment" in UK local government or the attempts to create "joint inspection" regimes in social services. Finally, there might be a "live with it and use it" strategy – which may take the form of either dysfunctional game playing (De Bruijn 2001) or as the complexity/paradox approaches would suggest, highly functional excellence producing strategies (Quinn 1988; Tirole 1994; Axelrod and Cohen 1999).

Seventh, conflicting performance "drivers" are not necessarily destructive – indeed some writers from an organizational theory perspective (Quinn 1988; Quinn and Cameron 1988; Collins and Porras 1994) and complexity theory approach (Axelrod and Cohen 1999) argue that conflicting imperatives can be positive if managed correctly. Tirole, examining the "multiple principals" problem inside government, from an institutional economics perspective, comes to a similar conclusion (Tirole 1994). The model would allow for examination of the relationship of actual performance, performance regimes, and managerial strategies to establish, if as these writers suggest, correct managerial strategies can produce excellent performance from conflicting external demands.

So the performance regimes framework permits the development of large-scale empirical studies that could be highly cumulative and informative about the real dynamics of performance in public services. Such investigations would have three types of possible outputs: theoretical, policy-relevant, and managerial.

In theory terms it would permit the development of an understanding of the dynamics and development of performance regimes and possible "configurations" or "pure types" (Mintzberg 1983a, p. 292). There are also possibilities for integrating a whole range of different theoretical perspectives around the model. In policy terms, empirical analyses of specific performance regimes and their evolution – and especially the conflicts within them – may allow possible policy responses to develop. In managerial terms such analyses could also help identify important environmental factors within which service delivery agencies have to formulate strategy (and of which they may not be fully cognizant), and also which sort of strategic responses may be most effective.

In Chapter 5, the types of interventions that are actually (or potentially) engaged in by performance regime actors are explored further.

5 Performance Regimes: Interventions

Chapter 4 explored the institutions that make up a performance regime, and how these may change over time. In this chapter we look at the types of interventions these various actors can and do make to try to steer or improve performance of public agencies.

By "interventions" is meant any exercise of power by performance regime institutional actors – executive government, legislatures, courts, auditors, etc. – which is intended to change, steer, or shape the performance of public agencies. Not all institutional actors have all the possible levers of power that may be available, and not all of them choose to use them anyway. Even where formal powers exist, they may not be used and conversely informal levers of power may be used that are not recognized in formal institutional analyses.

One approach would be to look at the possible tools, levers, or resources different sets of institutional actors might have at their disposal. As was suggested at the end of Chapter 4, there is a considerable theoretical literature on this topic. As a way of starting to unpack these issues it might be useful to begin with a widely used resource-based approach, the "tools of government" developed by Hood (1983; Hood and Margetts 2007) and subsequently applied in various ways by others.

Hood proposes four types of "tools" or levers available to public institutions in general:

- **Nodality** – the ability to compel acquisition of information from individuals and organizations and act as focal point for its analysis and distribution (or not). Thus, simply collecting and distributing (or not) some information can have an effect on individuals, groups, and organizations. In performance terms, this might mean collecting and publishing various forms of performance data – for example, the publication of comparative "league tables" of schools' performance.
- **Authority** – the ability of public institutions to compel individuals, groups, and organizations to comply with various laws, regulations, and ordinances – to do, or refrain from doing, certain things. In relation to performance this could mean several things – for example, imposing a duty to report publicly the performance of public agencies or bodies, through to establishing legal standards of performance and citizens'

rights to redress and enforcement. Authority can also be used to enforce systemic changes designed to enhance performance – for example, purchaser–provider splits and "market-type mechanisms" (MTMs). Authority can also be delegated to third parties – for example, the empowering of audit and inspection bodies.

- **Treasure** – the ability to compel the donation of resources (usually but not always money) to public institutions (fees, taxes, etc.) and then to use this money through direct expenditure on goods and services, or as subsidies and payments. The most obvious use of "treasure" as a performance-enhancing tool is through the granting or withholding of resources based on performance, including through contracts or quasi-contractual arrangements. It can also be used more indirectly, for example, through "voucher" schemes where resources follow the user, who in turn chooses providers on the basis of performance information.
- **Organization** – the ability of public institutions to directly control and organize human and other resources to produce goods, services, and other activities themselves. In relation to performance this would mainly mean direct interventions to try to "manage" the performance of public agencies (including things like capability enhancement – see later in this chapter) but it could also be about changing the status and governance of public bodies with the intention of improving performance.

This "NATO" framework (despite the confusing acronym) is a useful one to apply to the various groups of performance regime actors identified in Chapter 4 (see Figure 5.1). In this analysis "Y" means that the institution usually has such a tool or tools at its disposal, and "N" indicates they rarely have such a tool available. The "?" is used to suggest that this may sometimes be the case.

What this indicative analysis shows is that while the executive and legislative branches of government usually have all four tools available to utilize in "steering" the performance of public agencies, all the other institutional actors in the performance regime are in substantially weaker positions with only a limited range of options usually available.

Without going through every judgment suggested above, it is fairly clear, for example, that users usually have very little control over any of the tools, although they, or their representative organizations, could hypothetically receive delegated control over any of these tools. Judicial bodies also have very little control over anything except "authority" and even that would be contested between them and the executive and legislative branches of government.

The application of a "tools" approach also helps to illustrate differences between jurisdictions and over time. The growth of the "audit society" (Power 1997) in the United Kingdom, for example, has seen the growth of the power of auditors and inspectors, through the delegated use of "authority" and "nodality" tools, to steer performance.

	Nodality	Authority	Treasurcy	Organization
Core executive	Y	Y	Y	Y
Line ministries	Y	Y	Y	Y
Legislature	Y	Y	Y	Y
Judicial and quasi-judicial bodies	?	Y	?	N
Auditors and inspectors	Y	Y	N	N
Professional bodies	Y	?	N	N
Users	?	?	?	?
Partner organizations	?	N	?	N

Figure 5.1 Performance Regimes and Tools of Government

(*Note*: The judgments, above, have been made by the author for illustrative purposes. Further research is clearly needed to establish empirically what powers the performance regime actors actually have and use.)

Some types of intervention strategies utilize several of these tools in combination, so, for example, "market-type mechanisms" use "organization" to create purchaser–provider splits, and to disaggregate public agencies into smaller competitive units (Johnson and Talbot 2007*a*); "authority" to compel the establishment of contractual or quasi-contractual relationships between public bodies (Harden 1992); "treasure" by withdrawing the direct funding of "providers" and forcing them to get their resources through the competitive contracting process; and finally "nodality" to compel the supply and/or publishing of performance information on which services can be judged.

As other writers in the "tools of government" approach have illustrated (Salamon 2002), despite Hood's parsimonious typology there are in practice many possible ways in which governments can intervene and many of these apply to performance interventions. Although this theoretical approach is useful therefore in unpacking the particular "tool kit" deployed in any specific intervention strategy, it is these different strategies that are both theoretically and practically important. We turn now to trying to make some sense of this welter of intervention strategies and tactics tried by the United Kingdom and many other governments.

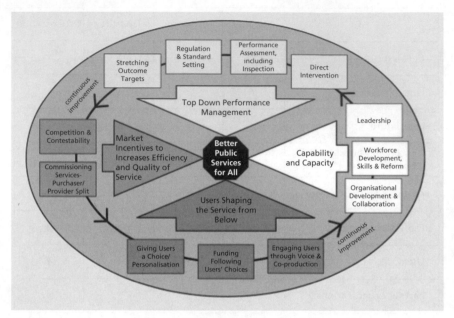

Figure 5.2 The UK Government's Approach to Public Services Reform
Source: Cabinet Office (Strategy Unit) (2006).

The UK government has, by way of example, attempted to provide a coherent explanation of the various types of interventions it has been making to improve the performance of public services and agencies (see Figure 5.2). This is a useful starting point, because, as some have pointed out, the UK government had thrown just about every type of intervention aimed at improving public services they could think of (Walshe et al. 2010b) so the framework is reasonably inclusive of most possible forms of intervention. To be sure, in the UK case these interventions may have been made with very little idea of impact, or sequencing, or interaction between them. And as Walshe and colleagues also rightly point out the UK government's comprehensive version of these interventions is very much a *post hoc* rationalization of a series of disconnected initiatives taken over more than a decade, with no evidence before the publication of this framework that there was any such forethought or grand plan behind each specific initiative. At best this is what can been called an "emergent strategy" – that is, one that is only discernable in hindsight (Mintzberg et al. 1998).

Despite its origins, this framework does form a useful categorization of types of intervention if each of the four central arrows is seen as a specific type of intervention strategy. We can reformulate them, and add in some forms of intervention that are not explicitly mentioned in this framework but nonetheless form a logical part of each strategy, as follows (using UK examples):

1. **Managerial-contractual interventions**: using direct, top-down, management control or more arm's-length quasi-contractual arrangements to enforce performance through imposed or agreed targets and enforcement. This can also include the delegation to third parties (audit and inspection bodies) the enforcement of minimum standards of performance. For example: "Next Steps" agencies and KPIs; Ministries and Public Service Agreements; etc.

2. **Market or market-like systemic change interventions**: systemic reforms to create competition at the organizational (business-to-business) level – resource- or status-based – between public agencies. This can include restructuring to create purchaser–provider splits; smaller and more providers (including nonpublic) to create greater competition; publication of "league tables" or "star ratings" of comparable agencies; contractual or quasi-contractual (service delivery agreements) relationships between agencies; etc. Often requires the establishment of market regulators and the empowerment of auditors or inspectors to publish independently performance data. For example: schools and hospitals (NHS Trusts) league tables; NHS internal market; social-care market; compulsory competitive tendering; outsourcing; etc.

3. **Giving users voice and/or choice through systemic interventions**: empowering users by either giving them formal rights to "voice" in shaping services; specific, enforceable rights and entitlements; or by providing choice of service provider, usually including a resources follows user approach. For example, patient choice in NHS and parental choice in education; formal "voice" through obligatory consultations in local and central government; former "Community Health Councils" which provided formal user representation; etc.

4. **Capability and capacity interventions**: focusing on providing aid to enhance capability of existing organizations either through development support, specific reforms, or restructuring. For example, direct support for leadership (creation of National Leadership colleges in education, health, universities, and many other sectors); replacement of leadership through "hit squads" in failing schools or hospitals; capability reviews in central government departments; some aspects of "Comprehensive Performance Assessment" in local government; reorganizations to enhance capability – for example, mergers: merger of Benefits Agency and Employment Service to create JobCentres Plus; merger of HM Customs and Inland Revenue; the whole "agency" program in UK central government, copied in many other countries; etc.

Having briefly outlined these four broad approaches to intervention it is useful to note a few things before having a closer look. All of these approaches are intended to improve performance, yet they all embed rather different assumptions (theories-in-use) about the best ways to achieve that. These differences make them, to some degree at least, incompatible. Indeed there may even be incompatibilities within each group of interventions – for example, voice and choice can work against each other, because if the most vocal and articulate users are allowed to exit from a specific provider (choice) this will in all probability weaken the voice of those left using the same provider.

In the next sections these four intervention strategies will be examined in more depth, including examining the theoretical assumptions and underpinnings associated with each, as well as some empirical evidence from the ESRC Public Services Programme (and elsewhere) about "what works" (and what does not).

It is worth mentioning one important contextual issue about the nature of the organizations that are the subject of performance interventions – particularly whether they are single, monopoly providers (e.g., a single national passport agency) or there are multiple units providing similar services (e.g., schools). We will return to this subject in Chapter 9, but it is worth noting here that the same performance intervention may have very different impacts depending on this factor – and indeed may be impossible if there is only one monopoly provider. So, for example, requiring a single passport agency to publish performance information (see next section) is likely to have a very different impact from the same requirements placed on several hundred very similar health or education delivery organizations.

Another complicating factor is that the same type of performance improvement intervention may well have more than one purpose – indeed performance measurement and management policies have nearly always been seen as serving multiple policy purposes (Talbot 2005a) and this also applies to very specific interventions. Thus, for example, requiring English NHS Trusts to produce a range of performance data about themselves and even the creation of composite indicators based on this data can be, and has been, used for multiple purposes:

- For managerial purposes to reward/punish managements or organizations.
- For competition purposes to inform purchasers within an internal market.
- For voice and choice purposes to enable patients to assess providers.
- For capability purposes to target "failing" organizations and intervene – for example, to replace the leadership, merge organizations, etc.

On a related point, not all interventions fall into these four categories – for example, some changes in the legal aspects of the performance regime do not easily fall into any of these categories, and they will be discussed after these four main groups of interventions have been examined a bit more closely.

Managerial-Contractual Interventions

The first type of performance intervention is top-down performance management. In a traditional public bureaucracy this would be a straight-forward managerial intervention, very close in nature to "management by objectives." It involves imposing objectives, measures, and targets on, or agreeing them with, subordinate units or individuals. The latter may or may not be formally part of a single organizational structure (e.g., a department or ministry) or they may be more arm's-length agencies, sometimes created with the specific aim of improving performance and introducing performance management systems (Pollitt and Talbot 2004; Pollitt et al. 2004).

PERFORMANCE REPORTING

The minimalist version of such interventions would be to simply impose a requirement on lower bodies to publicly report not only on their expenditures (an almost universal requirement, certainly in democracies) but also on some form of "results." The Government Performance and Results Act (1992) in the US federal government places such a requirement on federal agencies (it also goes further in requiring them to publish their own performance plans for the future).

In this US example, or similar cases, most of the organizations required to publish information are unique and any comparisons can only be made (often with difficulty) with similar organizations in other countries. However it is also possible to place such a requirement upon unique organizations, such as schools or hospitals. Most often, this has been done either explicitly or implicitly with the intention of enabling comparisons and hence competition between agencies (see below) – but simply requiring the publication of results does not automatically imply such comparisons and competition.

The Scottish and Welsh regional governments, for example, have specifically tried to retain some aspects of performance reporting for schools and hospitals but without the competitive "league tables" created by the UK government in England. UK central government itself requires all universities to publish various types of performance data, but does not create "league tables" as it does for schools or hospitals. In "nodality" terms this is using government's control of information flows to create or withhold "league tables" – however, even when they are withheld this does not prevent third parties (usually the media) from gathering locally published data together to create their own league tables (as has happened for Scottish schools or UK universities).

TARGETS

The act of publishing performance results – indicators or measures – does not by itself of course imply any standard or target level of performance to be achieved. It is a necessary, but not sufficient, condition for the setting of specific performance targets – but the two are regularly confused in the popular mind and media. A top-down requirement to simply publish results should not be confused with a top-down requirement to achieve a specific performance target.

A second source of confusion is between targets that seek to raise the performance of all organizations by setting so-called stretch targets and the setting of minimum standards of performance. Targets designed to increase maximum performance – often called "stretch targets" – are most often employed in situations of single service providers. Minimum standards targets are more likely in situations where there are multiple providers.

One area of debate around stretch targets is how far should they stretch performance? If they are set too high, there are almost certain to be some failures to meet the required targets, but if they are set too low they are likely to be too easily met. There has been some lively debate about this in policy-making circles (Bichard 1999; Alexander and Agency Policy Review Team 2002; Public Administration Select Committee 2003) but surprisingly little research. It raises important issue about the motivational impact of targets which has been widely researched in the individual performance area (Latham 2007) but very little in relation to organizational targets. Moreover, in the context of public agencies there are issues about what levels of "failure" to meet stretch targets would be acceptable to different actors in the performance regime. Some have suggested simply heuristics such as an 80/20 rule – targets should be set for organizations such that usually they are able to meet or exceed 80% of them (e.g., see Bichard's evidence in Public Administration Select Committee 2003). However, there does not appear to be much research to support such a proposition.

The issue of minimum standard targets is an interesting one – in public policy discourse "standards" have often been held up as an alternative to "targets," which of course they are not – they are merely minimum as opposed to maximum targets. Minimum standards, or "floor standards" as they are also sometimes called, have been used in several ways. One is a purely managerial use – defining minimum acceptable standards of performance to which all agencies are expected to adhere. These have been applied to services (outputs) as well as to internal processes. In the former case – services – they have also sometimes been used to introduce an element of competition through quality awards (see below).

PERFORMANCE BUDGETS

A further development of managerial performance interventions is to tie together the budgetary and performance systems. Most often performance systems have developed in parallel to existing budget processes, including budget setting, control, reporting, inspection (audit), and management systems. One effect of such parallel development has often been a disjunction between finance and performance systems – and indeed other organizational systems (Talbot 2000, 2004a, 2005a; Modell 2009).

One solution has been to try and integrate performance and budget systems to produce a single mechanism for allocating resources and performance targets, and reporting and managing both. This has, however, proved more difficult in practice than the rhetoric promoting the idea would suggest as studies of US states, where the practice is well advanced, have shown (Moynihan 2005; 2006).

QUASI-CONTRACTS

A final form of top-down managerial performance intervention is the imposition of some form of quasi-contractual arrangement. This is sometimes difficult to distinguish from the sort of performance budgeting reform described above – if there is a qualitative difference, it is probably in the notion of attaching some form of reward/sanction to performance budget and, although this is less crucial, the idea of some notional arm's-length separation between the contracting parties. The term "quasi" is used because these are rarely, if ever, legally enforceable contracts and the hierarchical nature of the relationship between the contracting parties means they are asymmetrical in nature – they can be enforced by the contracting party but not usually by the contractor (Common et al. 1992; Harden 1992; Lidbury and Petrie 1999). They have the appearance of contracts, but in practice are merely codifications of hierarchical relationships.

As the examples given above show, the focus of managerial–contractual interventions can cover the full range of aspects of performance – from (using simple definitions) inputs, through process and outputs to outcomes and including efficiency, quality, and other performance measures.

As the term "managerial" implies, this form of performance intervention is most usually undertaken by the executive branch of government but of course is a highly developed "separation of powers" such as in the United States this can, and often does, involve tussles between the executive and legislative branches. Indeed one criticism of this form of intervention, insofar as it is embedded in initiatives like GPRA, is that it assumes a simplistic hierarchy which does not apply in the United States (and some other) contexts (Radin 2000, 2006*a*).

However, other actors in the performance regime may make interventions of the type described here: professional institutes may, for example, set standards of individual performance for professionals that may, or may not, coincide with what other actors want from individuals. For example, in the United Kingdom the medical profession has sought to implement "risk-based" regulation of doctors, in this case with government backing (Lloyd-Bostock and Hutter 2008).

Partner organizations may seek to set quasi-contractual performance standards (as in, e.g., service-level agreements). There may also be circumstances in which the courts become involved in deciding upon conflicting or unclear minimum standards of service provision or deciding on standards for process, to ensure due process, equity, etc. So although in general these managerial measures are mainly implemented by the executive (and sometimes legislative) branch of government, they can potentially be used by many other institutional actors.

Capability Interventions

Whereas the previous set of interventions concentrated on defining and managing the results of organizational activities, another set of intervention strategies focus on those activities themselves and in many ways seek to "micro-manage" performance even more than imposing performance measures, targets, and quasi-contracts. These are interventions focused on the internal capacity of the organization.

CAPABILITY REVIEWS

As discussed later (Chapter 7) one aspect of the organizational effectiveness and performance measurement movements has been, for many years, whether to include the measurement of internal organizational factors in the "mix" of performance measurement. One solution adopted by multidimensional performance measurement models is to have two separate categories of performance assessment – one dealing with "results" and another with "enablers" or internal performance drivers such as leadership, strategy, resource, people, and process management as in the European "Excellence" model (again see Chapter 7). Even a cursory examination of the international literature on public management reform reveals that governments have made numerous interventions aimed at improving performance of public organizations by addressing one or other of these capability dimensions (Ferlie et al. 2004; Pollitt and Bouckaert 2004; OECD 2005).

There have been several attempts to assess overall capacity or capability in public agencies.

One recent example in the UK government has been the "Departmental Capability Reviews" (DCRs) conducted since 2006 that examined the dimensions of leadership, strategy, and delivery capability. Another UK example is the Comprehensive Performance Assessments (CPA) of local governments carried out by the Audit Commission, which looked at both results and capacity. Some other public sector performance frameworks, such as the Canadian "Management Accountability Framework" (MAF), the European "Common Assessment Framework" (CAF), the US Government Performance Project (GPP) and Federal Performance Project (FPP) (Ingraham et al. 2003), and the "Workways of Government" project (Davidson 2003), all contained substantial capacity assessments (see Chapter 6 and especially Chapter 8 for further discussion of these frameworks and models).

These interventions have come from a variety of sources: DCRs in the United Kingdom and MAF in Canada from within the executive branch of government; CPA in the United Kingdom from the executive branch, but via an audit and inspection body; the European CAF from a supra-national body (EU) coupled with a university (Speyer) and a foundation (EFQM); the US GPP and FPP initially from a foundation (Pew) and a university (Syracuse); and finally the "Workways" project from two think tanks (Brookings and the Governance Institute).

Despite all this apparent activity, comprehensive assessments of public agencies, capabilities, and capacities have been dwarfed by the amount of effort put into attempting to improve the various individual dimensions of performance capability. As has been recently pointed out in relation to the UK government (Walshe et al. 2010b) and to international reform efforts (OECD 2005), these efforts have often been disconnected from one another both conceptually and in practice, with often multiple overlapping reforms being implemented without any obvious thought to sequencing or links between them.

In order to make some sense of this welter of change efforts directed at improving performance of public agencies by improving their capabilities and capacities, in what follows we will use the "enabler" categories taken from the European "excellence" model as a convenient set of dimensions that capture a great deal of this activity: leaders, strategy, resources, people, processes, and innovation (the latter is not strictly a dimension of the "excellence" framework but has been an increasing focus of attention in capacity-building interventions). (More information about many of these efforts can be found in the various general surveys of public management reform (e.g., Ferlie et al. 2004; Pollitt and Bouckaert 2004; OECD 2005), so rather than repeatedly reference them here they are taken as "givens" in what follows and only more specific references will be made where appropriate.)

LEADERSHIP

A great deal of effort has gone into improving the leadership of public organizations (Brookes and Grint 2010; OECD 2001; Raffel et al. 2009*b*) and there is little shortage of research literature on leadership generically or in the public sector. Initiatives have come mainly from the executive branch of government and, internationally, have utilized a wide variety of approaches including national leadership colleges, tailored leadership development programs, succession planning, open competition, term contracts, performance reporting, performance-related pay, leadership replacement (in failure situations) – for example, so-called super-heads for English schools, etc. There is insufficient space here to do justice to the range of policy initiatives or to the theoretical difficulties with defining adequately the scope and content of leadership in general or in the specific context of public services. Leadership is something of an "umbrella construct" (Hirsch and Levin 1999 – for full discussion see Chapter 7).

STRATEGY AND PLANNING

Intervening to encourage public agencies to improve their strategies and plans has been a common feature on many public service reform programs. GPRA in the US federal government requires not just performance planning and reporting, but for agencies to produce more elaborate strategic planning documents, for example. Similar approaches have been adopted in the United Kingdom toward central government agencies (Next Steps Team 1995). Support has been offered, often through national public sector colleges, for developing better understanding of strategy and planning.

RESOURCES MANAGEMENT

Reforming the way in which public agencies manage resources has been tackled in various ways – changing accounting procedures to introduce resource or accruals budgeting and accounts, separating current and capital budgets, bringing in more specialist managers with resource and accountancy management skills, carrying out audits of assets and selling off unnecessary ones, sell and lease back schemes, private finance initiatives and public–private partnerships, devolving resource budgets, etc.

Ideas such as "business process engineering" (Hammer and Champy 1993; Hammer 1995), "lean thinking" (Womack and Jones 1996), "benchmarking" (Spendolini 1992; Bendell and Boulter 1993; Czarnecki 1999), and others have been fairly widely implemented as attempts to change and improve processes within the public sector (e.g., see Samuels 1997; Courty and Marschke 2004; Askim et al. 2007; Keehley and Abercrombie 2008).

PEOPLE MANAGEMENT

One of the biggest cultural shifts in public services has been the reform of the way in which people are managed – (allegedly) away from "personnel" to "human resource" management (Farnham and Horton 1996; Reichenberg 2006) with a shift in emphasis from process toward performance: term contracts, performance-related pay, performance appraisals, "right-sizing" and reconfiguring workforces, outsourcing, devolution of people management down to line managers, and many other initiatives.

INNOVATION

Probably the most recent additions to this panoply of capability-focused interventions are the ones aimed at improving "innovation capacity." Innovation has been very fashionable in the private sector and there is a large literature on innovation studies (Fagerberg et al. 2005), although most innovative change in the public sector has, until recently, been subsumed under the rubric of "reform" – although there are exceptions (Kimberly and Pouvourville 1993). More recently studies using the language of innovation have started to emerge (Abramson and Littman 2002; Rivenbark and Kelly 2003; Kelman 2005), paralleling and reporting on new policy initiatives in (some) governments – see, for example, the UK governments Public Service Reform Innovators Council.[1]

These types of pressures for increased capability in leadership, strategy making, resource management, and so on have come mainly from the executive branch of government although others have also contributed to both the pressure and offers of aid in developing some of these capabilities.

---

[1] http://www.hmg.gov.uk/innovation.aspx

(RE)ORGANIZATION

There is one further type of intervention to mention – reorganizations aimed at increasing the capacity of an organization to deliver superior performance. Reorganization – or "redisorganization" as one cynic called it – is one of the favorite past-times of governments (OECD 2005). We have seen waves of aggregation and disaggregation of public services delivery organizations (Johnson and Talbot 2007a) and of ministries (Pollitt 1984). The fashion for creating arm's-length "agencies" in many countries in the 1990s was one such period of a specific type of disaggregation in central government organizations. In the United States the (short-lived) agency policy was even called creating "performance-based organizations" and all such reorganizations were predicated on the notion of improving, in some way, the performance of the units involved (see Pollitt and Talbot 2004 for the general movement and specifically Graham and Roberts' chapter on the United States). More recently there have been some indications of trends back toward aggregation – mergers – as the best way of improving performance – for example, the creation of the Department of Homeland Security in the United States or the wave of mergers right across public services in the United Kingdom since 2000 (Johnson and Talbot 2007a). Very often the justifications for these reorganizations have included both a capability and a performance component – the new organizational configuration is supposed to be both more capable of, and will actually deliver, enhanced performance (however "performance" is defined). Sometimes the same justifications are deployed to support (often sequential) changes that go in completely opposite directions – thus breaking up civil service organizations into smaller agencies was, in part, justified as a way of achieving greater efficiency (Jenkins et al. 1988) and the subsequent mergers of many agencies into larger entities was also justified, in part, on the expected efficiency gains to be made (Johnson and Talbot 2007a).

Reorganization is also not necessarily just about size – it may also, or instead, be about the governance and status of the organization without necessarily changing its structure. In some of the "agency" programs pursued in many countries the principal reform was about changing the status of the organizations rather than carving them out of them from larger entities, for example. Privatizing agencies, which still continue to deliver public services and are fully funded by the public sector, is clearly the most radical of this type of change. But many intermediate reforms such as moving organizations onto a different status by making them into agencies, quangos, public interest corporations, etc., has been widely advocated and implemented (Pollitt and Talbot 2004; OECD 2005; Prabhakur 2006).

Recently there has also been an increased focus from policy-makers on what some have called "joined up government" – and in this context that specifically includes interventions aimed at changing the relationships between multiple public agencies to improve systemic performance (Frederickson and Frederickson 2006).

COORDINATING CAPABILITY INTERVENTIONS?

The primary issue to note here is that all these many and varied interventions can look much more systematic, thought-through, and coordinated, when set out in the above fashion, than they actually are. In reality they have often been messy, overlapping, sometimes contradictory, and often with only the flimsiest of links to any theory of improvement and performance. There is nothing surprising in this and public organizations have probably always been subjected to reform "tides" that emphasize different aspects of capability and results (Light 1997) and these are clearly more often than not "emergent strategies," as opposed to deliberate, thought-through-in-advance ones (Mintzberg 1994).

The present author has frequently used the above categorization of improvement interventions, derived from the Excellence model, with groups of senior managers to ask them to identify what improvement initiatives they were currently running in their own organizations and where they thought their main capability problems lay. The results were almost invariable (*a*) they were surprised by how many initiatives they already had in place and how uncoordinated these seemed to be, and (*b*) most often they thought there were serious areas of capability unaddressed. This is of course not research, but this anecdotal evidence certainly corresponds with what many researchers have said about these various capacity initiatives. Most of these very specific interventions, mostly emanating higher levels of government, have been informed, explicitly or implicitly, by theoretical assumptions as most researchers on the wider public service reform policies have stated. But, as these analysts have also pointed out, there are frequently slightly different, or more than one, theoretical assumptions underpinning reforms (Aucoin 1990; Pollitt 1993).

One further point, which is addressed more fully in Chapter 8, is do improvements in capability correlate with, and indeed cause, improvements in results? One obvious theoretical assumption underpinning all these initiatives, whether taken collectively or individually, is that improving all or any of these capability dimensions will lead to improved results. Unfortunately the research on this is equivocal at best.

Systemic Interventions I: Competition

MARKET TYPE MECHANISMS

We turn now to the first type of "systemic" intervention – by which we mean changes designed to alter the entire "rules of the game." One of the most widespread of these has been the attempt to introduce various forms of internal competition, or "market-type mechanisms" (MTMs), into public services. The explicit aim in these changes has been to improve performance, defined variously as efficiency, service delivery, quality, etc. Competition, however, does not have to be conceived in purely financial language, as terms like MTMs tend to imply. Competition can also take nonfinancial forms, as in competition for status ranking, for example. Systemic changes – especially of the competition variety – also often imply large-scale organizational changes to facilitate the workings of the new competitive system.

It has long been known that competition exists within classical bureaucratic hierarchies (Skok 1989). As one expert neatly put it "the currency of bureaucratic competition is currency" (Peters 1995, p. 217), that is the struggle for budgets although not just budgets, but for control of policy areas, etc. (Dunleavy 1991). However, this type of competition has nothing directly to do with performance, merely being about control. Competition aimed at improving performance requires very different structures from classical bureaucratic hierarchies, which are usually assumed to be fairly large, multifunctional, and monolithic. For performance-oriented competition to come into play one of two forms of disaggregation is needed.

The first disaggregation is to create multiple provider or service delivery units that can be compared in some way with one another.

Although things like "schools," "hospitals," and "universities" have existed as discernable units within even large bureaucratic hierarchies without some degree of formal autonomy and separation constructing any sort of competitive relationship between them, that is likely to impact on performance, is problematic (Pollitt et al. 2004; Talbot 2004b). Using the United Kingdom as an example – the creation of "Locally Managed Schools" and "NHS Trusts" in the education and health fields was a prerequisite for any sort of formalized (institutionalized) competition system within these fields (Common et al. 1992). This type of disaggregation is a prerequisite specifically for the type of nonfinancial competitive systems characterized as "league tables," or "benchmarking," which are discussed further below.

The second type of disaggregation is between "purchasers" and "providers." This can be used both for competitive and noncompetitive purposes.

In the latter case what is achieved is the sort of noncompetitive purchaser–provider quasi-contractual arrangements between a single purchaser and a single provider, symbolized by programs like the United Kingdom's "Next Steps" agencies and other similar agencification policies (Greer 1994; Pollitt and Talbot 2004).

But it is the former, competitive, type of systemic organizational change that concerns us at the moment. Here the change requires at least multiple, competing provider units and in many cases has included the creation of multiple purchaser units as well. One of the most well documented cases of this is the "internal market" within the United Kingdom (English) NHS during first the 1990s and then again in the mid-2000s. In the first case (under the then Conservative government) multiple District Health Authorities, and a small number of "fund-holder" GP practices, were the purchasers and NHS trusts the providers. In the second incarnation (under New Labour) the purchasers are primary care trusts (PCTs) and the providers are, once again, other NHS trusts (although considerably fewer in number than in the first iteration).

LEAGUE TABLES AND BENCHMARKING

The first competitive system to consider is the simplest – league tables. As the popular name suggests, this idea is based on a sporting analogy such as the National Football League (United States) or Premier Division of the Football League (United Kingdom) – groups of roughly equivalent teams who get rated on their performance and rank-ordered by performance within their league – hence league tables.

The performance aims of simple league tables are to firstly rank the various public agencies and secondly, hopefully, encourage them to strive to be nearer the top than the bottom of the rankings. Such league tables have proliferated enormously in recent years covering everything from local schools, hospitals, universities, police forces, local governments, national ministries, and even between whole national governments (see Chapter 6).

Some are not simple, or necessarily expressed as simple league tables and have adopted what could probably more properly be called a "benchmarking" approach. Notably some of the comparisons of different state (US) or local (UK) governments have been rather more complex. In the United States, the Government Performance Project (GGP) used multiple criteria to judge the performance of the fifty US states (Ingraham et al. 2003). In the United Kingdom, three different "benchmarking" approaches have been applied to local government in England, Scotland, and Wales – respectively the Comprehensive Performance Assessments, the Best Value Programme (BVP), and the Wales Programme for Improvement (WPI) (Downe et al. 2007).

Apart from the organizational prerequisites for such league tables or benchmarking programs discussed above, they also require a second important development – composite indicators of performance by which the various agencies can be ranked. Without a single aggregate metric – for example, points scored based on wins [3 points], losses [0], and draws [2] in English soccer – comparative tables would be impossible, or lack credibility. It would, of course, be possible to use just a single direct metric such as exam scores for schools, but in practice any meaningful comparison requires multiple measures aggregated into a single number to enable ranking. Even what can appear to be a single metric such as "exam scores" can actually turn out to be a composite metric, as various degrees of success have to be somehow aggregated to get a single number – just football leagues table ranks are determined by three separate sets of points awarded for wins, losses, and draws. This has developed so far that the OECD and European Commission have issued joint guidance to governments of constructing such composite indicators (OECD and European Commission 2008).[2]

It should be noted that the whole system of league tables, scoring systems, and any subsequent incentive systems linked to rankings are sometimes, but not always, developed by executive government. In England some league tables have been constructed by central government while others – like the local government league tables in England – by other bodies (in this case the Audit Commission). In the United States, Republican members of Congress developed their own league table of federal agencies using data from GRPA reports (during the Clinton Presidency), subjectively converted into scores by Congressional aids (Radin 2006*a*). In Ireland, central and local government collaboratively constructed them, while in Poland local governments have been developing their own, independently organized, comparative benchmarking system.

League table-based approaches do not usually have any incentives other than ones of status attached to them, although more recently some governments have attached nonfinancial incentives such as so-called earned autonomy and decreased regulatory burdens for some of the top performers.

OTHER FORMS OF COMPETITION

More actual competition is created where there are multiple purchasers and multiple providers, and the latter have to compete for contracts, and thus resources, from the former. Usually providers are expected to compete on price and quality criteria. This is expected to push up levels of efficiency and

---

[2] It should be noted that although composite indicators are a necessity for constructing league tables, they are not just used for this purpose, but can also be used for managerial and other objectives.

quality of service provision within provider organizations. Further competitive pressures can be added by allowing nonprofits and even profit-based organizations to move into the market.

There are other ways in which competitive pressures can be created that do not include whole organizations – by forcing organizations to subject some aspects of their service and/or back-office functions (such as personnel, finance, and estates management) to competitive tendering processes.

Of course there is a further step that can be taken, which is to shift whole organizations from the public to the private sectors and create regulated markets for public services, as happened with many utilities during the 1980s and 1990s. However, as this moves formal ownership of the public domain it removes these types of organizations from the scope of this book.

All of these types of systemic interventions seek to create competitive pressures – financial and nonfinancial – on public agencies to improve their performance. Strictly speaking they shift competition away from bureaucratic politics (which absent of performance management systems do not create any pressure for improved performance) toward more market or market-like forms of competition.

IMPACT OF COMPETITION ON PERFORMANCE

Evaluating how effective these types of systemic interventions are in actually improving performance is problematic, for several reasons. Firstly, they rarely occur in isolation from many of the other reforms/interventions described in this chapter. Secondly, because they often involve the disaggregation of bureaucratic hierarchies into smaller units, there is often a dearth of baseline data against which to judge performance trends. Thirdly, because the performance measurement systems that are applied are often relatively new they tend to have a high "churn rate" in what is measured, making longitudinal assessments difficult (Talbot 2004a).

Despite these barriers many attempts have been made to assess the efficacy of competition-based changes in improving performance.

One major study of the three UK systems (CPA, BVP, and WPI mentioned above) found that all three seemed from the evidence to have made a positive contribution to improving performance, perhaps most especially the English CPA program (Downe et al. 2007). However others within the same research ESRC Program have been more critical claiming that CPA was vulnerable to categorization errors and gaming, was inconsistent with other government policies, and failed to deal adequately with uncontrollable factors (McLean et al. 2007). Assessments of the effectiveness of league tables in health and education in the United Kingdom and the United States as tools for performance improvement have been the subject of similar long-running controversies.

Competition-based systemic changes can be implemented mainly by only either the executive or legislative branches of governments, but once in place a gamut of performance regime actors may become involved. The latter may both be involved in setting and refining the regulatory and competition environments within which competition is set to take place.

So, for example, the British government has changed the rules of the game for league-table-based competition in education several times, mainly through refining the basis of the league tables. These were initially based simply on measures of exam results (percentage of students gaining a certain level of examination results). But these have been changed to first include "value-added" (VA) elements (i.e., the difference between educational attainment levels of pupils before they enter a school and when they leave) and later also for environmental factors like poverty – "contextual value added" (CVA) (Leckie and Goldstein 2009).

However, once the competitive system is in place other actors such as auditors and inspectors may become involved – in the case of UK schools this includes, for example, inspections by Office for Standards in Education (OFSTED) and in principle any of the other performance regimes actors can become involved in trying to intervene.

(See also the next section, which shows how such a system can be extended to include elements of choice and voice.)

Systemic Interventions II: Voice and Choice

A second type of systemic intervention to improve performance of public services has centered around notions of "voice" and "choice" for users of public services – akin to the idea of a consumer in the private sector (Clarke et al. 2007). The idea is that public services are subject to "producer capture" and organized for the convenience of the workers that run them, rather than for the people who use them. Drawing on Hirschman's seminal text on "Exit, Loyalty and Voice" (Hirschman 1970) choice (exit) and voice are posed as the main ways in which users can affect the performance of services in their interests.

RIGHTS AND ENTITLEMENTS

One approach is to create defined rights, entitlements, or service standards that set out exactly what a user of public services can expect to receive and then create mechanisms through which these can be enforced or restituted for when they fail to be met. The most well-known government-level initiative in this direction was the Citizens' Charter initiated by the UK government in 1991 (Prime Minister and Chancellor of the Duchy of Lancaster 1991). This forced all central government bodies and some regulated and local services to produce "Charter Standards" – for example, the Taxpayers Charter and the Patients Charter – that set standards of service for each service. These "rights" were meant to be enforceable and users would be able to seek recompense when services failed to meet the stated standards (Harrow and Talbot 1993).

"Charter"-style reforms represent one form of "voice" – others include: encouraging or mandating consultation processes with users and/or stakeholders; encouraging or mandating regular surveys of user opinion of services; creating user fora – user boards, committees, groups – in which views about services can be expressed and that may even be given statutory rights to be consulted; etc.

These types of "voice" reforms can also be closely linked to the "league tables' " approach in the previous section – providing users with detailed comparisons of whether "their" service compares to a range of other, similar, providers and thus stimulating "voice" where services compare unfavorably.

There is of course a much older tradition of seeing failure to deliver services in an appropriate manner – the ombudsman approach (Rowat 1985). And of course in many public law traditions citizens have always had rights to appeal to the administrative courts about malpractices – but the focus of both of these was mainly on performance of due process, which is a very limited aspect of performance.

USER CHOICE

User choice is a much more radical solution – this changes the system so that users can choose their service provider. This may be a choice merely between competing public agencies or include nonprofit and private suppliers (see the section on "Competition" above). It is usually assumed that this only has any real impact if it is tied to resources in some way – such as resources follow users. This can take the form of simple bureaucratic transfers or even "vouchers" or "tokens." But it is at least arguable that even reputational effects may have an impact – for example, if a school which is seen as "excellent" has higher applications for entry than one which is seen less favorably, this by itself would reinforce the image of success.

As with "competition" on an organization to organization basis discussed in the previous section, although the executive and legislative branches of government will likely be the prime movers in establishing systemic changes like these, once established any or all of the stakeholders in the performance regime may become actively involved.

This brief tour of various methods of intervention to improve performance – managerial, capacity, competition, and choice and voice – is nowhere near exhaustive. It is merely meant to make the point that a wide variety of measures have been, and are being, tried by governments and others to intervene to improve the performance of public agencies, and not just through performance measurement and management, as the "performance movement" is usually restricted to as an analytic category. Focusing just on those things which are specifically labeled as "performance" misses the point that virtually all public management reforms and interventions are intended to improve some aspect of performance as conceived by those promoting the changes or interventions.

Performance Regimes: Institutions, Interventions, and Theory

What conclusions can we draw about performance from this and the previous chapter on performance regimes?

The first conclusion is that performance regimes matter – and is a neglected area of study. The configuration on institutional actors who may intervene to shape policy, what tools are available to them to intervene, and the way in which those tools are deployed (or not) are all important factors in shaping the environment within which performance of public agencies is made and judged.

Theoretically using a "tools-of-government" or "resource-dependence" perspective to understand both what constitutes – institutionally – the performance regime and also how the various groups factors actually seek to shape performance seems the most fruitful approach. Obviously these two sets of theories – "tools" and "resource-dependence" are not identical, although there is substantial overlap. But even within each there are substantial differences. Recent work on resource-based theories in strategic management, just to take one example, show that there are a substantial range of interpretations and approaches within this (supposedly) single approach (Barney and Clark 2007). Nevertheless, from a realist perspective, some synthesis of these ideas which provides a common analytical framework for understanding which institutions and interventions really "count" in shaping performance would seem the most fruitful direction to move in.

Asking, for example, whether or not a particular group of actors actually has any leverage through tools or resources is one path toward defining what constitutes the real performance regime for any public agency. If any "stake-holders" do not have any tools or resources with which to seek to shape performance, they are not part of the performance regime for that agency. This does not mean they are not "stakeholders" in the sense of being affected by the consequences of the agencies actions – on the contrary they may well be significantly impacted by those activities. But if there are no "levers of control" (Simons 1995), they have no power to shape performance.

A great deal more research is needed to establish what the real performance regimes are for various public agencies. This research needs to adopt reason-ably common approaches to be fruitful and allow comparisons across time and place. The specific model offered in Chapter 4 of the (possible) institu-tional groups of actors, and the attempts in this chapter to classify various types of interventions, may not be precisely the ones needed. The simple model offered in Chapter 4 is, for example, pitched at the level of central government and analysis of other tiers of government, or more complex governance arrangements would require significant modification. The exact range of "tools" or "resources" selected also changes the range of actors to be included or excluded. Including or excluding "nodality" means, for example, including or excluding the media as a significant actor in the performance regime. But the approach of trying to map institutional actors and the range of powers they have available to shape performance, and how they are deployed in practice, do at least start to point in the directions we ought to be looking in order to better understand performance regimes and their possible impacts.

The other major area for study is the impacts and reactions that the performance regime produces within public agencies. Do interventions pro-duce the desired results or do they produce unintended consequences as well (positive or negative) and maybe even resistance and gaming? One hypothesis would be that the greater the number of active constituents in the perform-ance regime, the more diverse their intervention tools and objectives, the more opportunity for gaming by the public agency would exist and the more real performance would suffer. Such a view, maybe not formulated precisely in this way, has often been expressed in the literature on performance.

An opposite view has also emerged – that complex performance regimes can be best suited for shaping the performance of complex organizations (such as public agencies). Unfortunately more has been written in terms of normative theorizing on these subjects than on good, solid, empirical work on what actually happens in the interaction between performance regimes and public agencies.

Not enough is yet known, empirically, about not just the overall perform-ance regime but also the effects of different specific types of intervention to shape and improve performance. Does competition, or choice, or managerial intervention actually improve and shape performance in the desired directions or not? While we have some evidence on some of these the cumulative knowledge base is surprisingly weak considering how much effort has been put into developing the approaches. And quite a lot of the "evidence" we do have has, unfortunately, too often come from partisan sources (including some academics) who are either "for" or "against" the performance movement or specific reforms.

Some of these issues will be further explored, in part, in Chapter 9 that will start to address how individuals, organizations, and managers respond to external pressures to shape and improve performance. Here some of the fundamental theoretical issues raised in the Introduction and in Chapter 3 cannot be avoided – what theoretical assumptions are used is crucial to explaining what actually happens in real organizations faced with performance challenges. Some of the assumptions adopted by quite a few researchers and other analysts can be shown to be deeply flawed and lead to quite misleading findings.

6 **Performance and Public Value(s)**

Value ... that unfortunate child of misery of our science.

Max Weber

The concepts of "value" and "values" have long been a subject of analysis with regard to both private and public organizations. But the ideas of value and values have been given renewed impetus in recent years – in both sectors.

The twin notions of value and values are closely intertwined but also generally regarded as subtly different. The literature on value and values tends to be separate – but it comes together, at least to some extent, in the field of organizations.

Value has its roots in classical economics, for example, the labor theory of value developed by Adam Smith, David Ricardo, and Karl Marx in the eighteenth and the nineteenth centuries. This can still be seen in the concept of "public value," at least as interpreted by some, as we will see later in this chapter. Thinking about values on the other hand tends to have originated in fields like philosophy, ethics, sociology, anthropology, and related areas. It is generally about the overall social values that people are thought to hold – how do we relate to one another in society and what aspects of behavior and things do we hold to be of value?

It is in the process of producing goods, services, and social outcomes – in both private and public organizations – that these notions of value and values become inextricably intertwined. How we assess the value of such activities depends crucially on how we hold and apply our values. If, for example, the only value we hold is one of personal self-interest – as Adam Smith apparently assumes in the following quotation explaining his version of a labor theory of value – then we adopt a fairly narrow definition of value:

The real price of every thing, what every thing really costs to the man who wants to acquire it, is the toil and trouble of acquiring it. What every thing is really worth to the man who has acquired it, and who wants to dispose of it or exchange it for something else, is the toil and trouble which it can save to himself, and which it can impose upon other people.   (Smith 2003 [1776] book 1, chapter V)

However, this was not the whole of Smith's views about what humans value. He also wrote in his *The Theory of Moral Sentiments*:

How selfish so ever man may be supposed, there are evidently some principles in his nature, which interest him in the fortunes of others, and render their happiness necessary to him, though he derives nothing from it, except the pleasure of seeing it. Of this kind is pity or compassion, the emotion we feel for the misery of others, when we either see it, or are made to conceive it in a very lively manner. That we often derive sorrow from the sorrows of others, is a matter of fact too obvious to require any instances to prove it; for this sentiment, like all the other original passions of human nature, is by no means confined to the virtuous or the humane, though they perhaps may feel it with the most exquisite sensibility. The greatest ruffian, the most hardened violator of the laws of society, is not altogether without it.   (Smith 2007 [1759], p. 1)

So, are human values limited to self-interest or do they also embrace other values such as sympathy and altruism? If so, how do we make some sense of the apparently bewildering array of possible values (Jorgensen and Bozeman 2007) that might apply to the performance of the public sector?

This chapter will look at some thinking on how these twin notions can be related to performance – in both the private and public sectors, but primarily the latter. The aim will be to point to some possible theoretical solutions to the puzzle of one value (economic self-interest) or an apparently limitless set of potential values. But first, we will examine some of the debates about value and values that have arisen in the past couple of decades in relation to organizations, starting with two from the private sector: shareholder versus stakeholder value and the culture and values movement.

Shareholder Value Versus Stakeholder Values

In the private sector, recent concern with "value" has emerged in the form initially of the "shareholder value" movement. The start of the shareholder value movement is widely attributed to a speech made by then CEO of the US giant GE, Jack Welch, in 1981, and the approach focused exclusively on financial performance of corporations – especially their discounted cash flows and share prices (Black et al. 1998).

Although the shareholder value movement was strong in the 1980s and especially in the 1990s, it was not without its critics and something of a countermovement toward stakeholder value, or value-driven management, started in the late 1990s and in the early part of the new century (Kennedy 2000; Pohlman and Gardiner 2000). It is worth quoting one pair of authors to get the flavor of this new movement:

Value takes many forms beyond simple monetary value...although there is a great disconnect between the way we measure the financial value of the firm – the maximization of shareholder wealth at a given point in time – and the way in which we measure the total value of the organization, which includes such things as its human assets and intellectual capital, its sustainability as a business entity, its place in the community and larger society, its creativity and resilience and flexibility, as well as its role in the creation of wealth in the society it serves.   (Pohlman and Gardiner 2000, p. 63)

Interestingly, the supposed initial champion of the shareholder value movement recently came to remarkably similar conclusions. Welch recently admitted, after the 2007–9 financial crisis, that the shareholder value was, in his words, a "dumb idea." "On the face of it, shareholder value is the dumbest idea in the world," Welch was reported as saying (*Financial Times*, 12 March 2009). He went on to add that "shareholder value is a result, not a strategy... your main constituencies are your employees, your customers and your product" (ibid). This is, of course, in direct contradiction of the central tenets of the shareholder value approach, which specifically rejects such "stakeholder" approaches (see, e.g., Black et al. 1998, pp. 12–15). Another critic of shareholder value attributes the earlier "dot.com" boom and bust to excessive focus on share prices not backed by serious value-creating corporations engendered by the shareholder value movement (Kennedy 2000).

What these debates between shareholder and stakeholder value highlight is a fundamental conflict over values. To be sure some of the conflict is technical and instrumental: the true value of a corporation lies not just in its dividends and share price rises but also in its human, financial, and physical assets, sustainability, etc. This is close to the resource-based theory (Barney and Clark 2007). But the notion that corporations are also to be judged by their "role in the creation of wealth in the society it serves" (Pohlman and Gardiner 2000) clearly goes beyond the simple material self-interest of the owners and managers of the corporations to much wider, more community and altruistic values (see also Plender 1997; Friedman and Miles 2006). Stakeholder theory has been described (Friedman and Miles 2006) as both normative (what should be) and descriptive (what is) and this is an important point in relation to values – values too, especially in the stakeholder literature, tend to veer between normative requirements derived from first principles and descriptive, instrumental, analyses of "what works." As Friedman and Miles point out, in practice these two approaches tend to reinforce and interact with one another in stakeholder theory and the same is true for value and values theories.

Organizational Culture and Values

As will be discussed in Chapter 7, the early 1980s saw the rise of a movement in performance theory and practice that focused on the values systems and cultures within organizations. This was symbolized most clearly by the success of *In Search of Excellence*, a book by two management consultants (Peters and Waterman 1982), which focused on cultural or "soft" issues, including values. Drawing on "total quality management" and other ideas from Japan (Pascale and Athos 1981; Oakland 1991), this movement saw managing the culture and values of an organization as a high-leverage variable in effecting excellence performance. It led to, for example, the ubiquitous "Mission and Values Statement," which invaded the majority of organizations in the late 1980s.

The movement also had an impact on the public sector, with the idea of managing organizational culture and values forming a key component of the "New Public Management" (NPM) (Pollitt 1993; Ferlie et al. 1996). In the United Kingdom, for example, a specific movement known as the "public service orientation" (PSO) became an important component in the late 1980s and the early 1990s public service reform movement in the local government directly inspired by *In Search of Excellence* (Clarke and Stewart 1985*a*, 1985*b*, 1986*a*, 1986*b*, 1987).

This movement – in both public and private sectors – however was one that proposed that culture and values was a high-leverage variable in achieving superior organizational performance without specifying what cultures or which values were important. To the extent that a choice of culture and values was theorized, it mainly took a "contingency" and functional approach. It was recognized that multiple possible cultures and values existed and that the criteria for selecting one or other culture and set of values was mainly determined by organizational context, the stage in its life cycle, and other mainly exogenous factors and some endogenous ones – the nature of the business (Harrison 1972; Handy 1985).

PUBLIC VALUES

As Bozeman has pointed out, the discussion of public values and public interest became deeply unfashionable in public management and administration with scholars "beating a hasty retreat" in the 1950s from a topic which appeared to some as "metaphysical and unscientific" (Bozeman 2007, p. 2). Nevertheless, the interest in public interest and public values has persisted and recently begun to become again the subject of research and theorizing (e.g., Frederickson 1997; van Wart 1998; Bozeman 2007; Loyens 2009; Steenhuisen et al. 2009; Vrangbaek 2009) to the extent that one pair of authors describe it thus: "public values are on a research front burner" (Davis and West 2008), while another calls it a "cardinal area of study for those interested in the changing world of public management" (van Wart 1998, p. 317).

Some of this interest has undoubtedly been generated by interest in the idea of "public value" (of which more is discussed below), but this is not quite the same as public values. The idea of some overarching public interests or values, as Bozeman (2007) and Frederickson (1997) point out, has an extremely long history in philosophical and political theory. More problematic is deciding what defines or constitutes public interests or values.

Van Wart (1998), for example, in an extended analysis derives public administration values from multiple sources: individual, professional, organizational, legal, and public interest values. He concludes that public values are subject to competition, complexity, and change (pp. 316–17). Values systems, he argues, are constructed to accommodate multiple interests and therefore inevitably produce competing values. In the public sector, in particular, the concerns of social equity, due process, propriety, openness, financial conservatism, fairness to employees, contribution to the common good, etc. all serve to create complexity in values. And finally, values change over time and are never static.

Jorgensen and Bozeman (2007) have attempted to produce an inventory of public values (see Figure 6.1)

What both the van Wart and Jorgensen and Bozeman analyses emphasize is the plethora of possible public values and this raises the problem of making some sense of them all. Indeed, after their analysis, Jorgensen and Bozeman conclude that:

Perhaps the greatest obstacle to analysis of public values is the interrelationship of so many values, so often stated ambiguously. If there is any single item for a public values research agenda, it is developing approaches to sorting out values and making some sense of their relationships.   (p. 377)

There are in fact several, remarkably similar theories that might provide some purchase on this sorting process – a topic to which we will turn after considering the idea of public value (singular).

PUBLIC VALUE

The more recent idea of "public value" (rather than public values) emerges from the work of Moore's book *Creating Public Value* (Moore 1995). This approach focuses on how public agencies can create public value and Moore suggests this comes from a combination of

- Delivering actual public services
- Achieving desired social outcomes
- Maintaining trust and legitimacy in the public agency

1. Accountability, adaptability, advocacy, altruism

2. Balancing interests, benevolence, businesslike approach

3. Citizen involvement, citizens' self-development, collective choice, common good, competitiveness, compromise, continuity, cooperativeness

4. Democracy, dialogue

5. Effectiveness, efficiency, employees' self-development, enthusiasm, equal treatment, equity, ethical consciousness

6. Fairness, friendliness

7. Good working environment

8. Honesty, human dignity

9. Impartiality, innovation, integrity

10. Justice

11. Legality, listening to public opinion, local governance

12. Majority rule, moral standards

13. Neutrality

14. Openness

15. Parsimony, political loyalty, professionalism, protection of individual rights, protection of minorities, productivity, public interest

16. Reasonableness, regime dignity, regime loyalty, regime stability, reliability, responsiveness, risk readiness, robustness, rule of law

17. Secrecy, shareholder value, social cohesion, stability, sustainability

18. Timeliness

19. User democracy, user orientation

20. Voice of the future

21. Will of the people

Figure 6.1 A Public Values Inventory
Source: Adapted from (Jorgensen and Bozeman 2007, pp. 377–8).

While accepting the need to satisfy these three types of results, an influential British Cabinet Office Strategy Unit paper also added that:

For something to be of value it is not enough for citizens to say that it is desirable. It is only of value if citizens – either individually or collectively – are willing to give something up in return for it. Sacrifices are not only made in monetary terms (i.e. paying taxes/ charges). They can also involve granting coercive powers to the state (e.g. in return for security), disclosing private information (e.g. in return for more personalised information/services), giving time (e.g. as a school governor or a member of the territorial army) or other personal resources (e.g. blood). The idea of opportunity cost is therefore central to public value: if it is claimed that citizens would like government to produce something, but they are not willing to give anything up in return, then it is doubtful that the activity in question will genuinely create value.   (Kelly et al. 2004).

So creating public value entails taking various resources from citizens (money, freedom, information, coproduction) and transforming it into something more than the inputs in terms of services delivered, social outcomes achieved, and trust and legitimacy (re)created in the public sphere.

One important point to note is that public value, in the sense discussed here, is actually not necessarily the sole product of public agencies. Public, private, nonprofit, and voluntary agencies can all generate (or destroy) public value (Bozeman 1987, 2007). Indeed, a key part of governments' policies has often been the imposition of regulations on private individuals and organizations to generate public value – by, for example, minimizing the undesirable externalities created by private corporations. The legalization of one of the key components of modern capitalism – the limited liability joint stock company – was actually opposed by the main mouthpiece of "free market" thinkers at the time as "socialism" (*The Economist*, cited in Micklethwait and Wooldridge 2005). It is easy to forget that the reason the main form of capitalist organizations are generally known as "public corporations" is not because they are publicly owned, obviously, but because they are created under public law (see also Bozeman 1987). Conversely, of course, actual public action can also create value – including private value – for such organizations. The basic governmental activity of regulating money, markets, property rights, and contracts all help to create private value as well as public. Recent events (2007–9) – with governments intervening on massive scales to prevent the collapse of financial markets and organizations – reinforce this point.

The above-cited Cabinet Office paper (Kelly et al. 2004) also recognizes that what constitutes "public value" is also shaped by public preferences, and these may be both private, self-interested preferences and also more common, or communal, altruistically focused preferences – the "public interest." However, other than recommending that the shaping of summative public preferences needs to be undertaken both by traditional representative democratic means and also through forms of deliberative democracy and participation, the paper (or Moore's work) tells us little about the content of actual public preferences.

We would argue that public value – in terms of some form of aggregation of public preferences – is actually constituted by multiple public values, as van Wart (1998) suggested above, and that the only way to make some sense of these multiple values analytically and theoretically is to have some framework for analyzing them and their interrelations.

It is to analytical frameworks that provide a way of making some sense of multiple, competing, complex, and changing public values that we now turn.

Values-Based Theories

There are several theoretical approaches that try to put some order onto multiple values in a social, institutional, and organizational context.

The simplest of these are those that challenge a simple unidimensional view of human values, especially those implied by the "rational utility maximizer" assumptions of neoclassical economics. The latter clearly implies two important assumptions about humans: first, that we all behave rationally; and second, that our overriding value consideration is self-interested utility maximization. Both of these have been radically challenged. The first need not detain us here, but we can simply note the challenges posed by "bounded rationality" (Simon 1983), heuristics (Gigerenzer 2000), behavioral economics (Thaler and Sunstein 2008), and others (Sutherland 1992; Ariely 2008).

The values-based challenge to neoclassical economic assumptions about self-interested values has come from several directions. One has been economics itself with some economists not only recognizing that altruism exists but that it also poses a fundamental challenge to the neoclassical model (Margolis 1982; Gintis et al. 2005; Meier 2006; Kolm 2008). Another challenge has come from evolutionary psychology perspectives, showing how, as Peter Singer (1999) famously put it, we were social before we were human and the impact this has had on our innate values of cooperation (Sober and Wilson 1998; Talbot 2005b; Henrich and Henrich 2007). A challenge from public policy perspectives has also emerged with Le Grand arguing that people behave as both "knights and knaves" – that is, both altruistically and self-interestedly (Le Grand 2003). Finally, it is also interesting to mention that public opinion researchers, examining attitudes to public services especially, in the United Kingdom were also forced recently to conclude that their respondents suffered from "cognitive polyphasia" – that is, they seemed to be able to think about the same issue in more than one frame of reference (e.g., selfishly and altruistically) simultaneously (Marshall et al. 2007 and personal communication – Ben Page, IPSOS MORI). (The term cognitive polyphasia originates in social psychology – see Moscovici 2000).

All this points strongly toward humans having more than one social value orientation, and not just self-interest. Surprisingly little of this has (yet) surfaced in the many discussions, analyses, and research outputs on performance. About the only place where it seems to have had any real impact is at the level of individual performance in the literature on "public service motivation" (Perry and Hondeghem 2008). Here it has long been recognized that individuals exhibit, at a minimum, both self-interested and public-orientated motivations. An attempt has been made to engage with these other fields including interestingly evolutionary psychology (Koehler and Rainey 2008). We return to the specific issue of public service motivation in Chapter 9.

There are several attempts at theorizing individual, organizational, institutional, and social behavior that assume more complex, but still parsimonious, models of values. We look at five of them here. Although all of those considered are apparently 'generic' – that is, they apply to the public and private sectors – they have a particular resonance and applicability in the public sphere. There is not much space here to mention all such possible theories so we will limit ourselves to these five: the four cultures or "gods of management" theory, cultural theory, competing values theory, relational models theory, and the reversal theory.

FOUR CULTURES THEORY (FCT – HARRISON AND HANDY)

The idea of there being just four fundamental and organizational cultures or "ideologies," as he then called them, was presented by Roger Harrison in a very early paper in *Harvard Business Review*, which predated the later "culture" movement by a decade (Harrison 1972). Harrison argued that peoples' personal organizational theories were in fact organizational ideologies, that is, unlike social scientists studying organizations who try to keep their own values out of the picture, people's views on organizations were very much value-driven. As Rogers put it: "if you change a man's organization theory, he usually ends up questioning his values as well."

The four organizational ideologies proposed by Rogers are given as follows:

- Power orientation – where the dominant value is the acquisition or maintenance of power through competition and conflict – both of the organization over its environment and within the organization between groups and individuals.
- Role orientation – where the dominant value is role-assignment, through rational and orderly processes and job allocation and where conflict and competition are severely limited by compromises and agreements.

- Task orientation – where the highest value is superordinate goal achievement – the goal(s) might be economic or noneconomic, but the overriding concern is their achievement.
- Person orientation – where the highest value is appreciation of and rewards for the people working within the organization, where authority and role adherence is discouraged and peer-to-peer-based consensus is the norm.

These four value-based cultures were popularized by Handy (1985) using the metaphor of Greek gods with Zeus representing the power-based organization; Apollo, the role-based; Athena, the task-based; and Dionysus, the person-centered organization. Harrison offered the normative view that real organizations ought not to be "monolithic structures that are ideologically homogenous" but that they would benefit from a degree of internal diversity, especially in terms of being able to adjust to complex external environments. Handy likewise recommends a "balanced mix," the balance being determined by a combination of intrinsic factors native to the organization type and extrinsic factors in the environment.

(Neither Harrison nor Handy gives an explicit title to their theory, so I have called it "Four Cultures Theory" for convenience.)

CULTURAL THEORY (CT – THOMPSON ET AL.)

"Cultural theory" takes its name from an influential text of that title (Wildavsky et al. 1990) that applied the "grid-group" theories of anthropologist Mary Douglas to public policy and administration and it has been particularly well developed in these latter fields (Thompson et al. 1999; Hood 2000; Verweij and Thompson 2006; Thompson 2008)

CT is avowedly social constructionist, grounded in the view that different cultures construct nature and social relations in radically different ways (Wildavsky et al. 1990). The basic dimensions of this construction are provided by the concepts of "grid" and "group." High "grid" societies rely on rules, regulations, and enforcement, whereas low "grid" societies emphasize discretion and negotiation. High "group" societies are ones where the collective prevails over the individual and low "group," where it is the individual who is paramount.

The grid–group matrix is used to produce four archetypes of organizations or institutions:

- Fatalist (high grid, low group) – low cooperation, rule-bound
- Hierarchist (high grid and group) – socially cohesive, rule-bound
- Egalitarian (high group, low grid) – high-participation, low-rules
- Individualist (low group and grid) – atomized, individualized, low-rules

There is a fifth archetype – the Hermit – that rejects social organization altogether.

COMPETING VALUES FRAMEWORK (CVF – QUINN ET AL.)

The competing values approach (usually called a framework) emerged from the organizational effectiveness movement (see Chapter 7) and in some ways represents its high point (Quinn and Rohrbaugh 1981, 1983). Through a process of trying to simplify and organize the many factors of organizational effectiveness that had been identified in the previous couple of decades, Quinn and Rohrbaugh (1981) and later also Cameron and others (Quinn and Cameron 1988; Cameron and Quinn 2006; Cameron et al. 2006) developed a highly structured, multilayered framework based on a pair of simple values dichotomies.

The two dichotomies are those between flexibility and control and between internal and external orientation. They result (Figure 6.2) in four organizational types (clan, hierarchy, market, and adhocracy); four organizational cultures (collaborate, control, compete, and create); and eight managerial roles (mentors, facilitators, monitors, coordinators, directors, producers, brokers, and innovators).

CVF also attempts to integrate four major trends in organization theory: human relations, internal process, rational goal, and open systems.

A very important point to note about CVF is that it emphasizes that it is not an either/or model based on a zero-sum approach where more of one quadrant automatically means less of the others. This point has been misunderstood by some scholars (Boyne 2003). The instrumentation developed for measuring managerial competences (Quinn et al. 1996) and organizational culture (Cameron and Quinn 2006), for example, both make this very clear – as does the various theoretical discussions on paradox and CVF (see especially Quinn 1988; Quinn and Cameron 1988).

RELATIONAL MODELS THEORY (RMT – FISKE ET AL.)

Relational Models Theory (RMT) emerged principally from anthropology, although with some input from other disciplines including sociology and social psychology (Fiske 1991). The basic tenets of RMT have two components – first, a definition of the (four) relational models that shape human social interactions and secondly the evolutionary origins of these RM, or "mods" as Fiske calls them, and their relationship to cultural compliments or "preos" (Fiske 2004).

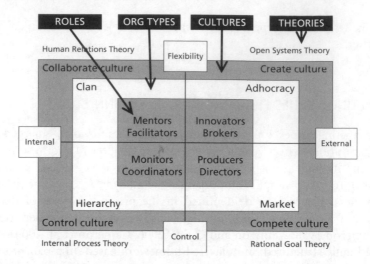

Figure 6.2 Complete CVF Model

Sources: Quinn (1988), Quinn and Cameron (1988), Cameron and Quinn (2006), Cameron et al. (2006), and Quinn et al. (2007).

"Mods" for Fiske are very similar to the supposed "universal grammar" that underpins our "language instinct" (Pinker 1994). "Mods" are cognitively modular open-ended generative potentials. They provide both the inclination toward, and the ability to, absorb culturally specific expressions that complement each mod – rather in the same way as any human can apply their language instinct to learn any human language. "Mods" by themselves are incomplete and rather like "wolf children" (Malson 1972) who have not been exposed to any language; failure to be exposed to appropriate cultural expressions of mods results in failure to express the mod at all. Fiske calls the cultural expression of a mod a "preo" – the class of paradigms, parameters, precepts, prescriptions, propositions, and proscriptions that turn each mod into a full relational model.

The four relational models are given as follows:

- Communal sharing (CS) – inclination to participate in an organization, community, or other social unit and contribute fully without expectation of equal reciprocal return.
- Authority ranking (AR) – the inclination to assign asymmetrical, linearly ordered authority or status to other individuals based on some criteria such as formal authority, charisma, election, appointment, etc.
- Equality matching (EM) – the inclination to match exchanges with others in an equal manner – hence coin-toss, voting, eye-for-an-eye, rotating credit, baby-sitting coops, etc.
- Market pricing (MP) – the inclination to trade or exchange on the basis of ratios, profits, rents, and prices that benefit the individual.

These are four independent relational models that may be triggered by a variety of factors, situations or conditions, or by personal inclination, and therefore the same circumstances could be reacted to through any one of them or sometimes more than one in close sequence or even muddled usage.

Based originally on intensive anthropological field work and an extensive literature review, RMT has since also been verified by a series of experimental and field studies (Haslam 2004).

REVERSAL THEORY (RT – APTER)

Reversal theory derives from psychology and the study of emotions, motivations, and personality (Apter 2007 [1989]). It argues that humans are inconsistent and changing – reacting in different ways to the same set of circumstances depending on the state of mind. This state of mind motivates us to act, react, and feel differently. However, these states of mind are not open-ended – a finite set of eight "ways of being," arranged in four contradictory pairs or domains, determine our current state of mind. We are in a combination of four such states (one from each domain) at any one time.

The states of mind (arranged in pairs) are given as follows:

The Ends-Means Domain		
Serious	vs.	*Playful*
Planning ahead, creating a sense of direction, realistic risk assessment, thinking strategically		Energy and enthusiasm, open to new experiences, creative, generating new ideas
The Rules Domain		
Conforming	vs.	*Rebellious*
Following procedures, being predictable and efficient, adhering to controls, standards, and ethics		Challenging assumptions and rules, desire for change and innovation
The Interaction Domain		
Mastery	vs.	*Sympathy*
Determination to achieve, confidence, taking charge, willingness to learn		Strong relationships, emotional support for and cooperation with others, open to feelings
The Orientation Domain		
Self-orientation	vs.	*Other-orientation*
Personal responsibility, work-life balance, realizing personal ambitions		Mentoring and coaching others, sensitivity to others' needs, team building

Source: Adapted from Apter (2007 [1989]).

For Apter, these "states of mind" are composed of values, feelings, style, and emotions (p. 49), but it is clearly the values part of the state of mind that is most relevant here. For example, the state of Conformist values "duty," whereas the Rebellious state values "freedom" (p. 126). Without elaborating all the other associated values, it is clear RT also offers a categorization of competing values that (in part) motivate attitudes and actions. RT has largely been used in personal psychology applications, particularly in areas like sports psychology and some clinical settings. Yet it clearly has implications for more collective arenas such as institutions and organizations.

SIMILARITIES AND DIFFERENCES

There are some very clear similarities, and important differences, between the theories briefly described above.

One surface similarity is the attempt to provide a parsimonious set of categories for different values – in all cases effectively just four sets (although RT does this as four pairs).

Much more substantively, the overlap in the proposed categories is quite striking. For example, the person culture (Four Cultures), egalitarian culture (Cultural Theory), clan culture (CVF), and communal sharing model (RMT) are obviously closely related. There are however also important differences. Categories do not all align and there are substantial differences between some. Probably more fundamentally the origins of these categories – ontologically, epistemologically, and methodologically – are radically different. Two – RMT and RT – are individualistic in origin and one (RMT) explicitly and the other (RT) implicitly have an evolutionary psychology explanation for their origins. The other three – FCT, CT, and CVF – are all much more systemic in nature and, by implication, see their categories as emergent properties of larger scale human collectives rather than as necessarily individual characteristics. Adherents of RT, in particular, would probably reject any individualistically based, or especially evolutionary, origins for their categories.

Before leaving the similarities and differences between these five theories, it is worth just mentioning a sixth – the current authors' own small attempt to produce a map of what I called "paradoxical human instincts" and corresponding values (Talbot 2005b). This work derived from a long-standing interest in CVF and especially a desire to answer the question which Quinn, Cameron, and colleagues do not – why should human organization be riddled with the sort of contradictory, paradoxical behaviors they analyze? My answer was evolutionary – because humans evolved as paradoxical primates with inherent contradictory social impulses or instincts. My hypothesized four pairs of contradictory instincts were aggression versus peace-making, selfishness versus altruism, conformity versus autonomy, and cooperation versus competition. Again, these categories are remarkably similar in character to those of RMT, RT, and CVF in particular.

Using RMT it is possible to map what otherwise appear as a bewildering set of public values. Using the listing of some of these values as compiled by Bozeman (2007), this sort of mapping starts to produce intriguing results (see Figure 6.3 Public Values Mapped onto Relational Models).

Communal sharing	Equality matching
Common good; public interest; social cohesion; altruism; local governance; citizen involvement	Human dignity; sustainability; future; majority rule; democracy; individual rights; user democarcy
Authority ranking Regime dignity; regime stability; political loyalty; accountability; responsibility	**Market pricing**

Figure 6.3 Public Values Mapped onto Relational Models

Bozeman speculates (p. 133) that what he calls "private values" may legitimately be viewed as public values also in some circumstances – but what this mapping exercise shows is that the listing of public values does not in practice cover such "private values" certainly insofar as they relate to private self-interest (the market pricing quadrant). This approach is further pursued in Chapter 10.

Shaping Public Values

Despite some differences in content and obvious major differences in origin, the similarities between these fives theories or frameworks is quite substantial and striking. Indeed it is all the more striking precisely because of the fact that they come from such different origins and yet have come to remarkably similar conclusions about some of the fundamental values structures shaping human behavior.

They clearly pose the possibility – and at this stage it is just a possibility – of constructing a unified model or theory of human values as applied to the performance of public agencies, as Figure 6.3 and the discussion above illustrate. Values lie at the core of any assessment of public sector perform-ance, so having some framework for understanding them is essential. How-ever, we should be duly cautious about the possibility of progress. More than thirty years ago one of the first writers to identify clearly the need to integrate values into our understanding of performance in the public sphere wrote:

Performance, at least as defined here, is effectiveness in securing collective goals by due process. We take administrative performance to be measureable not only by effective-ness, but by the question of effectiveness for whom, by what measure or indicator? Whose values or interests are reflected in the goals being pursued more or less effectively by public organizations? To which elements in the national or local community is the organization responsive, if any?   (Fried 1976, p. 15)

That we are still struggling today to integrate values into other aspects of performance suggests this is not an easy problem to resolve. Part of the explanation may lie in Thompson's interesting exposition on the varieties of social science that can emerge from the four categories of CT. He suggests that fifty different combinations of the four basic categories can be achieved by either selecting a subset or combining some categories. He gives many examples of the resulting social-theoretical possibilities (Thompson 2008, Chapter 8).

Interestingly for this book, Fried identifies – in the quote mentioned above and the rest of his book – the three core elements explored in the current book: the external constituency (or performance regime), the mechanics of production and delivery (or organizational performance models), and the values that infuse both.

What is clear is that it is not possible to divorce the issue of values from performance. While performance is in one sense objective – how efficiently and effectively organizations deliver public services is either better or poorer in reality – it is also socially constructed, at least to the extent that what the public values is crucial to which performances are important. This issue will be revisited in Chapters 8, 9, and 10.

PART III
PERFORMANCE AND ORGANIZATIONS

Introduction to Part III

As suggested in Chapter 1, the study of organizational performance, or effectiveness, or excellence, or greatness, or whatever it is called, has a long and interesting history. Unfortunately much of current research and theorizing about these issues at best neglects this history and at worst instead of "standing on the shoulders of giants" spends much of its time "reinventing the wheel." The chapters in this part (Chapters 7 and 8) seek to address some of this failure to accumulate knowledge by revisiting some of the modern (i.e., last half century or so) research and theory about organizational performance.

Chapter 7 looks at the generic, or rather in reality mostly private sector, literature on organizational performance. It starts with a recapitulation of the "organizational effectiveness" (OE) movement that lasted roughly from the end of World War II until the early 1980s. Highly quantitative, positivist approaches to seeking out the key variables that caused highly effective organizations to be so dominated this movement. However, by the late 1970s and the early 1980s it was running into severe conceptual and theoretical problems as it became apparent that the whole notion of "effectiveness" was problematic. No agreed definition of effectiveness could be arrived at, and worse some aspects of effectiveness appeared antithetical to others. In a period of intellectual crisis some scholars called for the abandonment of OE studies entirely, while others tried to resolve these problems by creating a multiple-models-in-a-single framework approach – the competing values approach already discussed briefly in Chapter 6.

The OE movement largely collapsed in the early 1980s, partly as a result of this internal intellectual crisis but also because of rejection of its quantitative, positivist approach by the newly emergent organizational culture and values movement, epitomized by the huge success of Peters and Watermans' *In Search of Excellence* and the McKinsey 7-S Framework which underpinned their approach (Pascale and Athos 1981; Peters and Waterman 1982). This new movement was clearly influenced by the newly fashionable ideas of social constructionism that emerged around the same time (Berger and Luckmann 1975). This new movement focused on culture, values, quality, and ideas like "mission." However, by the mid-1980s it also started to spawn a whole host of "quality" and "excellence" models, such as the Baldrige Awards in the United

States and the business excellence model in Europe. These multidimensional performance models (MDPMs), as they have been called, implicitly recapitulated some of the discussions of effectiveness models at the tail-end of the OE movement, but also went much further.

The third wave of organizational performance studies and practices began roughly in the early 1990s, and in some respects again repeated aspects of the OE movement – for example, an early emphasis on pragmatic measurement of various individual aspects of performance, not framed by any real performance model but rapidly moving toward discussions of models and specifically MDPMs. By the mid-1990s there was a virtual "new army of models" with many MDPMs emerging from the culture, values, and quality movement and also from the new performance movement. Some idea of the multiplicity of models is given in this chapter and some of their key aspects are analyzed, not least the similarity of many of them.

Chapter 8 turns to the public domain to examine how the performance of public agencies has been theorized. Not surprisingly, much of what has happened has paralleled wider developments. There have been many cases of simply adopting imported ideas from the more generic movements, but there have also been considerable adaptations of some of these ideas to the specific context of the public domain. There have also been a fairly large number of indigenous developments, especially of MDPMs, specifically for the public domain. The sources of these models are multiple – they have emerged from policy-makers, practitioners, consultants, and researchers. As with the wider literature and practices, these developments are analyzed and the multiplicity of public-sector models is examined.

In the final section, this chapter also takes a brief look at the emerging trend toward comparative performance measurement for more sectoral and governmental levels of the public domain such as the World Banks' World Governance Indicators. Full analysis of these developments is beyond the scope of the present book, but they are clearly important to note.

7 Theories of Organizational Performance

Theorizing organizational performance, as discussed previously (Chapter 1), has been around as long as people have studied organizations. It is endemic to the subject because – under the label of "effectiveness" or "performance" – it is the ultimate dependent variable when comparing different types of organizations (Cameron and Whetten 1983*b*, p. 310; Cameron 2005). Whether it is patronage-based public administration versus modern merit-based bureaucracy or M-form (multidivisional) corporations versus networked organizations, performance is the test that is used to evaluate these different forms. The same applies to management practices, such as leadership, quality management, business process reengineering, human resources management, etc.

In this chapter we will briefly sketch the history and trends in performance theorizing, roughly since the end of World War II up to the present. It is always hard – and perhaps unwise – to try and put too precise dating on movements, trends, or tides (Light 1997) in organizational theorizing of any type. Pick a date, or time frame, and someone will come up with numerous reasons why it is incorrect. So the time frames and trends offered here should be taken more as broad-brush outlines than exact analytic categories.

There have essentially been three "waves" of interest in organizational performance – by which we mean a specific focus on how organizational performance or effectiveness can be measured, and what are the key drivers of better or worse performance in individual organizations, rather than the more general interest in organizational analysis which has of course been around a lot longer.

The first wave is the organizational effectiveness (OE) movement, as the subject was then called, which occurred mainly in the United States from about the mid-1940s through to roughly the early1980s. OE studies focused on various factors or elements of performance and sought to establish links, patterns, and configurations between these using mainly quantitative techniques. Heavily influenced by quantitative planning techniques that had been used, apparently successfully, during the War effort, a new generation of researchers and practitioners turned to applying these to peace-time corporate performance.

OE studies experienced an internal crisis and an external challenge in the early 1980s and the term – if not the work – gradually faded from use. We will consider this in more detail below. Interest in these quantitative approaches to both financial and especially nonfinancial forms of performance assessment did not resurface until the early 1990s.

The next wave saw the emergence of a major new focus of interest in how to improve organizations – the movement toward "excellence, quality and culture," symbolized very precisely by the phenomenal success of *In Search of Excellence* (Peters and Waterman 1982). This approach specifically rejected the concerns on the quantitative OE and associated corporate planning movements of the preceding period (Mintzberg 1994) and focused instead on more qualitative issues like excellence, culture, quality, and values.

Interest in quantitative measurement of corporate performance did not disappear during this "quality" period – instead it fell back on very narrow definitions of financial performance – and especially the "shareholder value" approach that emerged in the early 1980s alongside – and in many ways in opposition to – the culture, excellence, and quality movement. But this approach eschewed the wider interest of OE in nonfinancial factors and their interrelationships. This particular line of research – especially the more esoteric efforts at financial measures (unfortunately associated with some of the financial instruments so widely seen as the cause of the 2007–9 financial crisis) – is of little or no real interest in studying public organizations, so it will not be further explored here.

Interest in research on the nonfinancial aspects of organizational performance or effectiveness also did not disappear, but it tended to concentrate on examining specific, individual factors of performance. A study of the performance literature in this period showed that articles examining each of the seventeen factors of OE identified in 1983 – only one of which was financial in nature (see Table 7.1 below) – continued. The number of articles published in total on these seventeen subjects, as individual items of study, remained more or less exactly constant between 1977 and 1994 (Hirsch and Levin 1999).

The third wave of what was now called "performance" studies, rather than organizational effectiveness, began in the mid-1990s. This third wave has been much more pragmatic and to some extent, at least in the first decade or so, fairly a-theoretical in its approach (Cameron 2005). One facet of this a-theoretical nature of the current movement is the almost complete disconnect between the literature on performance since the mid-1990s and the previous wave of OE studies This, despite the fact the current movement is (re)covering much of the same territory of trying to establish what are the main dimensions of performance and how they relate to one another. Yet despite the similarities between the OE movement and the current performance

Table 7.1 The Seventeen Elements of Organizational Effectiveness

1. Productivity	7. Control	13. Utilization of Environment
2. Efficiency	8. Conflict/Cohesion	14. Evaluation by External Entities
3. Profit	9. Flexibility/Adaptation	15. Stability
4. Quality	10. Planning and Goal Setting	16. Value of Human Resources
5. Morale	11. Information Management and Communication	17. Training and Development Emphasis
6. Growth	12. Readiness	

Source: Quinn and Rohrbaugh, cited in Hirsch and Levin.

movement, the latter rarely, if ever, refers to its predecessor. This is particularly disappointing because the earlier OE wave has a lot to tell us about theories of performance, in some ways more than the current performance movement.

The Rise and Fall of Organizational Effectiveness Studies

It has been argued that much of the early organizational studies were about effectiveness in one form or another, implicitly or explicitly. Whether it was studies of organizations as bureaucracy (Weber, Taylor, Fayol, and Perrow), cooperative systems (Barnard), as institutions (Selznick), as decision systems (Simon), or as human relations (Mayo), the ultimate dependent variable in all these studies was "effectiveness" (Cameron and Whetten 1983*b*) – however that is defined. But while this is implicit in much of the organizational theorizing that gradually emerged in the late nineteenth and the early twentieth centuries, it was not until the rise of the explicit OE research movement in the latter half of the twentieth century that this became much more explicit.

OE research as it emerged after World War II was highly positivist in approach, concentrating on defining dependent variables of performance and the independent variables that could be shown to correlate with and cause higher or lower effectiveness.

It should be noted that although the term "effectiveness" tended to strongly predominate in this period, "performance" was often used as an alternative, usually interchangeable, term. Despite this, the research effort into how good organizations were and what caused superior (or inferior) levels of achievement became firmly know as organizational effectiveness studies. The following analysis of articles on organizational performance and organizational effectiveness between 1977 and 1994 illustrates just how closely the terms were linked – although it should be noted how both declined and then organizational performance started to eclipse OE in the early 1990s (Figure 7.1).

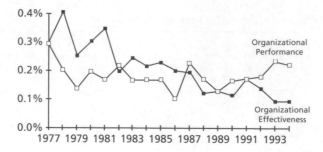

Figure 7.1 Percentage of Articles on Organizational Performance and Organizational Effectiveness (ABI/Inform)

Source: Hirsch and Levin (1999).

So well developed was this movement that as early as the late 1960s an ambitious attempt was made to summarize OE studies as learnt from a book entitled *Organizational Effectiveness – An Inventory of Propositions* (Price 1968). Reporting on forty previous studies covering the period 1944–66, an attempt was made to establish – in the form of formal propositions – what we "know about the effectiveness of organizations: what we really know, what we nearly know, what we think we know, and what we claim to know" (p. 1).

Unfortunately Price's attempt is deeply flawed and the flaws highlight problems with which organizational performance studies are still grappling. Price defines "effectiveness" as simply "the degree of goal achievement." (p. 3). However, he immediately goes on to recognize that goals are not easy to define, and adopts a distinction between "official" and "operative" goals. He then stipulates that he will use only achievement of "operative" goals as the dependent variable, even though he immediately admits that establishing "operative" goals is problematic and that most of the forty studies he has inventoried have failed to analyze them.

He also goes on to say that he often disagrees with the interpretation of the scholars who carried out the original research because they relied on "official" goals for their analysis, while he relies on "operative" goals. Leaving aside the issue of how he knew what "operative" goals were when they had not been systematically studied, it is easy to argue that achievement of both "official" and "operative" goals are legitimate aspects of organizational effectiveness.

Price's method slips even further into difficulties when he decides that alongside "effectiveness" (i.e., in his definition operative goal achievement) he will add five other variables: productivity, morale, conformity, adaptiveness, and institutionalization – none of which is adequately defined. Nor is it all clear whether these additional variables are measures of effectiveness (i.e., dependent) or measures of what drives, or contributes toward, effectiveness (i.e., independent).

As we will return to later, this raises a fundamental issue about aspects of organizational capacity, or rather capacities, and their relationship to effectiveness or performance. As we will see, many contemporary models of organizational performance – such as the "balanced scorecard" or the "European Excellence Model" – include measures of both capability and performance in their overall judgment of organizations' effectiveness.

It is hardly surprising then that Price's "propositions" turn out to be rather less than satisfactory. Firstly, many are qualified by aspects of organizational content or context – thus, for example (large) size matters, except where there is a high degree of professionalization (proposition 7.1) or that internal complexity is a determining factor in whether centralization of "tactical decisions is a good or bad thing" (proposition 3.3). In other words "it all depends," although precisely on what it all depends is unfortunately not systematically spelt out.

This is all extremely reminiscent of the "proverbs of administration" first explicated and then roundly criticized by Herbert Simon (1946) and then further explored in much greater detail half a century later (Hood and Jackson 1991). Again, what both Simon and later Hood and Jackson identified were a set of supposedly timeless propositions, but which can be shown to be contradictory and contextual, and the exact conditions under which they might never operate and the criteria for making choices are never spelt out by their promulgators.

Another, rather more serious attempt, was made to take stock of the OE literature in a 1977 edited volume that brought together some of the main researchers in the field (Goodman et al. 1977). In a scene-setting chapter, Campbell reviews the many theoretical approaches to OE and outlines some of the issues.

Campbell argues (as, subsequently do many of the main OE researchers) that the idea of "organizational effectiveness" is a "construct" that only makes sense within a particular theoretical framework:

An underlying assumption . . . is that no definitive definition of organizational effectiveness can be given. *The* meaning of organizational effectiveness is not a truth that is buried somewhere waiting to be discovered if only our concepts and data collection methods were good enough. As with theories in general, a particular conceptualization of organizational effectiveness may be useful only for certain purposes.

(Campbell 1977, p. 15)

Campbell continues that the usefulness of a particular formulation depends on both the values of the theory user and the "facts of organizational life." This is an important caveat which distinguishes this approach from pure constructionism – organizational effectiveness may be a construct; it may be dependent on a theoretical framework, which in turn has to be chosen on the basis of values – but the "facts or organizational life" that it then explores are really "out there" and not merely an artefact of the users perspective.

Nevertheless the idea of organizational effectiveness as a "construct" lies at the heart of the growing crisis within OE studies. It underpins the decision two years later by one of the editors of this volume – and a principle OE researcher – to assert that "there should be a moratorium on all studies of organizational effectiveness, books on organizational effectiveness, and chapters on organizational effectiveness" (Campbell 1979, cited in Cameron and Whetten 1983*b*).

The danger posed by viewing OE as merely a construct was precisely that of constructionism – that is, that ultimately all objectivity is removed from the idea and it becomes merely a social construct with "a potentially infinite number of value perspectives about the desired state of social arrangements on which theses [OE] judgements could be based. As a result, there are a potential infinite number of effectiveness models" (Zammuto 1984). This argument is faulty in two respects. Firstly, performance or effectiveness includes an element that is simply real – organizations either do or do not deliver services more efficiently or effectively. Secondly, how this is construed is also subject to values considerations (see previous chapter) but even then it is possible to put some limitations on the broad range of values that can be reasonably included.

OE studies died, or at least got terminally ill, in the period toward the end of the 1970s and the early 1980s. For a decade or more prior to 1983 the rise of publications – academic books and scholarly articles – on OE was substantial, reaching a peak in the late 1970s. A rapid decline set in thereafter and by 1993 publications using the term OE had declined to less than a quarter of its 1978 peak (Figure 7.2).

One powerful interpretation of what happened to the OE "construct" is provided by a seminal article by Hirsch and Levin (1999). They develop the idea of the "umbrella construct" – an idea or term which brings together in a fairly loose way an emerging stream of research activity. Recent examples would include things like "governance" or maybe "leadership."

Arguing that organizational studies are characterized by the emergence of successive umbrella constructs, they suggest that such constructs appear to have a life cycle, which is illustrated in Figure 7.3.

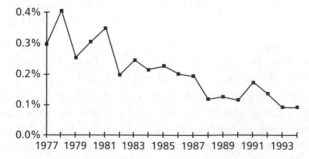

Figure 7.2 Percentage of OE Articles (ABI/Inform)
Source: Hirsch and Levin (1999).

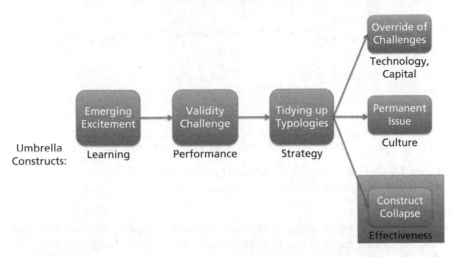

Figure 7.3 Proposed Umbrella Construct Process (with Contemporary Examples)
Source: Adapted from Hirsch and Levin (1999).

The critical part of this proposed life-cycle model is the point at which the "validity police" challenge a construct like OE. This usually results in an initial attempt to tidy up the construct by grouping different versions or interpretations into typologies. If this can be successfully achieved, the construct overcomes the challenge. If it fails this test, but refuses to go away as a construct (for various reasons), then it will simply continue as a challenged and controversial construct. It may also fail to such an extent it gets eliminated, which is what these scholars argue happened to OE in the early 1980s.

They offer five propositions based on this analysis:

1. The more the field lacks theoretical consensus, the more it is likely to rely on umbrella constructs.
2. Such umbrella constructs will inevitably, at some point, have their validity challenged.
3. The elements of construct that have collapsed often outlive the construct itself.
4. An umbrella construct that collapses often reappears later under a different label.
5. The more an umbrella construct has external (nonacademic) support, the less vulnerable it will be to validity challenges.

These propositions seem, at face value, a powerful explanation of what happened to OE studies. It was certainly true the field lacked theoretical consensus and relied on OE as an umbrella construct. It was also true this came under increasing attack from the validity police, to the point where some of its most prominent actors called for a moratorium on OE studies. It was also true that the elements of OE studies outlived its demise as an

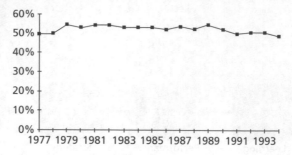

Figure 7.4 Continuing Research on Seventeen Elements of OE
Source: Hirsch and Levin (1999).

umbrella construct. Using seventeen elements of OE (see Table 7.1) that had been identified as common to many studies (Quinn and Rohrbaugh 1983), they show that research on these topics did not decline in the same way that the use of the OE construct did (Figure 7.4).

However powerful this approach is in partially explaining the crisis that overtook OE studies, it is incomplete in the application of its own framework and in the results that it produces.

The first omission is that it fails to factor in the issue of external support (proposition 5). What Hirsch and Levin do not include in their analysis is the almost complete withdrawal of external, nonacademic support for OE studies and its transfer to a new emerging umbrella construct of "quality and culture." During the period from the end of World War I until the mid-late 1970s the whole rationalist, strategic planning paradigm of management (of which OE was a subplot) dominated Western thinking on management (Mintzberg 1994). The combination of the economic crisis triggered by the 1974 oil crisis and the apparent rise of Japanese industry catalyzed an intense interest in Japanese management techniques that were apparently character-ized by attention to culture and quality, rather than structures, plans, and numbers.

The most successful management book ever – *In Search of Excellence* (Peters and Waterman 1982) – emerged from a team established within the huge consulting firm McKinsey & Co specifically to reexamine the whole issue of organizational effectiveness (p. 3).

This powerful external switch away from rationalist/numerical-based approaches toward more intuitive/qualitative frames of reference in large parts of the consultancy and practitioner communities, who had previously endorsed rationalist/numbers-based approaches like OE, coincided with the internal intellectual crisis within OE studies and sealed its fate.

The second error in Hirsch and Levin's analysis is the way it underestimates the possibilities for the "multiple models" and "multiple constituencies" elements that emerged from the wreckage of OE studies to provide an alternative. In his most recent reconsideration of that period, one of the principle protagonists argues that the multiple-models approach has weathered rather well since the collapse of OE (Cameron 2005). The specific approach he considers to have survived the "validity challenge" is the "competing values framework" (although as one of its principle originators and supporters this is hardly surprising). Nevertheless, Cameron strongly makes the point that the multiple-models approach has much to commend it.

Several categorizations of a parsimonious set of OE models emerged from this period ("tidying up the typologies"). At the time, Cameron and Whetten suggested five models: the goal model, the system-resource model, the internal process model, the strategic constituencies model, and the legitimacy model (Cameron and Whetten 1983b). In his later recapitulation, Cameron also offers the first four, but legitimacy is replaced by the human relations model (Cameron 2005). Boyne (2003) also offers five – the first four again being the same but instead of legitimacy he includes the competing values framework itself as the fifth.

Both Cameron and Boyne suggest two or more models can be combined into a single framework. Boyne excludes three of his five models as unsatisfactory in various ways, including, curiously, the one that does explicitly combine other models – the competing values framework (CVF). This might be in part due to a misinterpretation of CVF – Boyne argues that CVF "highlights that it is impossible for organizations to emphasize simultaneously control and flexibility, or to be responsive primarily to both internal and external stakeholders. Rather, movement into one box ... must be traded against movement out of another" (Boyne 2003, p. 220). Quite the reverse is actually the case – the proponents of CVF have argued again and again that "effectiveness is inherently paradoxical" (Cameron 2005) – that is, that organizations have to satisfy contradictory demands and values simultaneously to be really effective (see, e.g., Quinn and Cameron 1988; Cameron et al. 2006).

Despite the above misinterpretation, Boyne makes an important point and suggestion: by proposing the synthesis of the goal and multiple-constituencies models he points to the weakness of many of the models in being too inwardly (closed system) focused and failing to take adequate account of external factors. This is obviously not true for the systems-resources approaches, but their weaknesses lie elsewhere (i.e., a failure to systematically define the actual external sources of resources in such a way it can be properly analyzed).

CVF also includes an element of external focus – the right-hand side of the CVF model (Figure 7.5) is indeed an "external focus."

However, a weakness of CVF could be seen as the failure to incorporate adequately external stakeholders in all four quadrants of the multiple model, a point Boyne addresses by emphasizing the importance of multiple-constituencies models. We return to these issues later in the chapter and in Chapters 8 and 10.

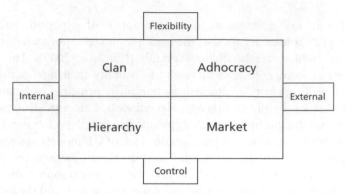

Figure 7.5 CVF Model

Source: Quinn (1988), Quinn and Cameron (1988), Cameron and Quinn (2006), Cameron et al. (2006), and Quinn et al. (2007). For the full CVF approach see Chapter 6.

The Excellence, Quality, and Culture Movement

Two facts seem indisputable: in the early 1980s the OE academic and practitioner movement went into terminal decline and that there simultaneously emerged a mainly practitioner/consultant-driven alternative in the culture and quality movement that at the very least had a big influence upon, if not dominated, both private and public sector thinking about organizational improvement for the next decade or so. The causes of these changes, and their interrelationship, may be open to discussion but the reality of changes seems indisputable. We turn now, therefore, to look at the roots and content of the excellence, quality, and culture movement.

As has already been mentioned, the new movement was most clearly symbolized, and given impetus, by the phenomenal success of *In Search of Excellence* (Peters and Waterman 1982), which impacted not just on the private sector but also heavily influenced some aspects of New Public Management (NPM) in the public sector (Pollitt 1990; Ferlie et al. 1996).

In Search of Excellence (ISOE) emerged from McKinsey & Co and their reconsideration of how they approached organizational effectiveness. But ISOU was not the only product of this reevaluation – a year before it was published, Pascale and Athos, also two senior McKinsey consultants, published a book entitled *The Art of Japanese Management* (Pascale and Athos 1981). Whereas ISOE portrays the new thinking as coming primarily from a study of "excellent" US corporations, Pascale and Athos' book depicts the new approach as coming more from ideas extant in Japanese management – especially their emphasis on "softer" issues of culture and quality as opposed to their western counterparts.

Both books drew heavily on the new McKinsey "7-S" Framework (Figure 7.6). The proponents of this new approach suggested that traditional

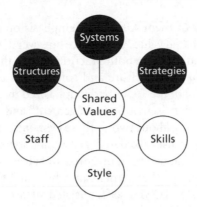

Figure 7.6 McKinsey 7-S Framework

western corporations tended to place their greatest emphasis on the issues of strategy, structure, and systems – the so-called hard-triangle. Popular management texts by gurus like Drucker and others tended to concentrate on these issues, and the influential academic texts did likewise. Alongside the OE movement described above, academics like economic historian Chandler were famously trying to create theories of historical determinants shaping the relationship between "strategy and structure" (Chandler 1991).

Interest in Japanese management practices seemed to emerge for several reasons: Japan's phenomenal postwar reconstruction and success; the penetration of US markets by Japanese companies, especially in the late 1960s in motorcycles; how Japan seemed to weather the mid-1970s better than most western countries; and so on. Japan, it was widely believed, was "different" but exactly how?

The conclusion that many seemed to come to was that this was a cultural phenomenon. Anthropologists like Benedict (2006 [1946]) had emphasized the unique and very different aspects of Japanese culture for western audiences. Other management experts echoed this approach in arguing it was aspects of Japanese culture that were responsible for the "Japanese miracle," but unlike Benedict, they thought it was possible to transport values and practices across national boundaries (Ouchi 1981; Pascale and Athos 1981).

The conclusion reached by the McKinsey consultants was that, in organizational terms, this was about concentrating on what they regarded as the neglected "softer" aspects of organizational life – the so-called soft-square of staff, skills, style, and above all shared value. A movement to study organizational, managerial, business, and "comparative capitalisms" also rapidly emerged during this period (influential texts from this period include Deal and Kennedy 1982; Schein 1985; Lessem 1990; Hampden-Turner and Trompenaars 1993; Johnson 1995; Hofstede 2003).

Several points need to be noted here – the formal McKinsey 7-S Framework did not abandon the "hard" elements of structures, strategies, and systems, but intended to complement them with equal emphasis on the four soft areas of staff, skills, style, and shared values. In practice however it was these last elements that gained the most attention in both practitioner and the academic literature.

Nor was this emphasis on culture and softer issues completely new – the human relations school of the 1930s had emphasized many of these issues and before that even Taylorian "scientific management" and bureaucratic scholars had had something to say about two of these elements, that is, staff and skills.

The emphasis on Japan also linked to a very specific approach to management – total quality (TQM) – that had been invented, or at least formalized, not by the Japanese but by Deming, the "American who taught the Japanese about quality" (Aguaya 1991). TQM itself consisted of a core philosophy about creating a "culture of quality" as the key way to improve organizational performance.

However, it should be noted that TQM and similar approaches say nothing about strategy, and this became a whole separate field of study and activity as Japanese companies were also sent to be better at strategy. Initially, the approach to analyzing Japanese firms' strategies was to apply Western strategic planning concepts to them but it soon became apparent these were not so easily applicable to the reality of the ways Japanese companies operated. A new interest in the role of the Japanese, and wider, martial strategic traditions emerged – translations and explanations of Sun Tzu's *The Art of War* and Miyamoto Musashi's *The Book of Five Rings* appeared in large numbers. Also studied was the role of intuition and Zen in Japanese corporate thinking.

The period from the early 1980s onwards was not solely one of quality and cultural management – it also saw the parallel rise of a new, almost univariate, managerial focus in the private sector, especially in the Anglo-Saxon countries, the shareholder value movement (Black et al. 1998). Shareholder value was not the only purely financial approach to assessing private sector corporate performance developed through the 1980s and 1990s – economic value added, earnings per share; return on investment, return on capital employed, activity-based costing, and many others have been used and extolled. (Many of these have limited relevance to public sector performance measurement.)

It is still arguable, however, that the predominant management research-practice movement during this period was the one associated with cultural and quality management (which often in practice was implemented in parallel with shareholder value and other management approaches, despite their contradictions). TQM spread rapidly through the private and public sectors (Aguaya 1991; Oakland 1991; Logothetis 1992; Morgan and Murgatroyd 1994; Joss 1995; Pollitt and Bouckaert 1995). One specific outcome from this movement was the almost ubiquitous mission and values statement that sprung up in organizations across the western world.

Figure 7.7 Organizational Excellence Model (Canada)

This period also saw the emergence of the first multidimensional performance measurement (MDPM[1]) models (Brignall 2002). The first (as far as I have been able to trace) was the Canadian Excellence Framework promulgated in 1982 (Figure 7.7).

The Canadian experiment was clearly inspired by notions of quality and excellence (as in ISOE and TQM) and only just predated the promulgation (in an Act of Congress no less) of the Malcolm Baldrige Quality Awards in the United States, which adopted a very similar structure (Figure 7.8).

A few years later the Europeans followed this basic approach with a similar award – the European Foundation for Quality Management (EFQM) Awards based on their own framework (also known as the "business excellence" or just excellence model at different times) (Figure 7.9) – although as will be discussed below there is at least one significant difference between the North American and European approaches.

There are a large number of other, very similar, national iterations of this basic idea – especially across Europe – that emerged in the late 1980s and the early 1990s. Some of this proliferation was undoubtedly due to the desire of national policy-makers and other actors to have their own "excellence" award/model – even when they were already covered by a multinational one like EFQM. There is no space, or much to be gained, by running through all of these national examples here (but see Table 7.2 Private Sector Performance Models at the end of this chapter for some more information and examples).

It is worth noting what they tend to share in common however:

- They all, rather obviously, emerged from the "excellence" and "TQM" movements of the early 1980s.

---

[1] The acronym MDPM is used throughout to refer to either multidimensional performance measurement model or multidimensional performance model interchangeably.

Table 7.2 Private Sector Performance Models

MODELS	ORIGINATORS	DATE	LOCATION
Statistical Process Control	Walter Shewhart and W. Edwards Deming	1950s	Japan
Deming Prize (for Company Wide Quality Control – CWQC)	Japanese Union of Scientists and Engineers (JUSE)	1951	Japan
Seventeen Multivariate Models	Various (see Steers 1975)	1964–75	USA
Corporate Social Performance Model	Carroll	1979	
Shareholder Value	Usually attributed to Jack Welch in 1981 but see (Rappaport 1979, 1981)	1979	USA
Competing Values Framework	Quinn and Rohrbaugh	1981	USA
McKinsey 7-S Framework	Peters and Waterman	1982	USA
TQM	US Navy (but based on Demming, etc.)	1984	USA
Canada Award for Excellence	Ministry of Industry	1984	Canada
Six Sigma	Smith (Motorola)	1986	USA
Baldrige Award	National Institute of Standards and Technology (NIST)	1987	USA
ISO9000 Quality Management System	International Standards Organization	1987 (with major revisions in 1994 and 2000)	International
(Business) Excellence Model	European Foundation for Quality Management (EFQM)	1991	Europe
Results and Determinants Framework for services	Fitzgerald et al.	1991	UK
The SMART Pyramid	Lynch and Cross (1995)	1991	USA
Balanced Scorecard	Kaplan and Norton (1996)	1992	USA
Burke–Litwin Organizational Performance and Change Model	Burke and Litwin (Burke 2008)	1992	USA
Business Process Reengineering	Hammer and Champy (1993)	1993	USA
Input–Process–Output–Outcome Framework	Brown (1996)	1996	USA
Simplified Value Management Framework	BS EN 12973	2000	EU
Performance PRISM	Neely et al. (2002)	2002	UK
Global Compact Performance Model	UN	2002	International

- They are all MDPM models, although their originators and supporters rarely use the language of performance. But they clearly embed several dimensions of performance and imply that if all these dimensions are managed well, the result will be enhanced organizational performance overall. These dimensions of performance owe something to both the excellence/TQM movement and also to the elements of performance identified in the preceding OE movement (see Table 7.1).
- Despite their origins in the excellence, quality, and culture movement, these MDPMs clearly owe something to the earlier OE studies on factors or elements of performance, many of which (see Table 7.1) reappear in

Figure 7.8 Baldrige Excellence Awards (United States)

these models. In some ways this generation of "excellence" models represent a fusion of some of the results of the earlier OE research with the focus on "softer" issues such as quality, values, and culture – something which the McKinsey 7-S Framework in fact makes quite explicit (see Figure 7.6) but most others do not.

- They are all "generic" models that claim to apply to all organizations – private and public, small and large, and industrial and service – regardless of time and place.
- By being generic they also claim to be comparable – that is, they can be used for benchmarking purposes and – as they have been in most cases – for making awards based on either comparable levels of achievement (i.e., the "best in class" get an award each year) or, as in a few cases, as standards to be attained.

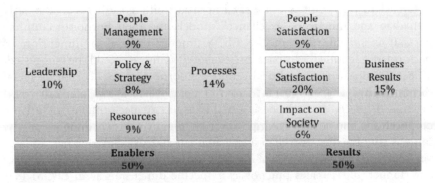

Figure 7.9 Business Excellence Model (Europe)

- In order to reach overall conclusions about an individual organizations' performance, they usually give weightings to the various dimensions of performance – as illustrated in the EFQM model where the percentage weightings are given (Figure 7.9).
- Within dimensions of performance a process of aggregation also takes place, often bringing together into a single "score" dozens of individual performance measures and indicators.
- They have all emerged from the somewhat gray area between practitioners, consultancies, policy-makers, and academia. All claim to be based on some sort of research – but this is rarely, if ever, published and thereby testable against existing research.
- All claim some sort of "official" or quasi-official status and most come with a whole infrastructure of institutions (e.g., NIST; EFQM; etc), awards processes, more detailed criteria and "how to" advice, databases of scores and best-practice case studies, and a coterie of specialist consultancies offering advice on how best to "do" Baldrige or EFQM or whatever national variant.

There are other, interesting, theoretical similarities between these and other multidimensional performance management models that will be considered later in this chapter, such as the nature of the multidimensional-ness, the problematic issue of "results" versus "drivers," their nonlinearity, and problems of weighting and aggregation of factors.

Despite their claims to universality, all these models keep changing – all of the main "excellence" models have been subject to successive iterations over the years since they have been established and while their basic structures remain similar in each case, there have been substantial changes to detail. This raises important questions about just how "generic" and "universal" – indeed how they sound – they were to start with and how we are to judge whether the current incarnation is merely another step along the way or the final, definitive, version.

Linked to this point is one very important difference between the early Canadian and American "excellence" models and their European counterpart. It is notable that in the EFQM model there is a dimension of performance entitled "Impact on Society." This, it could be suggested, reflects European socio-political-economic norms that see "corporate social responsibility" as an important factor. American liberal capitalism, it could be argued, placed less emphasis on this aspect of performance of private corporations and so the Baldrige Awards contain no such dimension (the same is true for the Australian and Canadian awards). Baldrige has, in later years, now incorporated some recognition of social responsibility (Porter and Tanner 2004) issues but not as a specific dimension as in EFQM (see also Talbot 1999).

Continuing Interest in Factors or Elements of Performance (Effectiveness)

Alongside these more holistic MDPMs, a strong interest in more limited, unidimensional elements of performance/effectiveness continued through the 1980s and into the 1990s and beyond (see Table 7.1 and Figure 7.4). For example:

- Item (1) productivity and item (2) efficiency seemed to be reinvented largely under titles like "business process re-engineering" and TQM.
- Item (9) flexibility/adaptation tended to be replaced with a new "umbrella construct" – organizational learning, that itself became one of the schools of strategic thought.
- Item (10) – planning and goal-setting – strategy emerged (again) as a major issue – it had in fact been around since the mid-1960s, initially under titles like "business policy" and "corporate planning" but it reemerged strongly in the 1990s under the title "strategy" with many competing schools of thought – some linked to the fascination with Japanese management (such as strategic learning and intuitive decision-making) – for a fuller account see Mintzberg (1994), Mintzberg et al. (1998), and Mintzberg and Quinn (1998).
- Items (16) and (17) – concerning human resources and training – tended to be absorbed into the new "human resource management" (HRM) movement that began in the early 1990s, which itself also has clear links back to the "skills' and "staff" elements of the McKinsey framework (Figure 7.5) and whole quality movement with its emphasis on staff engagement and empowerment.

The important point to note here is that these elements of performance, identified very early in the post-World War II OE movement, keep coming back again and again in different combinations, with slightly different emphases, and sometimes different labels – but this, admittedly slightly "fuzzy" set of issues has proved remarkably persistent over time. They have been embedded, to one degree or another, in most of the MDPMs examined above and below. Indeed, an analysis of the various "excellence" models shows a remarkable similarity in the factors that appear in them (see Porter and Tanner 2004, table 3.2).

Organizational Effectiveness Redux: The 1990s "Performance" Movement

The early 1990s saw a resurgence of interest in measurable, nonfinancial, organizational performance (Neely 1998; Neely and Waggoner 1998) more along the lines of the original OE movement than the excellence, quality, and culture movement. A symbol of the new movement, and effectively a starting pistol, was the influential "Performance Measurement Manifesto" published in the *Harvard Business Review* in 1991 (Eccles 1991). Numerous "how to" texts emerged as quantification of performance gained increasing favor, and academic studies of performance surged. The new performance movement was similar to the original OE movement in its emphasis on quantification, but rather less concerned with explicit theoretical issues – it seems to have been much more pragmatically driven.

This does not mean that it was not informed by theoretical ideas – merely that these were less explicitly, or rigorously, raised – especially in the first decade or so of this movement. For example, in terms of the various strands identified in the previous OE phase the new movement has seemed to be in some respects a reincarnation of the "goals" approach – focusing mostly on how to measure goal attainment. At first, the primary initial focus of the new movement was simply on measurement (e.g., Smith 1987; *Harvard Business Review* 1991; Lynch and Cross 1995). However, it has also taken on the idea of MDPM models in a very big way, with a veritable explosion of a new army of models, as will be discussed below.

One curious aspect of the "new" performance movement was its almost complete disconnect from the earlier OE movement. Thus, as an example, a keynote chapter on "Finding Performance: The New Discipline in Management" (Meyer 2007) in a major international collection of research papers does not mention the earlier work of the OE movement. Indeed, the whole volume of this "comprehensive review of theory and practice" totally ignores the earlier literature and research as if nothing much happened before the 1990s or the 1980s at best (Neely 2007). There is no reference to OE or any of the earlier generation of experts in the field. This might be, in part at least, because these types of books are aimed as much at practitioner as at research audiences and are subject therefore to the "tyranny of the new" (for a discussion of why this sort of thing happens, see Pfeffer and Sutton 2006).

THE NEW ARMY OF MODELS

The first phase of the new performance movement replicated in many ways the early days of the OE movement – counting everything that could be counted and, mostly, trying to relate this to organizational goals. However the indirect impact of the later years of OE and the search for multiple models of performance, coupled with the emergence from the excellence and quality movement of MDPMs, was not ignored and the new wave quickly turned to a focus on new models – of which dozens began to emerge, far too many to review in full here. A partial listing of such models is given in Table 7.2.

Some of these models were only partial in character – that is, they focused on one specific aspect of organizational performance; examples include those focused on human resources management (such as the "Investors in People" Awards in the United Kingdom) or on business processes (BPR – business process reengineering, some TQM models, and so on).

More holistic MDPM models however also began to proliferate. Probably the most famous is the "Balanced Scorecard" (Kaplan and Norton 1992, 1996, 2004), but others include the performance PRISM (Neely et al. 2002), the Burke–Litwin model (Burke 2008).

(As we will see in Chapter 8, this explosion of models was if anything even more pronounced in the public sector.

A NOTE ON LINEAGE

It is probably worth mentioning here the issue of lineage: to what extent do these models emerge independently of one another and to what extent are they based sequentially upon one another? To use evolutionary metaphors – are they simply examples of the parallel evolution of answers to a common ecological problem (like the wings of bats and birds) or are they actual "descendents" of prior models? In the case of the US and Canadian developments of excellence models it seems reasonable to assume they must have more or less simultaneously sprung from the quality and culture ideas emerging in the late 1970s and especially in the early 1980s mainly in North America. The later emergence of the European model, however, leaves more open the question of how far it was a purely local development and how far an imported adaptation of the North American models?

It is almost impossible to answer this question definitely without a huge research effort, and considering the multiple possible channels of communication and the probably questionable memories of key actors, even if it were possible, would it be worth it? Unlike evolutionary biology, it is not necessary to show that this particular fossil with early wing-like appendages actually is the progenitor of modern birds, rather than some dead-end off-shoot of such an evolutionary sequence. It is perfectly reasonable to assume for analytical purposes that if two models, to coin a phrase, both walk like a duck and quack like a duck, they are closely related. Moreover, in at least some of the MDPM models there are obvious links and anecdotal evidence sufficient to point to specific lineages, or at least influences, as a working hypothesis.

MDPM MODELS: SOME THEORETICAL ISSUES

It is worth now turning to some of the theoretical issues raised by, and embedded within, the MDPM models reviewed in the preceding text under

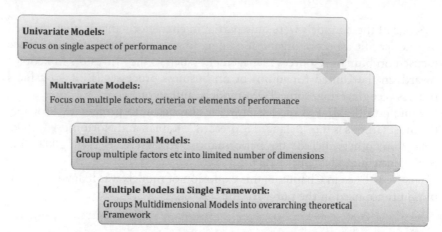

Figure 7.10 Suggested Conceptual Evolution of Models of Performance

both the excellence and quality and the new performance movement headings.

First, it is worth noting where MDPM models lie in a suggested conceptual evolution of performance models (see Figure 7.10). According to Steers (1975), citing Thorndike (1949), the very early OE movement of the 1940s tended to focus on a single "ultimate criterion" of effectiveness, such as productivity, net profit, mission accomplishment, or organizational growth and stability. An earlier analysis by Ridgway (1956) cites several early 1950s studies by Blau et al. of organizations that use univariate performance measures. A study by Campbell (1973) identified nineteen different such univariate measures used in different research studies.

These univariate models were superseded conceptually by multivariate models – of which Steers identified no less than seventeen that emerged between 1964 and 1975 (Steers 1975). The number of criteria used in these seventeen studies ranged from just two up to eight, the most common being adaptability flexibility (10), productivity (6), satisfaction (5), and profitability and resource acquisition (3 each). But there was thus a great deal of variation in the criteria being used – in ten cases the criteria were derived deductively and in the other seven, inductively.

MDPMs represent the next conceptual stage in development, as they tend to group together multiple criteria under several dimensions of performance. Thus, for example, the EFQM model (Figure 7.9) has contained anywhere up to around 100 criteria under its nine dimensions of "excellence."

The next stage in the conceptual evolution of performance models is, we would suggest, the development of multiple models within a single overarching theoretical framework – but this stage will be left until Chapter 10 for a full exploration.

It should be stressed at this point that although this conceptual evolution does more or less lie along a time dimension, the most recent (1980s and 1990s) explosion in MDPM models has happened mostly after the origin of multiple models within a single framework in the early 1980s.

Secondly, all of the MDPM models either implicitly or explicitly embed theoretical assumptions that are all too frequently not unpacked in the presentation of the finished article. This is partly due to their somewhat opaque origin at the interface of practice, consultancy, academia, and sometimes government policy-making (e.g., especially the various "excellence" models). The models are usually said to have "emerged" from a process of research (usually conducted by consultants rather than academics, and usually unavailable for inspection) and consultation with practitioner communities. So all that is usually available to analyze is the finished product and any theoretical assumptions underpinning them have to be imputed.

Multidimensional

The first and most obvious point is that these are all multidimensional models – that is they seek to incorporate a whole range of elements or factors of organizational performance under a number of dimensions – ranging from, for example, the four dimensions of the balanced scorecard up to the nine dimensions of the EFQM Excellence model. In most cases these multiple dimensions group many of the elements or criteria of performance identified in the early OE movement.

Many of the dimensions they incorporate are themselves the subject of a vast literature – both research and practice based – themselves. Thus, the literature on "people" issues – a fairly common element of many models – is itself probably as big, if not bigger, than the performance literature itself. As such the MDPMs are a sort of data reduction exercise, grouping large numbers of (potential) criteria into more manageable "chunks."

Models or Systems

These are "models" – in that they seek to arrange these various dimensions into some sort of relationship, structure, or system that purports to represent abstracted models of real relationships within real organizations. This is often just implied by the way the models are laid out diagrammatically – as with the EFQM model, for which there is relatively little explanation of the relationships between dimensions or why they are laid out as they are. The layout implies relationships, but it often only implies them. They all clearly owe something to systems theories in mapping complex causal links between multiple elements and dimensions.

Interestingly, despite this underlying systems approach, they nearly all appear – diagrammatically at least – as closed rather than open systems. This is especially notable given current concerns in management thinking and research with interorganizational networks and the so-called open business models (Chesbrough 2006). Networks, alliances, and open business models all pose important challenges to existing MDPMs because of their relatively closed organizational focus. As (or rather if, as this is not an unproblematic question itself) production, and therefore performance, becomes less organizationally bounded, and more driven by such networks, alliances, and open business models, then MDPMs would have to adapt to this new reality or be replaced by new models that incorporate these changes. This is an interesting new area of research which is only just starting to be addressed, and more in the public than in the private sector (see, e.g., Frederickson and Frederickson 2006) as will be discussed further in the next chapter.

Results and Drivers

Quite a few MDPMs have "solved" the problem of whether or not some performance criteria are really enablers or drivers of performance rather than actual results by dividing their models into "results" and "enablers" (again, EFQM, but also Baldrige, the Performance PRISM, the Results and Determinants Framework for Services, and several others). The implication is that high performance on "enablers" now will lead to high performance on "results" in the future, but at the present moment only past results can be measured. So "enablers" are said to be leading indicators of performance while present "results" represent lagging indicators.

MDPMs and Actual Performance

Research on the relationship between the use of MDPMs to shape and steer organizational performance and what impact is achieved is quite limited. Most effort has focused on the various quality and excellence awards and the evidence here is patchy. The most extensive research has been conducted on the US's Baldrige Award and the European Excellence Award and has included studies of whether Award winners had markedly different levels of performance to nonwinners, including financial performance (mainly share price).

The evidence for "excellence" MDPMs suggests there are benefits to applying these models to corporations. Improvements in various "enabling" dimensions have been noted and studies of share price movements suggest that there are benefits, although there are differences in the evidence about how big the benefits are; when they can be expected; and what other factors mitigate these results. For a summary of much of this research see Porter and Tanner (2004).

Most of this research has focused on the effects of using excellence MDPMs rather than on the validity of the models themselves. Only a few studies have actually examined the validity of the models themselves; for example, one has examined the weightings within the EFQM model (Eskildsen and Kristensen 2002) (more on this in the following text) and two have examined the validity of the relationships between the Baldrige criteria (Evans 1997; Pannirselvam and Ferguson 2001).

A major limiting factor for research on the various excellence MDPMs is that the sponsoring bodies often hold their own databases "in commercial confidence."

Correlations and Complex Causality

The next point relates to the complexity of, and causal relations between, different elements or dimensions of performance. For example, in a critique of the balanced scorecard, which could easily be expanded to include all MDPMs, Meyer (2002) argues that for MDPMs (he does not use that term) to work the various measures of performance proposed have to be uncorrelated – otherwise they (or some of them) are redundant. That is, if on a single dimension of bad to good to excellent two or more measures are strongly correlated – that is, they would all tell you the same thing about where an organization is located on this single dimension – then any one of them would suffice and the others are redundant. This of course assumes that there is such a single dimension of performance – the cumulative debates of the earlier OE movement about the nature of the "effectiveness" construct (see earlier in this chapter) suggest that there is not, nor can there be, in reality any such simple and one-dimensional construct of performance.

Moreover MDPMs, including the balanced scorecard, tend to imply complex, and not necessarily linear, causal links between different elements or dimensions of performance. To take an example, again using the EFQM model – virtually any dimension of this model can potentially interact with any other dimension. Even the connection between "enablers" and "results" is not necessarily a one-way link – current "enablers" drive future "results." Current results can just as easily influence current enablers, as when either positive or negative "halo" effects feedback into things like employee policies (Rosenzweig 2007).

These complex and sometimes iterative linkages, which can create negative or positive feedback spirals, are rarely discussed in the analysis of MDPM models. An exception being the study by Pannirselvam and Ferguson (2001) which attempts to map and test the causal linkages in the Baldrige model. While they broadly support the models internal coherence, some linkages, which purported to be important, proved to be very weak. Given that the mapping process was linear in nature this raises some issues about the internal coherence of the model.

Composite Measures and Weightings

The fifth point is that, as already mentioned above, all MDPMs implicitly raise the issue of compositing or aggregating performance measures and indicators; firstly within dimensions of performance and secondly (in some cases) by aggregating dimensions themselves. The balanced scorecard implies the first, but not the second, whereas EFQM explicitly does both. Indeed EFQM goes much further and assigns specific weightings to the different nine dimensions of performance it includes. It is however very unclear how these were arrived at and very little research has been conducted on the weightings (Porter and Tanner 2004).

Just to take one example: people management (9%) and people results (9%) are the two (one enabler and one result) dimensions relating to people in the organization. Should this be taken to imply that the two dimensions taken together amount to 18% of overall organizational performance? If so, on what basis? Some (now somewhat dated) research evidence suggests that individual performance can be enhanced by goal-setting by 16%, and when combined with material incentives by as much as 40% (Locke et al.1981). But this review of available evidence was at pains to point out that these results are highly variable and contextual. And, even if these results were correct and generalizable across contexts, how does this translate into organizational performance? In labor-intensive organizations, presumably it would have much greater impact than in capital-intensive ones?

Only one study seems to have been carried out to verify the EFQM ratings scheme – a survey of Danish companies (Eskildsen and Kristensen 2002). This empirical work showed that, for Danish companies at least, the weightings given to the various dimensions of performance were very different to those assigned by EFQM (Figure 7.11).

The differences between the EFQM and Danish managers' ratings of the different dimensions is quite different – the 50/50 split between enablers and results is shifted to a 70/30 split in favor of enablers and all the dimensions vary, in some cases dramatically – for example, the reduction in importance of "business results from 15% to only 6%." If the EFQM weightings had been derived by similar means – that is, a large-scale survey of European managers (there is no evidence of how they reached their weightings) – then these variances could easily be explained by cultural differences. But such an explanation

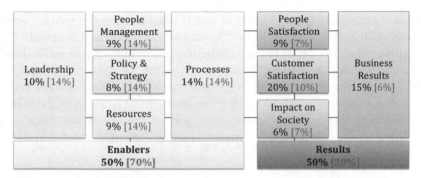

Figure 7.11 Empirically Derived Weightings for EFQM Dimensions [in square brackets]
Source: Adapted from Eskildsen and Kristensen 2002.

would raise important issues about the applicability of a single MDPM across culturally different settings – the final issue we will turn to in a moment. But first, it is worth noting that neither the Danish managers' nor the official EFQM weightings given to the dimensions of the Excellence Model have been shown in any way to relate to the actual performance of corporations.

Generalizability

This brings us to the final issue: how generalizable are MDPMs? Nearly all such models claim, or imply, universal application – that is, that they should apply to all organizations, everywhere and when. The exceptions are the explicitly sectoral ones like the services MDPM [Fitzgerald] and public sector MDPMs – see the next chapter.

In practice, and theory, this claim is difficult to sustain. Firstly, they cannot all be right – that is if one MDPM is a generalizable, universal model, then other MDPMs, being different, cannot be. This is easily demonstrated by the exclusion of any "social responsibility" dimension in the (US-based) Baldrige model but its inclusion in the (European-based) EFQM, mentioned earlier. They cannot both be "universal" models and in fact are both clearly culturally specific.

The MDPMs discussed in this chapter all claim to be generic, but in fact have their origins and theoretical underpinnings not in some generalizable world of organizations but specifically in the private sector corporate world. The existence of the many public sector MDPMs and the adaptation of the private sector ones, discussed in Chapter 8 on public sector performance demonstrates this.

This is not to say that one MDPM might not be a universal model, but it seems rather unlikely that any one MDPM could in fact capture the differences between sectors adequately. In other words, the "construct" problem which caused such an intellectual crisis at the end of OE movement (Campbell 1977; Goodman et al. 1977; Cameron and Whetten 1983*a*) once again rears its head. This will be discussed further in Chapter 10 of this book, which will examine the concept of multiple models in a single framework, as suggested in Figure 7.10 above. In many ways, addressing this problematic issue lies at the core of performance theory and without some sort of resolution the chances of avoiding another "umbrella construct collapse" (Hirsch and Levin 1999) seems a distinct possibility.

8 Theories of Performance of Public Organizations

This chapter addresses theories about the performance of public organizations or agencies.

First, a word about terminology – by public agency I mean any public organization that is engaged in the delivery of public services or goods. I use the word "agency" rather than "organization" for the simple reason that public organizations are always accountable to some body (or bodies) outside of themselves, and indeed depend on this "authorising environment" (Moore 1995) or "performance regime" (Talbot 2008c) for their very existence. The term "agency" helps to remind us of this, but in other respects the terms "agency" and "organization" are used interchangeably.

For the sake of analysis in this chapter we will, despite the above, treat public agencies as if they were discrete entities along the lines of private companies or corporations. This means looking at whole entities – not subsystems or parts, but the whole. Again, in some public domain systems defining these internal boundaries is problematic because organizations are often "nested" – for example, in school age education do we treat as an agency a ministry or department (much of Europe), a school district (United States) or education authority (United Kingdom), or an individual school, or for different purposes maybe all of them?

Treating public agencies (however delineated) as equivalent to private sector corporations has been done in much of research and theory of generic, public, and private organizational performance or effectiveness discussed in Chapter 7. This has resulted in a fair degree of crossover, especially from the private to the public domains, in organizational performance models.

However, the first phase of the modern performance movement that started around the mid-1980s was, like its private sector cousin, concerned more with issues of measurement unframed by specific models of organizational performance (Jowett and Rothwell 1988; Cave et al. 1990; Rogers 1990; Carter et al. 1992; Jackson and Palmer 1992; Holloway et al. 1995; Jackson 1995; Halachmi and Bouckaert 1996; Mayne and Zapico-Goni 1997; Hatry 1999). Much of this literature was primarily concerned with the sort of technical and definitional problems of measurement discussed in Chapter 2.

Nevertheless, multidimensional performance measurement (MDPM) models or frameworks (see Chapter 7 for discussion of MDPMs) both predated this movement and ran in parallel to it. We can distinguish between three types of models of organizational performance that have developed in the public sector, depending on their provenance:

- **Adopted imports** – these are generic (in reality usually mainly private sector models) that have simply been adopted, unchanged, by the public sector – these would include examples like widespread adoption of the Baldrige, EQFM, and other quality-originated models and the balanced scorecard (BSC) discussed in Chapter 7.
- **Adapted imports** – these are versions of the above-mentioned types of models that have been specifically changed in some way to make them more applicable in public sector contexts.
- **Indigenous innovations** – new models that have been specifically developed for the public sector only.

There are of course many other ways of parsing the many MDPM models that have emerged, or been utilized, in the public sector over the past decades, especially more recently. Later in this chapter, we will examine some of these other possible classifications, but for the moment these three will help us get some better idea of the range of developments. The importing, by simple adoption, or more sophisticated adaptation, of private sector management ideas was also not limited to performance models. Many other more partial or functionally focused techniques and ideas were imported over this period, including the following:

- Total Quality Management (Dickens 1994; Morgan and Murgatroyd 1994; Gaster 1995; Kirkpatrick and Matinez Lucio 1995);
- Human Resources Management (Farnham and Horton 1996; Farnham et al. 1996);
- Business Process Reengineering (Linden 1994)
- Transformational Leadership (Raffel et al. 2009a; Brookes and Grint 2010)

These are just a few examples of initiatives that were also undertaken in the hopes of improving public organizational performance. Performance models are important, however, because they represent the espoused theories of policy-makers and practitioners, and to some extent also of researchers.

Adopted Imports

The adoption of MDPM models of organizational performance developed primarily for private sector organizations by the public sector should be not a great surprise for several reasons.

The first is that it goes with the grain of the "New Public Management" (NPM) movement of the 1980s and the 1990s that specifically favored the importation of private sector management techniques into the public sector (Aucoin 1990; Hood 1991; Pollitt 1993).

Secondly, NPM was not entirely novel in recommending the import of private management approaches – this has been a long-term aspect of public management reforms (Hood and Jackson 1991; Light 1997).

Thirdly, some of these models – especially the "quality" ones – had official government sponsorship as part of government policies aimed at productivity and innovation improvement in the private sector. It would therefore have been odd if the same governments had not at least encouraged, if not imposed, the importation of these officially sanctioned models into the public sector.

Fourthly, ironically some of the early work on organizational effectiveness and performance that eventually led to the emergence of many performance models actually occurred in the public sector (see Appendix 8.1), or at any rate a mixture of public and private organizations – for example, CVF (Quinn and Rohrbaugh 1981, 1983) and work on some of the quality models mentioned above.

For some of these reasons, the first wave of private sector imports was the various "quality" models that originated in the 1980s – for example, the Baldrige Awards framework, Canadian Quality model, EFQM Excellence model, and so on. In the United Kingdom, for example, government departments and agencies were strongly urged to adopt the EFQM Excellence model (Samuels 1997, 1998) and the practice spread to other parts of the public sector.

The second major wave of importation was the BSC (Kaplan and Norton 1992, 1996) that has been widely adopted across public services, certainly in the United States and the United Kingdom and elsewhere too (Griffiths 2003; Kerr 2003; McAdam and Walker 2003; Niven 2003; Radnor and Lovell 2003a, 2003b; Wilson et al. 2003; Chan 2004; Gueorguiev et al. 2005; Holmes et al. 2006).

Adapted Imports

More often than not, despite the supposed generic nature of many performance models in both theory and practice, there are good grounds for suggesting they simply do not fit easily into the public sector context – the public sector really is different in important ways that affect how we theorize performance (Fried 1976; Denhardt 1993; Moore 1995; Frederickson 1997; Behn 2001; Denhardt and Denhardt 2003).

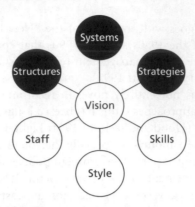

Figure 8.1 Audit Commission Framework
Source: Audit Commission (1984).

Where generic models have been imported they have therefore often also been heavily adapted.

A particularly telling example of this was the adaptation of the McKinsey 7-S Framework (see Chapter 7) by the UK Audit Commission in 1984 for its handbook on *Improving Economy, Efficiency and Effectiveness in Local Government in England and Wales*. In this unacknowledged "borrowing" from the McKinsey model (there is no reference to the McKinsey model in the handbook), the framework is adapted by replacing the central category of "shared values" with "vision" (see Figure 8.1). Because there is no acknowledgment of the source of the framework, there is also no explanation given as to why this change was made. We are left to construe the reasoning from the facts of the change. The implication is that "shared values" is not appropriate to an elected local government context because the whole nature of politically elected assemblies is that of contested, rather than shared, values – at least in important areas relating to what sort of services should be provided, for what purpose, and by raising what taxes? So shared values is replaced by "vision," which is defined as "what the Authority is seeking to be or to achieve" – which is essentially the same as saying what is the program of the ruling party or coalition? Indeed, this was the conclusion drawn by one contemporary authority who, after examining the Audit Commission version of the 7-S Framework, stated: "[the] organization must have a clear vision of where it is going based on *the shared values of the elements of the dominant coalition* in the organization" (Tomkins 1987, p. 80 – emphasis added). For the Audit Commission to have stated this view would, however, have been far too "political"; hence, it simply avoided the issue.

The BSC concept, for example, has been probably more widely adopted than the actual categories of the BSC itself. In one study in the United Kingdom involving nine diverse public sector agencies, all had adopted

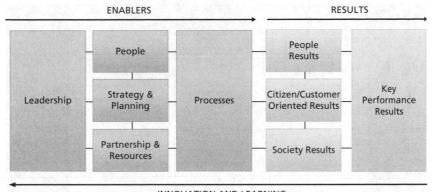

Figure 8.2 EU Common Assessment Framework
Source: EIPA web site www.eipa.eu.

some form of BSC, and drew on the BSC's conceptual framework for inspiration, but in none of these cases were the actual BSC categories used – instead the organizations involved devised their own categories ranging in number from 4 up to 8 (Talbot and Johnson 2005).

Similarly, other performance models have been adapted or in some cases become the inspiration for new models. The European "Common Assessment Framework" (Figure 8.2) for public services was explicitly created through a merger of the EFQM Excellence and a framework used for many years for the University of Speyer Awards for public sector innovation and excellence[1].

In Canada, for example, the Management Accountability Framework (MAF) (Figure 8.3)[2] was created from an amalgam of both generic (private) models such as the Canadian Excellence Framework and other public sector models (Heintzman 2009) including the current author's Public Service Excellence Model (Figure 8.4), which was used by the Treasury Board in developing MAF.

The Public Service Excellence Model was also created in a reassessment of, and in response to, the applicability of the EFQM Excellence model in public services.

The strong influence of generic or private sector developments is evident in all of the above models, but so too is a strong desire to introduce dimensions of performance that are specific to the public sector. These include things like social "outcomes" (CAF, PSEM, and MAF); public/customer service orientation (CAF, PSEM, and MAF); and public service values (MAF). These types of

[1] http://www.eipa.eu/en/pages/show/&tid=67 – accessed August 2009.
[2] http://www.tbs-sct.gc.ca/maf-crg/implementation-implementation/history-historique-eng.asp - accessed August 2009.

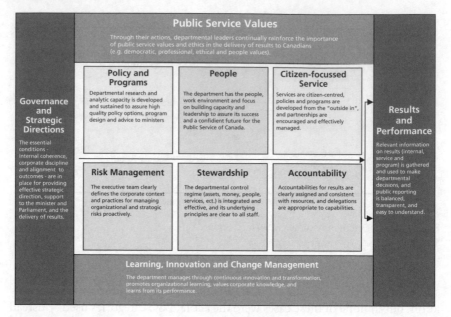

Figure 8.3 Management Accountability Framework (Canada)
Source: Treasury Board web site (www.tbs-sct.gc.ca).

concerns are even more evident in the "homegrown" MDPMs invented specifically for the public sector.

Indigenous Innovations

One of the earliest MDPM for public organizations that I have uncovered so far[3] is the "Three Ethics" approach developed by Fried in a book on *Performance in American Bureaucracy* (1976). This early example identifies many of the themes to arise in later discussions about public sector performance. Fried's main concern is that performance, in the context of American public administration, is very different from that of private organizations. Another is that performance, rather than mere existence, is "the most interesting aspect of bureaucratic behavior" (p. V) – which is similar to the point made in Chapter 1 about performance being the ultimate dependent variable. Fried (somewhat optimistically) comments that:

The task of building a theory of administrative performance requires not only that we are able to describe and evaluate performance, but that we are able to

---

[3] It is worth noting that in this field as soon as you identify "the" earliest example, another, earlier, one inevitably emerges.

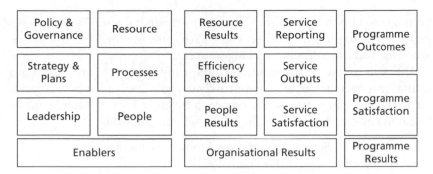

Figure 8.4 Public Service Excellence Model
Source: Talbot (1998, 1999).

explain it, particularly if wish to improve it. Knowing what we like and don't like is one thing; knowing how to increase performance we like and eliminate performance we dislike is another. Such explanatory theory is only now beginning to be sketched.   (p. 14)

For Fried, performance in bureaucracy is characterized by three dimensions, or as he calls them "ethics":

- **The Democratic (or Responsiveness) Ethic** – which is concerned with the widely held values and norms; responsiveness to whom and about what?
- **The Legal (or Liberalism) Ethic** – which is concerned with adherence to ground rules (due process) in responding to community demands for action; with equal rights; limited jurisdictions; compliance; and so on.
- **The Work (or Effectiveness) Ethic** – which is concerned with production (delivery in modern parlance), efficiency, and achievement (outcomes).

Interestingly, Fried adds a fourth concern, that is, survival, which is remarkably similar to the concept of trust and legitimacy in public agencies in the much later "public value" approach of Mark Moore (1995). Fried argues that classic Weberian theories of bureaucracy and public administration are static and stress goals, and he contrasts this with a Darwinian view that stresses only survival. What is needed, he suggests, is a theory that encompasses both (pp. 76–8). (See also Chapter 3 of this book on evolutionary perspectives on organizations.)

Finally, Fried stresses the possible trade offs and contradictions between his democratic, legal, effectiveness, and survival imperatives. The American system of government, especially the institutionalized separation of powers, he argues helps to maintain the balance between these sometimes complimentary and sometimes conflicting principles (p. 79). (See Chapter 6 on values conflicts.)

While Fried's MDPM model – for that is in effect what it is – offers a remarkably well-developed approach, it somewhat inevitably seems to have been ignored by the many other attempts to create frameworks or models of performance in the public sector. These have come mainly from two places – academia and official/policy-making sources.

Although as previously mentioned, the early (current) wave of the performance movement focused on relatively straightforward issues of measurement and reporting, it was not very long before a host of MDPM models began to emerge. Academic examples include the following:

- University of Speyer Public Sector Innovation Awards
- "Significance" model (Denhardt 1993)
- Public Value model and Scorecard (Moore 1995, 2003)
- Comprehensive Public Sector Productivity Improvement model (Holzer and Callahan 1998)
- "Three Pillars" model (Ingstrup and Crookall 1998)
- Stakeholder Influence and Performance Dimensions (Jann and Jantz 2008) adapted from Brignall and Modell (2000)
- "Logic of Governance" model (Lynn et al. 2001)
- Public Sector Scorecard (Moullin et al. 2007)
- Government Performance Project model (Ingraham et al. 2003)

In addition to these academically derived models there have also been a series of officially inspired ones, for example:

- European Public Sector Award – (successor to the CAF) (Europe)
- Program Assessment and Rating Tool (PART) (United States)
- Comprehensive Performance Assessment (CPA) for local government (England)
- Municipal Compass for local government (Sweden)

Neither of the above lists is anywhere near exhaustive and is just intended to give some flavor to the amount of work taking place in this arena. Nor do they include some of the models emerging from consultancies – for example, the "Unlocking Public Value" approach (Cole et al. 2006). There are also a large group of performance frameworks or models that have been developed for specific services, often to satisfy the need for "league table"-type interventions discussed in Chapter 5 (see, e.g., Chang 2007). There are also a group of models that only address specific aspects of performance – for example, the UK Charter Mark model that only looks at service standards.

As has already been indicated in the discussion on imported and adapted models, there has been a great deal of "policy transfer" between countries and sectors in the development. It will probably never be possible to trace the full lineage of all these models (see Chapter 7 for a similar discussion about private-sector-only models) but it does help orientate the discussion to at least have a broad idea of timelines and interactions.

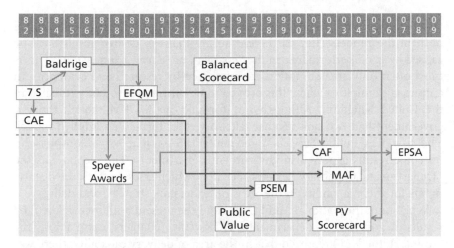

Figure 8.5 Partial Mapping of Links Between Models

The above map (Figure 8.5) makes an attempt at showing some of the lineages of various models where they have emerged from, or begat, further models (with private sector models at the top and public sector ones below). Just tracing one set of transfers shows just how complex these processes are. The Baldrige Awards in the United States clearly derived from the general emergence of the quality and excellence movement, including in part the earlier Canadian framework and the McKinsey 7-S Framework. The influence of Baldrige then crossed the Atlantic to influence the European (EFQM) Excellence Model. This in turn crossed the sectoral divide to produce the Public Service Excellence Model. Finally, the influence of EFQM and PSEM both crossed the Atlantic to have some impact on the development of the Canadian Government's Management Accountability Framework.[4]

There is obviously not sufficient space to devote to going through a detailed analysis of all of the approaches listed above. There are however some commonalities that should be emphasized in the overall line of attack, or configuration, of the various models.

Most of them are clearly and emphatically public sector models, incorporating aspects or dimensions of performance that would not apply to the private sector such as public sector values, external reporting and accountability, and social impacts.

They are all MDPM models suggesting in every case multiple dimensions from a minimum of three dimensions and ranging up to over a dozen (we analyze some of the commonalities in dimensions below).

---

[4] The current author was directly involved with the Canadian Treasury Board in these developments, including presenting the PSEM approach to them.

Most make some distinction between "results" and "enablers" but include both in the model. They all thereby imply that the desired results will be caused by good performance in the "enabler" or "driver" dimensions. This is most often only an assumption, unsupported by research and evidence. An empirical example of where this proved to be untrue was recently revealed in the United Kingdom. Although not formally an MDPM model, the UK government had two policies that taken together formed an implied model. The first was Public Service Agreements (PSAs) that set to output and outcome results expected in government departments. The second was the "Departmental Capability Reviews" (DCRs), which assessed the same departments for their capability in the areas of leadership, strategy, and delivery.

When both the National Audit Office and the present author correlated the results of government departments' DCRs (the "enablers") and PSAs (the "results"), the NAO reported that in the area of delivery capability, there was a -0.02 correlation between the DCR and PSA scores (Comptroller and Auditor General 2009). My own additional calculations showed that for "leadership" capability there was a moderately strong negative correlation of -0.44 and for "strategy" capability a weak negative correlation of -0.13. Overall, the correlation between the PSA and DCR scores was -0.35 (Talbot 2009 (Feb 29)). In other words what was assumed to be the drivers of performance (the capability measures) turned out to have zero or even a negative correlation with actual performance (as measured by PSAs).

This does not, of course, "prove" that the dimensions themselves are wrong, or that they do not have a causal relationship, but it raises serious questions and possibilities. The first is there is a fundamental conceptual error in the "model" of capabilities and results – that is, these "capability" dimensions (however measured) do not cause improvements in the results (likewise however measured). The second possibility is operationalization error – that is, that the model itself is sound, but the specific ways of measuring capabilities, or results, or both, are erroneous. The third is that there were measurement errors – that is, the data collection was flawed. There is indeed strong evidence that a good proportion of PSA data collection has been of poor quality (Comptroller and Auditor General 2005, 2006b, 2006c, 2007a). Whatever the reasons, this sorry tale does illustrate the perils of making what might appear to be reasonable assumptions about causal linkages in performance models.

The models all also imply some sort of causal linkages between the various individual dimensions, although these are rarely made explicit. Most often simply the layout of the model or the position of the linking arrows is the only indication of the implied causal linkages. The same comments apply here as to the links between "enablers" and "results." It is worth noting however that some models also imply recursive, iterative, or nonlinear linkages between dimensions, that have major implications for investigating the actual effects of such dynamics (see Chapters 3 and 7).

They all also imply, or explicitly include, the idea of "composite measures" of performance. Each dimension is, by implication, made up of a subset of possible elements, measures, and indicators of performance. Indeed so much has this aspect come to the fore that recently official guidance has been issued on how to construct such composite indicators (OECD and European Commission 2008). In some cases the underlying measures or elements are specified (e.g., PSEM had around 100 such more specific measures). In others, the dimensions are treated more like the four foci in the BSC – "black boxes" to be filled in by the organizations themselves. Whichever approach is adopted, composite or aggregate measures are not without their critics (Meyer 2002; McLean et al. 2007). Nevertheless it is difficult to see any realistic alternative – composite measurements are common in economics and other social sciences. As long as there is care and transparency in their construction and due caution in their use, it is difficult not to agree with the OECD/EC guide in concluding that they are on balance a "useful tool" (see Figure 8.6).

Pros:	Cons:
Can summarize complex, multi dimensional realities with a view to supporting decision-makers	May send misleading policy messages if poorly constructed
Are easier to interpret than a battery of many separate indicators	May invite simplistic policy conclusions
Can assess progress over time	May be misused, e.g., to support a desired policy, if the construction process is not transparent and/or lacks sound statistical or conceptual principles
Reduce the visible size of a set of indicators without dropping the underlying information base	The selection of indicators and weights could be the subject of political dispute

Figure 8.6 Pros and Cons of Composite Measures
Source: Adapted from OECD and European Commission (2008, p.13).

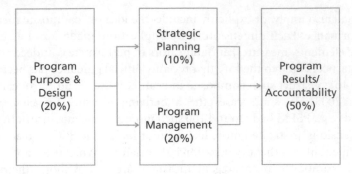

Figure 8.7 Program Assessment and Rating Tool (PART – USA)

The models also generally imply the weightings to be given to different dimensions of performance – and sometimes these are made explicit – for example, Program Analysis and Reporting Tool (PART) in the US federal government (see Figure 8.7) or EU Common Assessment Framework and European Public Service Awards.

Finally there are clearly recurring themes in these models and frameworks of what are considered to be the appropriate dimensions of performance to be included, although there are also substantial differences. An initial, admittedly superficial, analysis of all the above models that looks for commonalities (where two or more address the same dimension of performance) yields the following list:

- Values (endogenous and exogenous)
- Aim, mission, goals, or mandate
- Legitimacy, trust, responsiveness, sustainability
- Governance arrangements (including accountability and democratic control)
- Strategy, integration, and alignment
- Structures
- Partnerships, joined-up working, networks
- Leadership
- Resources management (including economy and efficiency)
- People management (including equality and diversity)
- Process management
- Customer/service focus and responsiveness
- Risk management
- Innovation and learning
- Service delivery, outputs, quality of outputs
- Social impact, outcomes, results

This is a daunting list of dimensions of performance and a thorough analysis of these and other models would probably add to this list. This serves to emphasize that any simplistic modeling of performance in the public sector, while appealing to some, is likely to be theoretically sound. Public services and agencies are very complex organizations working in complex and demanding environments and the resulting dimensions of performance are therefore likely to be complex and multiple.

It is also interesting to note how some dimensions have waxed and waned over the decades. "Partnerships, joined-up working, networks," and "leadership" have both come to the fore in recent years while "quality" seems to have been demoted from an overarching issue in the early 1990s (Gaster 1995; Joss 1995; Kirkpatrick and Matinez Lucio 1995; Pollitt and Bouckaert 1995) to a relatively minor aspect of service delivery today. Some "up-and-coming" possible dimensions also do not yet appear – for example, the issue of "co-production" of public services with service users (Alford 2009).

Performance of Governments and Sectors

This chapter has focused on public organizations or agencies – individual units. However, before leaving the topic it is probably worth mentioning the more recent exponential growth in various forms of "whole of government" and sectoral performance comparisons.

A feature of the modern performance movement which links back to previous eras is the focus on reporting on social, economic, and other outcomes. Governments have, in modern times, always claimed beneficial effects of policy on these types of outcomes and have usually published data about them (i.e., unemployment, educational, health, crime, and other data). The greater prominence given to these issues and public reporting linked closely to input and policy issues has generated more interest in "whole-of-government" or "whole sector" reporting and especially comparisons. It has also generated interest in the context of these performances – for example, in differences between political-institutional arrangements and their (possible) impacts on outcomes.

Since the World Bank's (re)discovery of the importance of democratic public administration and institutions (World Bank 1997), efforts have developed to measure what has sometimes been called "good governance" specifically through the World Governance Indicators (Kaufmann et al. 2007; World Bank 2008). This has now been joined by the Bertlesmann Institute's "Sustainable Governance Indicators" for OECD countries (Bertlesmann Stiftung 2009). The WGIs and other measures have been the subject of much methodological criticism (Van de Walle 2006; Hood et al. 2008; Pollitt 2009*b*) but they seem likely to continue to develop. Recently the more studies on comparisons of the performance of national administrations have begun to emerge (e.g., Boyle 2007; Accenture 2008).

This specific aspect of performance in the public domain – the performance of government institutions focusing on both due process and outputs and outcomes at the highest level of a polity – is a specific, albeit relatively isolated, stream within the performance movement. Despite its relative isolation, the effort that has gone into this specific subset of performance measurement has been considerable.

Apart from the World Bank's work – which has largely focused on establishing criteria for evaluating the performance of developing states – and the more recent Bertlesmann studies, the most well-known research effort in this field has been that of Lijphart which has focused on the relative performance of different democratic forms (e.g., Lijphart 1999). A more recent study has looked at the impact of political institutions on policies (Roller 2005).

There has also been a growing concern from statisticians and economists with the way in which the public sectors' economic performance and contribution to national economic statistics is assessed. The problem has been that the public sector contribution to GDP was measured simply by comparing one set of inputs with another set of inputs, meaning that in effect the public sector never gained (or lost) in productivity. Led by the United Kingdom, several governments have now begun to address this problem. The UK's Atkinson Review, and more recently the Office of National Statistics, has undertaken a large-scale program of establishing measures of output for public services (Atkinson 2005; Simkins 2008). Somewhat embarrassingly for the UK government, the latest assessments from this work have shown a decline, followed by a slight recovery, in UK public services productivity over the past decade – only passing its 1998 level in 2006 (Office of National Statistics 2009). (For a discussion of the relationship between efficiency and productivity see Chapter 2.)

Internationally there has also been a growth in measures of outputs and especially outcomes for specific sectors – for example, health, education, and criminal justice. Some of these – such as the PISA[5] education assessments – have received greater acceptance for being reasonably robust (Pollitt 2009b).

Within national jurisdictions there have also been several efforts at comparative assessment of lower tiers of government, such as the unofficial Government Performance Project covering US state level governance (Ingraham et al. 2003); or at the local government level, the officially sponsored "Comprehensive Performance Assessment" system in the United Kingdom; or the "Municipal Compass" in Sweden. Some of the ESRC projects have relevant data and theorizing to add here: for example, on the links between

[5] http://www.pisa.oecd.org.

various quality-of-life indicators (Jacobs); on international comparison metrics and methods (Rice); and developing a "report card for Britain" (McLean 2008–9).

Alongside these large-scale, cross-national jurisdiction comparative efforts, there have also been attempts to study the effectiveness of institutions within specific countries – for example, the effort of the Brookings Institution to study the "workways of government" in the federal US context (Davidson 2003).

Assessment of policies and programs has traditionally been the domain of evaluation studies. A remarkable feature of the performance movement has been the almost complete mutual disengagement – or when they do engage the open hostility – between "performance" and "evaluation." These two camps have been living almost completely in parallel universes with little contact between them – with a few honorable exceptions. Despite Blalock's plea for "useful engagement" almost a decade ago in a leading evaluation journal (Blalock 1999), a cursory perusal of the pages of the same journal in the decade since would reveal an almost complete absence of discussion of the performance movement.

There are many reasons for this estrangement. Evaluation has a concern with policies and specific programs, which often cut across organizational boundaries, whereas performance measurement has been mainly focused organizations. Evaluation is usually concerned with time-limited assessments and is therefore episodic, whereas performance measurement is intended to be more permanent and periodic. The performance movement has many objectives and justifications, but the predominant one has been its managerial use, whereas evaluation studies are more directed at policy-makers. Linked to this the commissioners, analysts, and implementers of performance and evaluation systems are often to be found in different parts of the public domain, in policy arenas, public organizations, and in the academy, from one another.

None of the above really justifies the continued estrangement of these siblings – both are concerned with assessing in different ways the success (or otherwise) of public domain activities. To the degree to which the performance movement is moving into the territory of "outcomes," as many policy-makers assert (Molen et al. 2001; OECD 2005), the potential for fruitful engagement between performance and evaluation would seem to be both greater and more imperative.

It has not been the intention here to fully analyze, much less critically, these developments in the performance movement that spread into international comparisons of governments, sectors, institution, policies, and programs – but merely to illustrate how far the performance movement is now spreading and some of the challenges this is throwing up. They are, mercifully, beyond the scope of this book to fully analyze, but that will surely come.

Appendix 8.1 Some Public Sector Performance Models and Frameworks

Performance model	Place or origin	Originators	Year
"Three Pillars" model	Canada	Ingrestrup & Crockall	1998
Management Accountability Framework	Canada	Treasury Board	
PMG	Chile	Chile Finance Ministry	
Common Assessment Framework	European Union	EU, Speyer Institute, EFQM	
European Public Service Awards	Germany	Bertlesmann Foundation	
The Municipal Compass	Sweden	Association of Local Authorities and Regions	
Unlocking Public Value	UK	Accenture (Cole and Parston)	2006
Comprehensive Performance Assessment	UK	Audit Commission	
Public Service Excellence Model	UK	Talbot	1998
Public Benefit Model	UK	New Economics Foundation	2007
Strategic Process Model	UK	Joyce	2000
"Significance" model	USA	Denhardt	1993
"Logic of Governance" model	USA	Lynn et al.	2000
"Three performance ethics" model	USA	Fried	1976
Government Performance Framework	USA	Ingraham et al.	
Program Analysis and Reporting Tool (PART)	USA	Office of Management and Budget	
Public Value Model and Scorecard	USA	Moore	1995/2003
Strategy Change Cycle	USA	Bryson	2004
Dolphin™ Assessment Process (linked to EFQM Excellence Model)	UK	Centre for Management and Policy Studies (now called the National School of Government)	2001

PART IV
RESPONSES AND CONCLUSIONS – SHAPING PERFORMANCE

Introduction to Part IV

In this final section one further issue is explored and then some attempt at synthesis is made – bringing together the theory, evidence, and approaches developed through the preceding chapters.

The main further issue explored is how, and why, do individuals and organizations react the way they do to both exogenous and endogenous pressures for performance improvement? But how other actors in the public domain are also considered.

One especially disheartening aspect of the current wave of the performance movement has been the partisanship displayed by many analysts, including academic researchers who really ought to know better. Commentators – politicians, consultants, practitioners, and academics – have all too frequently adopted a stance toward performance measurement, reporting, and management and then sought evidence to support this view. The most classic example is the issue of "gaming," in the broadest sense of any manipulation of performance data, or performance itself, not in the interests of actual performance improvement but of enhancing the reputations and possibly rewards of the organizations or individuals doing the gaming.

Does gaming happen? Certainly it does, but what is interesting is not that it happens but that it happens inconsistently. Take any population of public agencies, subjected to more or less the same performance regime, and you will find a wide distribution in how much actual gaming goes on – ranging from the very bad to the completely pure. Any objective analysis of what evidence is available tends to suggest that gaming is a minority activity in most cases, but this of course does not prevent those who are opposed to the performance movement claiming it is endemic and proof that all this "weighing the pig doesn't make it any fatter" (a favorite expression of opponents). At the other extreme, overenthusiastic proponents of performance systems minimize the dis-benefits of gaming, overemphasize the benefits of performance systems, and also fail to ask the really important questions.

A realist analysis would ask – how much gaming actually goes on? Why do some organizations and individuals react differently to essentially the same set of circumstances? What motivations cause these differential reactions? Does the level of gaming, and its dysfunctional consequences, outweigh the benefits generated by performance systems – in other words what's the cost–benefit analysis of performance systems? It is remarkable just how little these types of questions have generally been posed, even by academics who ought to be taking a more balanced, measured approach.

Drawing on some of the ideas initially explored in Chapter 6 about competing public values, some thought experiments are suggested about mixed motivations and their effects on responses to performance drivers. Thus, for example, if people have mixed selfish and altruistic motives, how does this play out in relation to performance? Posing these questions suggests a wholly different approach researching performance systems that allows for, and seeks to comprehend, these complexities.

Chapter 9 also explores what all this performance information is actually used for, both within and around public agencies? Many normative assumptions are made in the development of performance policies about how performance data will be used to shape all sorts of decisions – by political executives, parliamentarians, practitioners, the public, etc. However, it is becoming increasingly obvious that these normative expectations are rarely met in full, and we need to know a great deal more about how, and how much, performance data is actually used.

Chapter 10 summarizes what has been explored throughout the book, especially the three central issues of performance regimes, organizational models of performance, and public values. However, before it does that, it restates the basic proposition that a realist view of performance is that it is both about "brute facts" and how these are socially construed – any analysis has to accommodate both these aspects.

Building on the analysis presented in Chapters 7 and 8, this chapter reviews what we already know about models of organizational performance in the public domain. It suggests, very tentatively, the idea that a multidimensional performance model (MDPM) can probably be constructed based on existing knowledge and offers an example. Unfortunately, such a model will probably be more complex and less parsimonious than some would like, simply because the important dimensions of performance are multiple. The same, incidentally, is probably true for any MDPM for private sector organizations – although there are some additional dimensions in public sector MDPMs.

While we may have a reasonable approximation of the dimensions, we have little really serious evidence or theory about the relationships and dynamics between these different factors. Most research has tended to focus on the relationship of a single dimension – like leadership, for example – and isolated (or attempted to isolate) it from other factors.

Whether or not any single model of public agencies performance will ever actually emerge as dominant is a rather more tricky question – while it may be scientifically feasible (and there are those who will doubt even that), the nature of the public domain – its national boundaries, its value and politics laden character, etc. – means that such an approach would be difficult to achieve.

Performance regimes are crucial to understanding performance dynamics in the public domain and the approach outlined in Chapters 4 and 5 starts to move toward a more systematic, and theoretically grounded, approach to understanding them. There is however still an immense amount of work to be done to begin to record how performance regimes have evolved over time and comparatively between different jurisdictions. Much of the interplay between actors within the institutional performance regime remains obscure. Understanding of the multiple types, and sources, of interventions is also weak.

The issue of public values, and what we mean by public value, is the final piece in the jigsaw that shapes performance in the public domain. The approach outlined in Chapter 6 is further developed and it is suggested that there may be a way, based on approaches like relational models theory and competing values, to create a framework for understanding public values that is parsimonious (using only four dimensions) but also allows for the complexity evident in real systems of public values. Again, this is an area of research that is in its infancy in many ways – especially when it comes to trying to understand the links between public values and what the public sees as valuable about the performances of public agencies.

Bringing these three themes together – regimes, models, and values – provides a road map to the areas of performance that need greater attention in theory and evidence generation. Of course there are many areas not necessarily covered by these three themes – but, it is argued, without a firm grounding in these three areas progress on some of the more complex issues – like multilevel governance and networks for example – will be difficult.

The chapter concludes with a brief summary of the necessary areas where progress needs to be made, and some assessment of the theoretical and practical difficulties of making such progress.

9 Performance Responses

This chapter will examine how various actors within the public domain respond to imperatives for increased or improved performance. Our general understanding of the impact of various performance policies is poor. As indicated in Chapter 5, a vast array of types of performance policies and interventions has been applied to public services. Veritable mountains of performance data have been generated – in the United Kingdom, for example, literally tens of thousands of data points of performance information are published annually, a figure matched by Japan where 10,000 policy evaluation reports are produced every year as a result of the Government Policy Evaluation Act (Talbot 2006).

All of this effort is meant to produce action to improve performance. As has recently been observed, translating data or knowledge about performance into action and actually improved performance in this area has proved problematic at best (Walshe et al. 2010a). There have been, as we will explore below, some perverse or unwanted results of this effort. But there have also been major areas of real improvement. The real problem – theoretically and practically – is to understand how and why these variations in the reactions to the performance drive have occurred. The empirical data on this is not at all complete; despite the vast amounts of performance measurement available, connecting the dots between measurement and improvement is still weak. Nor are our causal theories very well developed, with some (on both sides of the arguments for and against the performance movement) bordering on the crude and ideological. Several broad areas need addressing.

First, and most crucially, is how and why do public agencies and the people who work within them respond to increased pressures for performance and the various ways these are applied? There is quite a lot of evidence about this, and it will form the bulk of this chapter.

Second is how and why do policy-makers and politicians, who mainly but not exclusively drive the new performance regimes, utilize the performance data generated by the new systems? We have relatively little evidence about this, but what we do have will be examined.

And thirdly, what do the public – as both users and citizens – make of both the data about and the actuality of the performance of public agencies? Again, there is surprisingly little evidence in this area, but what there is will be analyzed.

In all three cases we will utilize a combination of empirical data and theory to explore what we know, and what we do not yet know, about these responses.

Public Sector Staff and Organizations

Throughout this book it has been emphasized that it is impossible to make any sense of discussions about performance in the public domain without questioning "on what fundamental assumptions is this position based?"

One of the most basic of these assumptions, we would argue, are those about human behavior at the individual level (Perry and Hondeghem 2008). Are we all rational utility maximizers; or socially constructed from blank slates; or indeed altruistic, other-oriented? Or is there something in-between, or combining, these very different perspectives that explains both the universal and particular aspects of human behavior (see Chapter 6)?

The next set of assumptions is about how individual behavior relates to organizational or institutional arrangements. Are the latter merely expressions, writ large, of underlying human behavioral traits or do the cultural, organizational, and institutional arrangements shape these behaviors? Or, again, is there some rather more complex and iterative process by which individuals and organizations both shape and are shaped by each other? And do organizational- or institutional-level structures contain "emergent" elements – as complexity and systems theorists would suggest – that are not present at the individual level (Emery 1969)?

A concrete example of how this relates to the performance of public organizations is the predictive hypotheses adopted by many writers on the subject. A typical argument would be as follows (although usually not spelt out quite so explicitly):

1. Human beings are always, and everywhere, rational utility maximizers (RUMs) who will seek to gain the greatest personal benefit from their choices.
2. Public sector employees will thus respond to pressures for improved performance by either (a) responding "positively" to incentives if correctly designed and/or (b) seeking to "game" the system for maximum advantage.
3. Individual behaviors will be replicated at an organizational or managerial level so...
4. Organizational units can be treated as if they are also RUMs, so the same responses will apply.

Most of the analyses of public sector performances that have explicitly, or implicitly, adopted something like the above set of assumptions have tended to focus on the negative "gaming" consequences of RUM-reactions (as in 2(b) above). A typical list of the effects of this type of response is given as follows:

(a) Ratchet effects: where managers, knowing that next year's performance targets will be set higher than this year's actual performance, deliberately restrain performance below what is possible in order to avoid too high targets in the future.

(b) Threshold effects: where performance is designated as a minimum standard, those below tend to try to improve to reach the minimum but those above the minimum level tend to reduce performance to the minimum because there is no benefit in over-performing.

(c) Cherry-picking effect: where, in order to meet a target or minimum standard, concentration is placed on those cases where the target or standard can be most easily met and "hard" cases are neglected.

(d) Output distortion effect: deliberate manipulation of results by various forms of "cheating" – for example, keeping patients in ambulances rather than Accident and Emergency rooms, so as to avoid "starting the clock running" on waiting times.

(e) Output tunnel vision effects: where the targets or standards become the only focus of performance and other areas of services not covered by them are neglected.

(f) Output suboptimization: similar to the above but where focusing only on targets or standards performance actually directly damages other outputs or outcomes – for example, achieving faster throughput of benefits claims but as a consequence increasing error rates.

(g) Performance myopia: excessive focus on short-term performance goals at the expense of longer-term goals and improvements.

(Adapted from Bevan and Hood 2006*b*; Jann and Jantz 2008.)

All of the above assume a RUM-type reaction to performance imperatives. But it should be recognized that the types of adverse reactions listed above are merely hypotheses, not facts, and propositions that need supporting evidence to sustain them. When the evidence is examined however, these hypotheses turn out to be only moderately predictive of actual behavior, at best. It is interesting that proponents of this type of criticism rarely draw on the available data from official – especially independent audit – sources, but prefer to rely on, usually selectively chosen, secondary analyses by academics that bolster their assumptions (e.g., Van de Walle and Roberts 2008, which cites no official data on the perverse effects they postulate).

Any examination of the official data sources – especially those produced by independent audit bodies – soon produces a rather different, much more mixed picture from the hypothetical presupposed one generated a priori from some fairly narrow theoretical assumptions. Independent audit sources are useful for several reasons. First, they are independent. Second, they usually have access to vast amounts of data not directly available to academic researchers. Third, they have access to the systems that produce the data and can audit its reliability. All of this make their studies particularly valuable sources of knowledge, which makes the choice of some to virtually ignore them curious.

So it is useful to examine some of this data on the actual performance of public agencies and on the levels of detected aberrant behaviors as proposed in the above list of "gaming" activities.

Most of the comparative analyses of actual performance of public agencies, such as hospitals, schools, and police forces, have been conducted by either governments themselves or by audit and inspection bodies (academics have shown remarkably little interest in this rather fundamental question). What these analyses – such as CPA results in local government or league tables in schools and hospitals – have generally shown is something approximating a normal distribution curve in the range of performances (Figure 9.1). Sometimes these are skewed in one or other direction, but always there is a distribution curve with some agencies doing well and others doing badly, but the bulk being usually somewhere in-between, on whatever metrics are used.

As all these organizations are similar and comparable to one-another, and all are subjected to the same "performance regime"; how do we explain why some seem to choose to react or perform positively whilst others seem to fail and/or try "game" the system (Walshe et al. 2010*b*)?

The evidence on various types of "gaming" is likewise at best equivocal. Studies of data quality by the main audit bodies have revealed serious levels of error in performance reporting and elements of gaming. The National Audit Office has studied performance reporting by agencies and departments, reporting of Public Service Agreements, of Efficiency program results, and

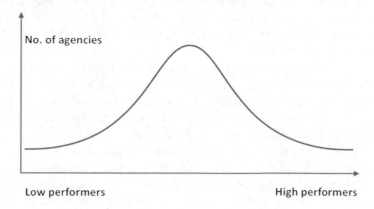

Figure 9.1 Normal Distribution of Performances

Departmental Capability reviews (Comptroller and Auditor General 2000, 2001, 2005, 2006*b*, 2006*a*, 2006*c*, 2006*d*, 2007*a*, 2007*b*, 2009). Whilst in virtually every case there have been problems, they are always in a minority of cases and there is always a tendency to improve over time, though interestingly apparently never to absolutely disappear.

The Audit Commission has studied data quality in the National Health Service (NHS) and come up with very similar results. Performance measurement in the NHS has been on a vast scale – with latterly strong financial incentives attached to some measurements – but even here the levels of error are obviously concerning, but not quite as large as is often supposed. A major study of the quality of performance data by the Audit Commission, over three years, found that "the overall level of accuracy is sufficiently robust to enable reasonable judgments to be made about national trends in the number of people waiting and the length of time for which they have been on the list" [one of the main performance targets] (Audit Commission 2004). A later study, also by the Audit Commission, of the quality of data for the "Payment by Results" systems – which obviously have major financial implications – examined 50,000 episodes worth £73 million to judge the accuracy of reporting. The finding is worth quoting:

An average . . . error of 9.4 per cent was identified, with a range across [NHS] trusts from 0.3 per cent to 52 per cent. These errors contributed to a gross financial error of approximately £3.5m, approximately 5 per cent . . . In most cases, the net financial impact is close to zero, indicating little evidence of systematic and deliberate upcoding or gaming.   (Audit Commission 2008, p. 7)

There are many other audit and inspection reports, from the United Kingdom and internationally, that replicate this pattern: significant but minority levels of error and in some cases blatant manipulation of data, improving and diminishing over time but never entirely being eliminated. Given the types of problems in measurement discussed in Chapter 2 this is hardly surprising. The obvious parallel here is the reporting of financial data by public organizations. Across the OECD countries this has improved immensely over time but it is never perfect and has often taken years if not decades to achieve current standards.

A simple RUM-based logic cannot explain this behavior in actual performance or in levels of "gaming" satisfactorily. It may have, and indeed has, identified some important tendencies toward certain types of behavior, but in no case has it explained anywhere all, or even a majority, of the behaviors observed in reality. This does not, of course, stop exponents of such theoretical positions from claiming any evidence of "gaming" and other such behaviors somehow "proves" their assumptions are correct.

Another, equally plausible set of hypotheses could be constructed from rather different assumptions – for example, those propounded by researchers on the so-called "public service motivation" (PSM). Whilst it would be wrong to suggest that PSM researchers assume a purely altruistic set of motivations of public sector staff, they do conclude that "it is the inherent nature of people to want to provide benefit to others, a premise critical to the public service motivation construct" (Koehler and Rainey 2008, p. 50).

We know also, however, that individual public-service staff do not behave in uniformly altruistic ways and that such a "strong" assumption of pure PSM is not any more explanatory of actual behavior than RUM assumptions (ibid, pp. 50–53).

At this point it is useful to start conducting some thought experiments to see how we might begin to make some sense of this. Thought experiments are a powerful tool in the development of theory – they played a crucial role in Einstein's development of Special and General Relativity theory, for example (Miller 1987). What follows is a series of thought experiments applied to both theoretical assumptions and empirical evidence about performance.

In these thought experiments we are going to use the device of considering what sort of distribution patterns in behaviors we would expect to see if certain assumptions are adopted about individual and organizational behavior. Using simple distribution graphs aids understanding of what these patterns might look like. There is also an assumption here that we are largely dealing with "natural systems" in which we can expect to see something at least approximating normal distributions; so, using (hypothetical) distribution curves is a useful approach that throws up some interesting ideas.

In this exploration we will limit ourselves to the behavior of individual public sector staff. This is not to imply any "methodological individualism" but simply for exploratory and expository purposes. We will return later to the issue of how individual behavior within organizations does, and does not, relate to higher-level performance by the organization itself.

Let us start by assuming a simple dichotomy between selfish RUMs and more altruistic PSMs, or as Le Grand pithily put it between "knightly" and "knavish" behavior (Le Grand 2003). This is not to suggest that such a simple dichotomy exists in reality. As has already been suggested (Chapter 6) slightly more complex models of behavior (such as "competing values" and "relational models") are rather more likely candidate theories than a simple dichotomy between selfish and altruistic behaviors. But for the purposes of exploring some initial ideas about the implications of paradoxical behaviors this simple contradictory pair is useful.

So, let us start by assuming that in any given population most individuals will have some combination of both RUM and PSM motivations and decision-making. Let us also assume that these two contradictory imperatives are normally distributed – that is, there will be a few extreme RUM-motivated people and a few extreme PSM-motivated people and the majority will be somewhere in the middle. Such a situation is illustrated in Figure 9.2.

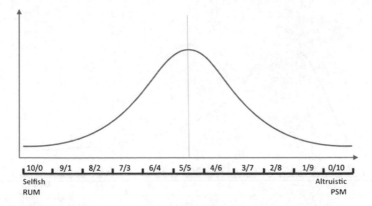

| 10/0 | 9/1 | 8/2 | 7/3 | 6/4 | 5/5 | 4/6 | 3/7 | 2/8 | 1/9 | 0/10 |

Selfish   Altruistic
RUM   PSM

Figure 9.2 Normal Distribution of RUM Versus PSM Behaviors

The numbering here is meant to suggest that in any given ten decision-making situations at the left-hand end of the spectrum a small minority would make "perfect" RUM-type decisions (ten out of ten times), whereas in the middle individuals would split evenly, making RUM-type decisions in five out of ten cases and PSM-type decisions in the other five. Most individuals in a normal distribution like this would make relatively balanced RUM–PSM decisions. It should be stressed immediately that we are not suggesting such an evenly balanced normal distribution actually exists – it simply serves as a useful starting point to consider what various theoretical constructs and assumptions would lead us to.

In this purely hypothetical state of a normal distribution of RUM and PSM decisions by individuals it would be very easy to be misled by data into trying to "prove" or "disprove' either strong RUM or strong PSM assumptions. There are certainly plenty of examples in the literature where, for example, researchers point to some RUM-selfish "gaming" of performance systems to "prove" such systems do not work. If the above distribution were actually true, we could expect nearly all the population to engage in RUM activities at least some of the time and half to engage in predominantly RUM-based decisions. For some this would "prove" that RUM-type reactions to perform-ance regimes were strongly supported. In reality it would of course be just as easy to "prove" the opposite – that PSM-type reactions were likely. With a few honorable exceptions most researchers on the topic have tended to explicitly or implicitly adopt one or the other assumption (for some exceptions see contributions in Perry and Hondeghem 2008).

We do not know however whether there is such a balanced normal distri-bution of RUM and PSM characteristics in any given population. It seems unlikely. It could be, for example, that in a "natural" case the distribution of behaviors would look more like Figure 9.3, – that is, with a distinct "skew" in favor of RUM-type behaviors.

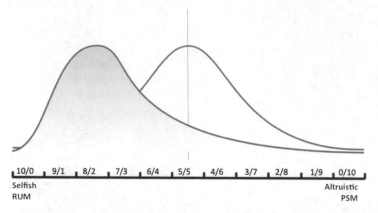

| 10/0 | 9/1 | 8/2 | 7/3 | 6/4 | 5/5 | 4/6 | 3/7 | 2/8 | 1/9 | 0/10 |

Selfish   Altruistic
RUM   PSM

Figure 9.3 RUM-Skewed Distribution?

Such a skewed distribution would explain why RUM-based research has had some, but nowhere near complete, success in predicting behaviors (Green and Shapiro 1994). But this is speculative at best.

If we accept the hypothesis that in any given real socio-geo-temporal situation subjects will have been affected by local culture and history, it becomes impossible to establish such a "natural" state with any certainty – we could only ever hope to approximate what the balance of behaviors in a natural state of affairs would be between altruistic and selfish, or RUM and PSM, behaviors.

We do have some evidence that actual public sector staff, at least in the limited sets of data we have, are more prone to PSM-type decision making than the general population or private sector employees (Perry and Hondeghem 2008). If the natural distribution of RUM versus PSM behaviors in a population were as in Figure 9.2, then the distribution in public organizations might look more like that in Figure 9.4.

And, incidentally the remainder of the working population would be then skewed in the opposite direction. Given on average public sector employment accounts for only about [20%?] of the total in OECD countries, then the effect on the rest of the working population would be small but noticeable.

We will leave aside for the moment the question of how such a distribution (Figure 9.4) within public sector organizations might come about and simply assume that something like this is actually the case. The implications for performance are interesting.

Firstly, we could expect that the majority of staff would tend to react more positively to pressures for improved performance provided these appealed to their PSM motivations. This latter proviso is however an important one – even in this PSM-skewed distribution most individuals would be prone to some RUM reactions. We know that it is relatively easy to trigger differently

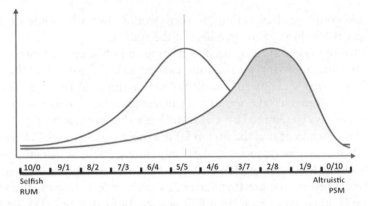

Figure 9.4 RUM Versus PSM Distribution Within Public Sector Organizations?

framed responses based on sometimes quite small differences in the way in which decisions are presented to individuals as both behavioral economics (Thaler and Sunstein 2008) and relational models researchers have shown (Haslam 2004). Some policies may even – inadvertently – trigger exactly the opposite of the desired response. Thus if appeals for higher individual performance are couched within a RUM framework – including for example performance-related pay incentives – rather than appealing to a predominant PSM framework, such appeals and policies might actually invoke exactly the opposite reaction to that intended.

The example cited by Thaler and Sunstein (2008) of such a perverse reaction is that of parents who arrived late to collect their children from kindergarten. In this case, in order to incentivize the parents to turn up on time the kindergarten management decided to fine latecomers. The result – more parents turned up later, treating the fine as a "payment" for extra time. In this case there was no experiment to see what would happen if the problem was "framed" differently and parents were encouraged by more altruistic incentives – for example, a very personal appeal from the staff about the impact on their welfare of the persistent late collections. In a very different context – tax collection – there is evidence that appeals to more altruistic, public-spirited motives do have a positive effect (Schwartz and Orleans 1967).

Secondly, even without the above "unintended consequences" policy problems mentioned above, in the distribution of behaviors implied in Figure 9.4 it is still the case that a substantial set of behaviors will be based on RUM type frameworks. In research terms this would mean it would be necessary to take into account that any empirical studies would show a substantial element of RUM-type decisions throughout any given population of public sector staff. The dangers of misreading this are obvious. It could mean, for example, that even with well-designed performance policies with carefully balanced RUM- and PSM-related incentives it would be likely a significant number of agents' decisions would be dysfunctional – there would always be some degree of (attempted) "fiddling" and "gaming" of the system.

This has always been recognized in relation to public sector finances, even where the predominant motivations can be safely assumed to be PSM-skewed. External and internal audit, as well as internal financial controls, has been developed to take account of the fact that some people, some of the time, will always be tempted by RUM-motives to behave unethically. Yet most analysts would accept that the reason for the success of most OECD countries in mostly eliminating financial misbehavior among public sector employees is due to strong PSM-type cultures rather than controls and audit systems – PSM-type cultures that are themselves linked to, at least in part, the type of individuals attracted to work in public service. But extreme RUM behaviors would still exist and this would also imply that a degree of internal control and internal and external audit of financial systems would always be a necessary ingredient.

In performance terms this would also mean that policies would need to take account of both RUM and PSM motivations among employees, whatever the balance between them, because even in a PSM-skewed distribution RUM behaviors would still be a significant factor. Focusing on one or the other exclusively could prove counterproductive for a substantial number of individuals.

There are many other possible areas of possible reactions of organizations to external pressures for improved performance that could be considered, and the range of possible pressures is vast (see Chapter 5). How organizations respond to managerial, capacity, competitive, and choice interventions may well vary by type of intervention as well as by organization's own nature. Moreover there is evidence that organizations themselves generate endogenous movements toward enhanced performance. The dynamics of this whole situation are poorly understood.

One thing we do know is there has been an increase in the use of multidimensional performance models by organizations themselves (Business Intelligence and Public Futures 2004; Talbot and Johnson 2005) (and see Chapter 8). Part of the explanation for this is the exogenous pressures for increased performance in several ways – firstly, the mere existence of these pressures forces organizations to look for "quick fixes" to improve performance and tools like the Balanced Scorecard can seem like a way to achieve this; secondly, some of these models have been specifically promoted by important performance regimes actors (e.g., British government support for EFQM); and thirdly, these models offer a way of trying to integrate the various (sometimes un-congruent) external pressures into some sort of coherent internal strategy (Talbot and Johnson 2005).

Finally, recent research taking a knowledge-based perspective tends to show that those organizations suffering from failure or poor performance may be the most problematic in terms of "absorptive capacity" – that is, the capacity to take in knowledge about how to improve and change and actually implement it (Walshe et al. 2010*b*).

Policy-Makers and Politicians

Performance policies have, by common agreement, become a central instrument of public policy in many jurisdictions – and yet the whole issue of "performance" is rarely approached as a policy issue that is tackled with the tools, methods, and theories that have been developed to analyze other types of policy decisions and their implementation.

To use a distinction developed in the area of policy tools, for example, policy instruments can be seen as both effectors (i.e., deployed to change something) and as detectors (i.e., ways of finding out things) (Hood 1983; Hood and Margetts 2007). Much of the analysis of performance policies has however concentrated on the former rather than the latter – that is, how performance policies are used to try and change things, and the impact of those attempts, rather than on what the resulting performance data tell decisions-makers and what they are used for within decision processes (Pollitt 2006). This despite the fact that in most cases gathering performance data for decisional purposes is alleged to be a principle reason for introducing performance policies.

We still know comparatively little about how core executives actually use the performance data generated from the implementation of performance policies, and probably even less about how other institutional actors – such as parliaments – in the performance regime utilize such data (Chapter 5). Perhaps a bit more is known about auditors' and inspectors' use of data, simply because their work is more out in the open than some other actors.

Government executives' use of performance data is at best patchy according to OECD surveys (OECD 2005, Curristine 2007). Whilst most OECD countries now produce performance information at the national level, and 40% have done so for more than ten years, the most recent OECD study found that links to budgeting and other decision-making processes were usually loose:

Countries experiences have shown that the existence of a procedure to integrate performance information into the budget process is a necessary but not sufficient condition to ensure its use. (Curristine 2007, p. 12)

And later rather more bluntly "Most OECD countries continue to struggle with these reforms" (ibid, p. 68). The report cites issues such as institutional structures ill-suited to adopt performance-based systems, political challenges, and the detailed policy approaches adopted as all creating difficulties. They note that the countries that have driven these reforms hardest and most top-down, particularly the United Kingdom and New Zealand, have experienced problems with perverse incentives and gaming. On the other hand, a number of countries have implemented the reforms largely in name only, with little enthusiasm or drive.

Some of the common challenges, whatever the strategy, they identify include:

- Improving measurement
- Finding appropriate ways to integrate performance information into budgeting processes
- Gaining the attention of key decision-makers and changing the behavior of politicians
- Developing institutional capacity to deal with performance information
- Improving the quality and presentation of performance information (ibid., pp. 68–71)

To complement this rather dry and somewhat sanitized account by the OECD of the problems, a fascinating "insider" account of one aspect of these sorts of problems has been written by the first head of the Prime Ministers Delivery Unit (PMDU) in the United Kingdom (Barber 2007). The PMDU focused on taking performance data, analyzing it, and coming up with critiques and proposals for improvement in four major areas – education, health, criminal justice, and transport. They coordinated (initially) quarterly "stock-take' meetings between the Prime Ministers' Office, Treasury, and the four-line ministries involved. Barber records the intense battles and difficulties experienced in implementing even this simple aspect of the performance agenda. He also notes the frequent disjunctions within Whitehall between various core actors – especially the Prime Ministers' Office and the Treasury.

The second main governmental actor is the legislative branch of government – parliaments, legislatures, and congresses. Within the rhetoric of the performance movement these are sometimes assigned a prominent role – for example, in the United Kingdom the introduction of Public Service Agreements (PSAs) within Whitehall was supposed to lead to a fundamental change in the accountability of government to parliament (Chief Secretary to the Treasury 1998). In some instances the impetus for the introduction of performance-reporting policies in the central government has indeed emanated from the legislative branch (France and the United States, for example).

Despite all this the evidence for engagement by Parliaments and Congresses is weak. The OECD study found that engagement was low (Curristine 2007) while a more detailed analysis of the response to the availability of PSAs to Parliamentary scrutiny committees (Johnson and Talbot 2007b) also found relatively low levels of engagement. In Japan, officials from the Parliament likewise admitted that parliamentary scrutiny of the vast number of policy implied by a variety of existing theories that have sufficient overlap to suggest there is a parsimonious set of underlying human social values that can help to explicate the public values attached to public performance.

These three aspects of public performance have to be brought together to make any real sense of the current, and any future, performance movement. They also have to be based on the same philosophical and theoretical bases to produce any real advance in our understanding.

A Realist View of Performance: Brute Facts and Social Construction

We begin by making a reformulated statement of how a realist philosophical and theoretical approach might apply to performance. A realist stance makes the following assumptions:

First, that ontologically the performance of public agencies is "real" regardless of observation or social construction. That is, public agencies take real resources (money, staff, physical resources, contributions for users, and so on) and turn them into real outputs (services) that in turn affect real social outcomes. Organizations do this better or worse than other similar organizations, or their own past performance, and this can be measured through many individual elements or dimensions of performance. Although performance does include a socially constructed element, no amount of social construction can change actual, real processes and products of public agencies – they either do generate more outputs more efficiently or with greater effect or they do not.

A failing, or succeeding, organization cannot be socially (re)constructed as its opposite. Even organizations that appear to be "permanently failing" (Meyer and Zucker 1989) are actually succeeding on some dimensions of performance sufficiently for some key stakeholders to want to keep them in existence. But they are still actually failing on most dimensions of performance, otherwise they would not be considered as "failing organizations."

Second, that epistemologically actually measuring performance is made more difficult because what is accepted as important in the multiple elements and dimensions of performance, and how each of them is measured, is not just an objective exercise but is also, in part, socially constructed. However, with Searle (1995), we would assert that these social constructions are themselves epistemologically real, or can be treated as such. That is, they are positions, attitudes, and beliefs held by real groups and individuals that are discernable through research, although such research is more problematic than simply measuring some of the more easily observed and counted aspects

evaluations was absolutely minimal.[1] In the United States, Congress did engage, early on, in using data generated by the Government Performance and Results Act (GPRA) but in a very partisan and political way (this was a Republican initiative aimed at Democrat President Bill Clinton) (Radin 2003).

In contrast to Parliaments, there is ample evidence that auditors and inspectors have responded to the performance movement by huge efforts to expand their engagement with the issues (e.g., Hood et al. 1999; Pollitt et al. 1999; Hood et al. 2004; Campbell-Smith 2008). As already mentioned at various points in this book, auditors have developed an array of performance assessments and evaluation techniques and have often been the driving force at this more technical end of developments (see also Chapter 4).

Finally, and in many ways most importantly, how have the public responded to the performance movement and its various outputs and changes? The evidence here is again mixed.

The first possible public response is in the general, democratic accountability mode – has performance reporting affected the way citizens judge elected politicians and public institutions. Data from opinion poll surveys show mixed results in the United Kingdom; for example, these surveys have identified a common trend for citizens to think that national performance of public services, especially health and education, is worse than the local services they actually experience (Marshall et al. 2007). However, recent data collected through the British Social Attitudes Survey on health show that public satisfaction levels have risen overall between 1997 and 2007 (Appleby and Phillips 2009). However, given performance measurement and reporting started in the NHS in the early 1980s the picture is clearly more complex – because public satisfaction rates generally fell between 1983 and 1997 before starting the post 1997 steady rise.

There is some indication that the public response to performance is not linear – at least as far as giving political credit is concerned. Research evidence comparing local government performance (as measured by Comprehensive Performance Assessment scores) and the electoral fortunes of incumbent politicians shows that poor performance is electorally punished but that excellent performance is not rewarded (James and John 2006). This suggests that performance might be a type of "hygiene" factor – the public expects minimum standards of performance, but after that other factors eclipse performance in political importance.

The other area where performance information might be important for the public is in choice, where it is available (see Chapter 5). Here the evidence is extremely limited – although the recent British Social Attitudes survey data shows that whilst the majority want choice in public services, they are far less

---

[1] Interviewed by the author, 2006.

content with competitive markets – suggesting that choice is a very limited value for the public (Curtice and Heath 2009).

Generally then, the uses to which the public at large use performance information seems very limited, but the evidence is too incomplete to come to any real firm conclusions.

Conclusions

This chapter has hopefully demonstrated that there are substantial problems in understanding the responses of individuals and organizations to pressures for performance improvement. These problems are of two, interrelated types: empirical and theoretical.

Theoretically, many of the studies of performance responses start from weak or distorted theoretical assumptions about the behavior and motivations of individuals and organizations. Many researchers from apparently diverse theoretical perspectives tend to assume rational self-interest motives and behaviors, including dysfunctional "gaming," in trying to explain responses to performance pressures. Other theoretical accounts of motivation – such as PSM and public values – are simply ignored. This is unfortunate in that it biases much research and theorizing, producing unbalanced theoretical propositions.

Secondly, empirical evidence: this is adversely affected by the preceding unbalanced nature of theorizing performance motivations. Far too many academic studies have gone in search of "gaming," for example, and not surprisingly have found it. However, they have ignored the pretty strong evidence that alongside gaming and other undesirable effects, there have also been significant gains in real performance and service delivery. The evidence for this in independent audits is strong, if not complete. There are also significant empirical lacunae such as evidence about how performance knowledge is really used by organizations themselves and especially by external performance regimes' actors such as the executive government, legislatures, and citizens/users of public services.

10 Shaping Public Performance

This chapter will seek to summarize what has been argued in this book and point toward those areas of future development of our understanding performance in the public sphere that seem most promising.

It begins, unapologetically, with a restatement of the fundamental approach that would seem the most fruitful in this and other areas of social enquiry – a realist approach. Realism in this context is the view that performance is composed of both "brute facts" and socially constructed meanings attached to such facts. Proper understanding has to embrace the complex reality of the construction of this social reality from both actual, real things as well as social values.

It then suggests that any comprehensive and consilient theory of public performance has to address, and integrate, three issues.

Firstly, any model of organizational performance is likely to be of the multidimensional performance models (MDPMs) variety discussed at length in Chapters 7 and 8. A great deal of progress has already been made in establishing what the key dimensions of performance have to be. A crucial part of this conceptualization is the separation of the "enabling" dimensions from the "results" dimensions – a development that came primarily from the emergence of quality models in the 1980s. Whilst such models provide a "skeleton" of the key dimensions of performance, they do not provide, necessarily, the details of what should go into each dimension.

Secondly, any theory of public performance has to embrace the fact that public organizations – even more so than private ones – are inevitably enmeshed in a performance regime: governance networks of key institutional power-holders who can utilize various tools, resources, or levers to try to shape performance of public agencies. It is crucial here to have a sound theoretical and empirically verifiable basis for identifying both the key actors and the resources they can deploy within any particular performance regime, in a way which is portable across sectors, jurisdictions, and time.

Thirdly, both the performance model and the performance regime will be suffused with a (current) balance of public value(s) that will shape the way in which performance facts are given weightage. The argument advanced is that a possible model or framework for understanding public values seems to be implied by a variety of existing theories that have sufficient overlap to suggest there is a parsimonious set of underlying human social values that can help to explicate the public values attached to public performance.

These three aspects of public performance have to be brought together to make any real sense of the current, and any future, performance movement. They also have to be based on the same philosophical and theoretical bases to produce any real advance in our understanding.

A Realist View of Performance: Brute Facts and Social Construction

We begin by making a reformulated statement of how a realist philosophical and theoretical approach might apply to performance. A realist stance makes the following assumptions:

First, that ontologically the performance of public agencies is "real" regardless of observation or social construction. That is, public agencies take real resources (money, staff, physical resources, contributions for users, and so on) and turn them into real outputs (services) that in turn affect real social outcomes. Organizations do this better or worse than other similar organizations, or their own past performance, and this can be measured through many individual elements or dimensions of performance. Although performance does include a socially constructed element, no amount of social construction can change actual, real processes and products of public agencies – they either do generate more outputs more efficiently or with greater effect or they do not.

A failing, or succeeding, organization cannot be socially (re)constructed as its opposite. Even organizations that appear to be "permanently failing" (Meyer and Zucker 1989) are actually succeeding on some dimensions of performance sufficiently for some key stakeholders to want to keep them in existence. But they are still actually failing on most dimensions of performance, otherwise they would not be considered as "failing organizations."

Second, that epistemologically actually measuring performance is made more difficult because what is accepted as important in the multiple elements and dimensions of performance, and how each of them is measured, is not just an objective exercise but is also, in part, socially constructed. However, with Searle (1995), we would assert that these social constructions are themselves epistemologically real, or can be treated as such. That is, they are positions, attitudes, and beliefs held by real groups and individuals that are discernable through research, although such research is more problematic than simply measuring some of the more easily observed and counted aspects of performance. This complicates the overall performance measurement process and renders simplistic reductionist strategies ineffective.

Models of Performance

The emergence of MDPMs in the 1980s and the 1990s marks a distinct step forward in theorizing the performance or organizations, public and private. But this approach still leaves many problematic issues to be resolved, some generic and some specific to the public sector.

First, let us examine why MDPMs represent an advance. Prior to their emergence there was a great deal of work – mainly in the organizational effectiveness movement (see Chapter 7) – on the various elements and dimensions of performance, but these were rarely put together into any sort of coherent model or framework which tried to identify the relationships between the various elements or dimensions.

The MDPMs that emerged from the quality movement (Baldrige, EFQM, and so on) were not put forward as multidimensional organizational performance models, but that is in effect what they were. They were also highly normative in character, specifying not only the dimensions of performance (or quality as they would put it) but the specific weights to be attached to each dimension and the implied set of causal relations between them. Further they also usually specified the detailed elements, measures, or indicators of performance within each dimension.

Particularly important to fully emerge with these models was a more formalized notion of the relationship between those dimensions that could be regarded primarily as "drivers" of performance and that focused on "results." During the organizational effectiveness (OE) movement there had been much debate about whether endogenous elements and dimensions like "staff morale" should be counted as a dependent or independent variable in measuring effectiveness. The answer given by the "quality" MDPMs was in effect that they should be counted as both dependent and independent variables. They were seen as indicators of both current/past performance and predictors of future performance. The key causal assumption was that the "driver" dimensions would produce better (or worse) performance on the "results" dimensions *in the future.* So an assessment against these "driver" dimensions contains both a current/retrospective component and prospective component.

Public sector MDPMs, and other similar models, exhibit some distinctively public sector features and some obvious parallels with their private sector or generic counterparts. Some of these differences relate to public agencies' positions within a performance regime (of which more below) and some are to do with the public values that they are expected to pursue and embed (again, more is given later). Such issues almost certainly mean that a public-agency MDPM would require a different set, and even configuration, of performance dimensions to those for private sector MDPMs.

Based on Bryson (1995) and other work it has been in the past suggested that the key extra dimension in the "driver" or "enabling" part of such an MDPM would be something on the governance and policy framework – or as Bryson calls them the "mandates" – of each public agency (Talbot 1999). Based on the analysis in this book, these have been separated and relabelled as "Governance" and "Aim."

Some would argue that governance and aims are not under the control of the agency – they are usually imposed externally by executive governments and/or legislatures – and therefore cannot, or should not, be counted in any performance assessment. However, with Moore (1995) it can be argued that it is part of the responsibility of public agencies to help at least try to shape their mandates and governance arrangements to the objectives they are established to achieve. Moreover, with Carpenter and Lipsky (Lipsky 1980; Carpenter 2001) it can be suggested that this is in any case what happens, at various levels, within public agencies and it is better to recognize and manage it rather than try and pretend that public agencies are merely Wilsonian implementers (Wilson 1955 [1887]).

The second area where public sector MDPMs should or could differ from private sector ones is in the "results" dimensions. A good example of this is the EFQM Excellence Model, which does include a specific dimension of "impact on society." In the EFQM approach this is clearly about what is now called "corporate social responsibility" – that is in effect a tangential rather than primary organizational result and this is reflected in the weighting it is given (see Chapters 7 and 8). However, "impact on society" is a primary goal for public agencies – achieving social, economic, technical, environmental, and other outcomes are key reasons public agencies and activities exist (Talbot 1999). So including a more central social impact or outcomes dimension to performance would also seem a crucial difference for a public sector MDPM.

Not all generic or private sector MDPMs are the same and there is a very critical difference between the various quality awards and the other highly successful MDPM – the balanced scorecard. The quality MDPMs are highly normative in laying down not just the performance dimensions but also, within each dimension, specifying in some detail precise criteria of what constitutes "good" performance. Thus, for example, they do not simply identify "leadership" as a key performance dimension but in spelling out precise criteria, which themselves embody theoretical assumptions about what "good" leadership constitutes, they set normative standards for leadership.

The approach of the balanced scorecard (BSC) is very different. It is also an MDPM but it clearly differs in many respects from the quality movement-originated MDPM – not least in its parsimony in adopting only four performance dimensions. That is not the main difference that interests us here though – it is rather the "scaffolding"-like nature of the BSC that is of interest. The BSC's four dimensions of (or perspectives on) performance – financial, customer, internal business process, and learning and growth – are each "empty boxes." That is, they specify only that these dimensions of performance are important but not what the elements of performance are that make up each dimension. Deciding which elements are important is seen as a contextual problem and, unlike the quality MDPMs, not specific content of each dimension is specified. This allegedly gives the BSC both a universal and a specific nature (Kaplan and Norton 1996).

This raises important theoretical possibilities and issues. Is it possible to construct an MDPM that captures the key dimensions of performance without specifying precisely the content – elements – of performance that go to make up each dimension? If so, what is the real nature of a "performance dimension" and how can they be empirically verified if they cannot be more precisely operationalized? If, for example, different organizations utilize different variables in each dimension are they really doing anything comparable (Meyer 2002)?

Both the quality MDPMs and the BSC's approach are, in different ways, flawed. The detailed elements of performance measurement adopted by the quality MDPMs have little, if any, apparent theoretical or empirical justification. On the other hand the BSC's failure to specify any elements of performance for its different dimensions of performance raises serious issue about how the dimensions themselves could ever be validated.

A more reasonable approach would seem to be to try to iteratively validate both the dimensions of performance and their detailed content. The preliminary analysis of the common dimensions of performance conducted in Chapter 8 points toward a possible list. Of course, a great deal more work would be necessary to verify and complete such a list of dimensions, so we cannot in any sense be certain these are the correct set of dimensions. Despite these uncertainties it is worth – as a tentative exercise – constructing a model based on this analysis. If the sixteen dimensions are mapped along the lines of many of the above models, then we get something as shown in Figure 10.1.

It must be stressed immediately that this is not a proposal for yet another performance model for public organizations – merely an attempt to indicate the sort of logically structured comprehensive model that it might be possible to construct. There does not seem to be any overriding theoretical reason why such an endeavor should be impossible. To be sure it would take a large-scale research effort to collect and analyze sufficient data from a sufficiently large and diverse set of organizations to test such an approach. There are obvious

Figure 10.1 Possible MDPM for Public Organizations?

methodological challenges to overcome – but these are all practical rather than theoretical problems.

Taking this as a preliminary guide it is clear that we now have a great deal more evidence and theory about most of the dimensions proposed, at least individually. What we emphatically do not have is any sense of whether these are the correct dimensions, in the correct relationships to one another. A great deal of further work would be needed before any robust MDPM for public agencies could be created and, as Chapter 8 demonstrates, there is still a fair degree of uncertainty and still less consensus about what the main performance dimensions should or could be. And some of the dimensions proposed above have been subject to relatively little research as yet (e.g., values).

It is being suggested here that the above MDPM, or something like it, could be taken as a starting point. That is beyond the scope of this book but it does seem to be a reasonable way for this aspect of the performance question in the public sector to be pursued.

It is fairly apparent that a great deal of academic, policy-maker, and practitioner effort has already gone into developing the many public sector generic and subsector or nationally specific variants on the MDPM theme that are reported in Chapter 8. There is at least sufficient commonality in these various attempts to suggest that constructing a standard MDPM might be at least a possibility. There are of course major obstacles of a theoretical and practical nature to such an enterprise. Practically it is fairly clear that policy-makers and practitioners tend to have a penchant for creating "their" model, even when they are adopting essentially the same approach as others – see, for example, the discussion of the Canadian MAF in Chapter 8. Academics are not immune from such pressures either – as Huff put it, management researchers exhibit a "strong desire for independence" from other management researchers and that "[c]umulative activity is further weakened by journals that encourage claims of independent discovery" (Huff 2005, p. 346, already cited in Chapter 1).

Performance Regimes

The second aspect that needs to be included in any comprehensive attempt at theorizing public agencies performance is the performance regime within which they operate. Chapters 4 and 5 began the process of trying to consolidate what we know about performance regimes and how they might be better theorized.

In terms of what we know, the answer is far too little. As was argued in Chapter 4, many if not most theorizing about performance have tended to neglect the political and institutional context within which this occurs in the public sector. All too often a simple principal–agent chain that goes something like voters–government–ministries–agencies is assumed. As a few recent scholars have pointed out this ignores the complexities of governance in modern states. The question of the performance regime is however now beginning, at last and slowly, to emerge as a key topic for investigation.

Any attempt to theorize performance regimes has to make some assumptions about what to include and exclude and what criteria to use in making such choices. A common fault in much of the stakeholder literature is to have no theoretical foundation on which to build a robust model of who stakeholders are and how or why they matter to the organization.

What was proposed in Chapters 4 and 5 was to use some variant on resource-based theory to both select what power-holders can have an influence on the organizations and how they might exercise such power. The term power-holders is preferred to stakeholders, because every individual and corporate body in any particular jurisdiction has some interest in what public agencies do – as citizens and taxpayers if not as users – so the stakeholder concept can become fairly meaningless. And "power-holders," as a concept, also assume that some model of what power they hold has to be employed.

The concept of a variant of resource-based theory, as a way of analyzing power relationships, is coupled with an attention to the structures of institutions, in the rather old-fashioned sense of parliaments, governments, courts, and so on. This builds on the institutionalist assumption that structures do matter (see Chapter 3) and that variations in these structures across time and place will have significant effects on the performance regime. Indeed one strategy for governments or legislatures wanting to alter the performance regime is to alter this institutional framework – for example, by empowering audit and inspection bodies, as in the "audit explosion" (Power 1994, 1997).

One important issue needs to be mentioned at this point that differentiates the "performance regimes" approach from the "multiple-stakeholder" theories that have also been employed to analyze the context that shapes performances in the public sector (e.g., see several contributions in Boyne et al. 2006). The multiple stakeholders approach includes internal stakeholders – staff, managers, professionals, and so on – within the analysis of stakeholder impacts. The performance regime approach however excludes internal "stakeholders." Internal stakeholders are in a qualitatively different position to external stakeholders and are better considered, not in the analysis of the context of performance, but in the internal modeling of how performance is produced within the organization.

This has a distinct advantage analytically because it allows for the separation of exogenous and endogenous variables when assessing organizational performance. In any case, in a great deal of the stakeholder literature (at least as applied to public services) although the internal stakeholders are often mentioned, they are rarely included in the actual analysis, which almost invariably focuses on the external stakeholders. Also, many MDPMs implicitly adopt this approach – for example, the "people management" and the "people results" dimensions in the EFQM Excellence Model focus on not just the organizational need for human resources but also on issues like staff views, morale, opinions, desires, and needs. What is this if not an analysis of the impact of internal stakeholders?

The analysis of performance regimes contained in Chapters 4 and 5 only takes us so far. A fundamental question still to be answered is what aspects of resource-based theories are crucial to understanding the performance regime and what are secondary or even unimportant. This is a theoretical-empirical question that could only be answered by multiple studies of performance regimes over time and place to establish what are the key variables. Very few such studies have yet taken place and there is as yet no theoretical or methodological consistency to them that would allow such the accumulation of such theory and evidence.

Another aspect of performance regimes that has yet to be seriously studied is the interaction between various components of the regime. It is fairly clear, for example, that the interaction between legislatures and the executive branch of governments is in some instances (e.g., the United States) a very important aspect of the performance regime, the dynamics of which have hardly been explored yet. In other cases the creation of new institutions, as the massive growth in numbers of, and turnover in, such bodies in the United Kingdom is an important aspect of the evolving performance regime that has also, as yet, been under-explored (although such work has started – see Hood et al. 1999). Just to give one small example: the policies of the UK Audit Commission with regard to what performance indicators it set for local government has mirrored fairly closely central government policy on performance measurement over a decade and a half – yet there is no study, to my knowledge, of how the relationship between the Audit Commission and its "parent" ministry (it is technically a quasi-autonomous government body) exists and how and why the AC policy so closely aligned with government policy?

Performance regimes are, then, emerging as a key aspect of understanding performance in the public domain but we are a long way from having a satisfactory, or widely accepted, theoretical conceptualization of what exactly is a performance regime and how, therefore, it should be investigated. Hopefully the chapters on the topic in the current book make some contribution and at the very least point in a broad way to approaches that might begin to get some real traction on the issue.

Public Values

In Chapter 6 the issue of multiple public values was explored, and especially various theories that might make some sense or place some ordering upon them – Cultural Theory, Competing Values, Relational Models, and so on. However, the discussion was left somewhat hanging with the suggestion, but only the suggestion, that it might be possible to apply one of these theories (or some synthesis) to the problem of ordering public values.

The current author has made several attempts to do this recently, mainly by applying Competing Values to the analysis of public value (Talbot 2008*a*, 2008*b*, 2008*d*; Talbot and Wiggan 2009). For various reasons, these attempts seem unsatisfactory, so a different approach is suggested here. Relational Models Theory (RMT), with its four relational models of Communal Sharing (CS), Authority Ranking (AR), Equality Matching (EM), and Market Pricing (MP), seems to offer a better "fit" to the range of values considered in Chapter 6.

A tentative application of RMT to public values is offered in Figure 10.2.

Communal Sharing (RMT) is translated into public values that focus on social solidarity, community cohesion, redistribution (through taxes, benefits, and services), coproduction or services, and so on. This is clearly a major theme in public values – especially in debates about "the community" and at what level collective decisions should be taken, as well as what constitutes citizenship. It includes altruistic motives and self-sacrifice for the good of the collective.

Authority Ranking translates as desires for stability, reliability, security, regulation, efficiency in delivery of services, and enforcement of norms by "the authorities." In popular parlance this is the appeal that "the authorities should do something" whenever some crisis occurs or threat to the community arises. It is a fundamental appeal to hierarchical structures to "take charge" of the collective and impose order.

Equality Matching is the value of being treated equally, with due process and reciprocity. The most obvious implementation of these values is in the idea of "one person, one vote" in democratic societies and equality before the law. In public services the values apply to setting standardized norms and providing for equal treatment in equal circumstances. It extends to a desire to be consulted or participate in more direct forms of decision-making.

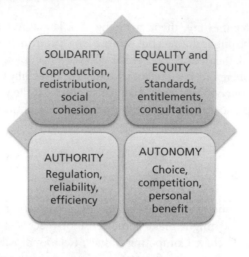

Figure 10.2 Competing Public Values?

Finally the values associated with Market Pricing are those that focus on personal benefit for the individual (or their immediate family) especially through choice and competition. These are the values that have been said to have informed much of the current reform movement in public services – the "New Public Management" and more recent developments like personalization in services.

Before turning to some of the tensions between and applications of these four aspects of public values, it is important to note that the values as described above are all what would widely be seen as positive, or legitimate, in nature. However, as the originator of RMT has pointed out, each of the basic relational models has a "dark side" (Fiske 2004).

Communal Sharing depends on defining "in-groups" and "out-groups" and can lead to withdrawal of communal benefits from those considered to be outside "the community" and battles over defining what "the community" consists of. Many separatist movements within existing states are driven by perceived wrongs committed by one community against another and a desire to redefine communal boundaries.

Authority Ranking and the desire for order and stability can obviously give rise to the abuse of power, unwarranted infringements on individual liberties and rights, and in the worst cases corruption and authoritarian rule. Equality Matching may give rise to over-bureaucratic and rigid systems and at its most extreme can also be translated into principles of revenge – an eye for an eye – and vendetta. Finally, Market Pricing can lead to an overconcentration on the needs of the individual and distortions and bias in collective activities to benefit specific individuals or groups against others interests.

These negative aspects of each relational model also serve to highlight some of the possible tensions between them. Authority-based values may clash with equality-based ones, over issues such as civil liberties, and similar issues, for example. Or excessive focus on market pricing and individuals' personal benefits may undermine communal solidarity principles, or equity in resource allocation, or authority through corruption, and so on.

These possible negative tensions suggest strongly that in any particular community it is what is collectively considered to be the appropriate balance between competing public values at any particular time that is important, whilst recognizing that all four dimensions of values will always to some degree need to be addressed. An interesting example of this is in national country differences. Using competing values framework (CVF) rather than the RMT theory, a survey of civil servants in Thailand revealed that they had a different values profile to that of western (mainly North American) public servants (see Cameron and Quinn 2006 for data on public servants' CVF profiles). Most notable was that Thai civil servants' "clan" quadrant values (the equivalent of Communal Sharing in RMT) were significantly higher than their western counterparts, a probable reflection of the Buddhist-influenced national culture (Jingjit 2009).

The dynamics of such tensions between competing values, especially in an organizational context, are explored more fully in the CVF theory than in the RMT (see especially Quinn 1988; Quinn and Cameron 1988; Cameron et al. 2006). This approach especially emphasizes the point that the four competing values quadrants in CVF are always in dynamic tension, and whilst a particular organization may have an unbalanced profile in one direction or another, this is always likely to change.

The approach to structuring public values offered here is not by any means meant to be definitive. The approach to cataloguing public values undertaken by Bozeman (2007; Jorgensen and Bozeman 2007) is clearly a start but a taxonomy of the type suggested here is needed to make more progress, as Bozeman himself points out. This particularly suggestion to use RMT may or may not be the correct one, but RMT does seem to have the necessary structure and underlying theoretical precision, methodological tools, and empirical evidence to support using it as a fruitful approach.

Bringing It All Together – Regimes, Models, and Values?

What this chapter, and this book, concludes with is the suggestion that what is needed is advance in theory and evidence on three fronts: performance models, performance regimes, and public values (Figure 10.3).

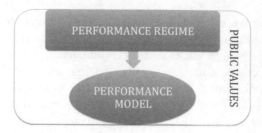

Figure 10.3 Shaping Performance?

Some progress has been shown in the research literature in all three areas and some of the analysis in this book has hopefully made a modest contribution to taking these advances further. But we still have a long way to go.

As was argued in the introductory chapter and throughout the book, what is also needed is a strong orientation toward consilience in developing our understanding of these three aspects of performance in the public domain, and how they interrelate.

At the start of this chapter, it was suggested in a fairly vague way that public values will suffuse the performance regime and performance model of organizations and affect the way in which the "brute facts" of performance are interpreted. Let us explore this a little further, because public values have a more profound impact than just interpreting performance measures; they will also, for example, shape the institutional context – performance regime – in which performance occurs.

Bozeman argues, "a theory of public values is *not* a theory of government and politics. There is no necessary correspondence between public value and either public policy, politics, governance, or markets. Individuals, groups, and institutions can ignore, serve, thwart, or achieve public policies." (Bozeman 2007, p. 133, his emphasis). Whilst there is clearly no simple deterministic relationship between individual values and institutions, to that extent Bozeman is correct. However, it would be misleading to think that any public institutional superstructure of society could stray far from the underlying substrate of individual public values for any prolonged period, without generating intense political upheaval.

Using the CPV framework suggested above (Figure 10.2), it is possible to discern links between underlying public values as held by individuals and the institutional superstructures of democratic societies. Thus, the democratically elected executive core of government, plus its permanent civil service, reflect the public values of authority. Not exclusively of course, as each institution of governance embeds all four competing public values to some extent, but government (in the executive sense) is above all about authority. The separation of powers that exists to some extent in all democracies, whether presidential or parliamentary, reflects mainly the underlying value of solidarity – with the legislative branch (Congress or Parliament) usually seen as the representative expression of the commonwealth – especially in times of national crisis – for example, wars. The pluralistic and representative nature of democratic assemblies is clearly framed by the underlying idea of communal sharing and solidarity. The democratic and legal apparatus of the state – elections and courts – can be seen as representing primarily the underlying values of equality and equity. And finally the competition for power through politics, political parties, pressure groups, and so on can be seen to incorporate predominantly the public values of autonomy, personal choice, competition, and personal benefit.

This is obviously somewhat simplistic – each of the institutions mentioned above includes all the public values captured in the CPV framework to some degree. This is a question of emphasis, not deterministic one-to-one relationships. But it does suggest that the evolution of the modern democratic state has, to some degree as least, been shaped by and sought to accommodate the competing public values of individuals, groups, and societies.

Progress and the Future

To recap, probably the most work has been carried out in the area of organizational performance models. Unfortunately this work has almost always led not toward consolidation but toward a multiplication of models of performance in both the private and public sectors. Although there is a fair degree of commonality in the basic approaches to constructing multidimensional performance models and to the dimensions to be included there is no consensus nor even any real coalescing around a specific model or models. As time goes on we get more, not less, MDPMs.

Yet as is suggested in this final chapter, if the commonalities in approach and substance are drawn out, it does not seem impossible to construct an MDPM for pubic agencies that is reasonably robust and rationally should command a fair degree of consensus of, or at the very least acceptance by, a substantial community of researchers and policy-makers. The overall construction of an MDPM – that it should be multidimensional to capture all the major areas of performance; that it should separate drivers and result; that it should be configured to suggest causal relationships (but not necessarily linear ones); and lastly what the dimensions should be – all this seems achievable. Much of the work is already there and although the specific attempt here (Figure 10.1) is a very tentative, and necessarily provisional, summary of what has already been proposed it serves to illustrate what is possible.

Progress on performance regimes has also been substantial, but probably even less integrated than for performance models. Whilst many specific aspects of performance regimes have been examined intensely there have not been the numerous attempts at model construction that characterize the organizational performance literature. The use of "third-party" audit and inspection has especially been subjected to much analysis and research (although not a great deal of theorizing). Other aspects of performance regimes have only just started to be investigated – the relationship between core executives and legislatures being the most obvious. Other aspects, such as the role of judicial and quasi-judicial interventions have hardly been explored at all. The kinds of interventions carried out by performance regime actors have likewise been the subject of a great deal of research and analysis, but again of a very unintegrated nature. We know quite a bit about certain types of interventions (league tables, targets, internal markets, specific capability interventions, and so on), but this has rarely been pulled together into any understanding of the range of interventions or their interactions. Hopefully the approach suggested in this book could help to make some progress in this direction.

The most problematic area is clearly public values – discussion and research of this area is remarkably underdeveloped. As has been suggested some empirical work has emerged and some theorizing, but as yet there is little evidence of either the intensity of some of the research on aspects of performance regimes and virtually none of the model construction that characterizes organizational performance.

At the very least, then, we ought to be able to make some rapid progress toward consensus around a fairly robust model of public organizational performance – although clearly more work is needed. Progress on performance regimes is also possible – especially attempting to bring together the wealth of empirical evidence and creating some sort of analytical framework to enable us to fill in the gaps and analyze the relationships within regimes. Is any of this likely to happen? It is difficult to predict, but if current trends persist the answer is probably no.

The pressures amongst policy-makers against consolidation and consensus are fairly obvious and to some extent understandable – they all want their own, preferably "new," models, approaches, and innovations for "their' national, community, political, or other reasons. This is clearly a major factor in the proliferation of public organization performance models. Nor are they especially interested in examining performance regimes – any serious research would start to expose the serial initiative over-kill and inherent confusion, ideological blinkers, and institutional actors' turf-wars that characterizes so many real performance regimes. Serious analysis of public values is also far from their central concerns – values are for mobilizing not analyzing (Hirschman 1991). Despite all this there are small signs for optimism. The emergence of transnational initiatives like the EFQM Excellence model, or the Speyer institute awards spreading from Germany to Austria and Switzerland, and the subsequent merger of the two to form first the EU-wide Common Assessment Framework and thence the European Public Service Awards – all these speak towards the possibility, at least, of consolidation and consensus around at least some aspects of the problem.

The likelihood of gaining academic consensus is another matter – if our research communities were guided by the scientific principles that most of us espouse then it ought to be possible to make progress. As we have seen however the academic community is fraught with the philosophy of science paradigm wars, and divided by disciplinary boundaries. Even where paradigmatic and disciplinary divisions do not exist, the dominant culture is one of individual (or small group) rivalry and the "tyranny of the new" rather than a drive towards consilience and consensus. As E. O. Wilson joked – the one thing about the social sciences is that they are not social. All this militates against progress, but the story is not wholly negative. The growing interest in multidisciplinary studies; moves toward more large-group social and organizational research; and a growing movement toward awareness of unhelpful disunities and the need for more scientific integration are all apparent. Some of the cutting-edge findings from areas like cognitive science are forcing reappraisals in many areas – not least economics with the rise of behavioral economics.

So if we were to draw up a scorecard for performance research and theorizing in the public sector it would probably have to read something like: "some good progress, with emerging understanding in some areas – but a need to gain a more comprehensive understanding and work more effectively with others. Could do better."

⬚ REFERENCES

Abramson, M. and I. Littman, Eds. (2002). *Innovation.* Lanham, MD, Rowman & Littlefield.

Accenture (2008). *An International Comparison of the United Kingdom's Public Administration (for the National Audit Office).* London, National Audit Office.

Aguayo, R. (1991). *Dr Deming – The American Who Taught the Japanese About Quality.* New York, Fireside (Simon & Schuster).

Alexander, P. and Agency Policy Review Team (2002). *Better Government Services – Executive Agencies in the 21st Century* (The Agency Policy Review – report and recommendations). London, Cabinet Office.

Alford, J. (2009). *Engaging Public Sector Clients – From Service Delivery to Co-Production.* Basingstoke, UK, Palgrave.

Allison, G. T. (1971). *Essence of Decision.* Boston, MA, Little, Brown & Co.

Ansell, C. (2006). Network Institutionalism. *The Oxford Handbook of Political Institutions.* R. Rhodes, S. Binder, and B. Rockman. Oxford, Oxford University Press.

Appleby, J. and M. Phillips (2009). The NHS: Satisfied Now? *British Social Attitudes – 25th Report 2008/09.* A. Park, J. Curtice, K. Thmson, M. Phillips, and E. Clery. London, Sage/National Centre for Social Research.

Apter, M. (2007 [1989]). *Reversal Theory – The Dynamics of Motivation, Emotion and Personality (2/e).* Oxford, OneWorld Publications.

Ariely, D. (2008). *Predictably Irrational – The Hidden Forces that Shape Our Decisions.* London, Harper.

Askim, J, A. Johnsen, et al. (2007). "Factors behind Organizational Learning from Benchmarking: Experiences from Norwegian Municipal Benchmarking Networks." *Journal of Public Administration Research and Theory* 18(2): 297–320.

Atkinson, T. (2003). *Atkinson Review: Interim Report.* London, HMSO.

—— (2005). *Atkinson Review: Final Report Measurement of Government Output and Productivity for the National Accounts.* Basingstoke, UK, Palgrave Macmillan.

Aucoin, P. (1990). "Administrative Reform in Public Management: Paradigms, Principles, Paradoxes and Pendulums." *Governance* 3: 115–37.

Audit Commission (1984). *Improving Economy, Efficiency and Effectiveness in Local Government in England and Wales – Audit Commission Handbook.* London, Audit Commission.

—— (2004). *Information and Data Quality in the NHS.* London, Audit Commission.

—— (2008). *PbR Data Assurance Framework 2007/08 – Finding from the First Year of the National Clinical Coding Audit Programme.* London, Audit Commission.

Axelrod, R. (1990). *The Evolution of Co-operation.* London, Penguin.

—— (1997). *The Complexity of Cooperation – Agent-Based Models of Competition and Collaboration.* Princeton, NJ, Princeton University Press.

—— and M. D. Cohen (1999). *Harnessing Complexity – Organizational Implications of a Scientific Frontier.* New York, The Free Press.

Barber, M. (2007). *Instruction to Deliver*. London, Politicos.

Barkow, J. H., J. Tooby, et al., Eds. (1995). *The Adapted Mind – Evolutionary Psychology and the Generation of Culture*. Oxford, Oxford University Press.

Barney, J. B. and D. N. Clark (2007). *Resource-Based Theory – Creating and Sustaining Competitive Advantage*. Oxford, Oxford University Press.

Bartlett, W. (1991). "Quasi-Markets and Contracts: A Markets and Hierarchies Perspective on NHS Reforms." *Public Money & Management* 11(3): 53–61.

Behn, R. (2001). *Rethinking Democratic Accountability*. Washington, Brookings Institution.

Bendell, T. and L. K. Boulter, J. (1993). *Benchmarking for Competitive Advantage*. London, Pitman.

Benedict, R. (2006 [1946]). *The Chrysanthemum and the Sword: Patterns of Japanese Culture*. Boston, MA, Mariner Books.

Berger, P. and T. Luckmann (1975). *The Social Construction of Reality*. Harmondsworth, UK, Penguin.

Bertlesmann Stiftung, Ed. (2009). *Sustainable Governance Indicators 2009 – Policy Performance and Executive Capacity in the OECD*. Berlin, Bertlesmann Stiftung.

Bevan, G. and C. Hood (2006a). "Have Targets Improved Performance in the English NHS?" *BMJ* 2006(332): 419–22.

——— (2006b). "What's Measured Is What Matters: Targets and Gaming in the English Public Healthcare System." *Public Administration* 84(3): 517–38.

Bichard, S. M. (1999). *Performance Management – Civil Service Reform: A Report to the Meeting of Permanent Heads of Departments*, Sunningdale. London, Cabinet Office.

Black, A., P. Wright, et al. (1998). *In Search of Shareholder Value – Managing the Drivers of Performance*. London, *Financial Times*/Prentice-Hall.

Blalock, A. B. (1999). "Evaluation Research and the Performance Management Movement: From Estrangement to Useful Integration." *Evaluation* 5(2): 117–49.

Boschken, H. L. (1994). "Organizational Performance and Multiple Constituencies." *Public Administration Review* 45(3): 308–12.

Boston, J., J. Martin, et al. (1996). *Public Management – The New Zealand Model*. Auckland, Oxford University Press.

Bovens, M. (1998). *The Quest for Responsibility*. Cambridge, Cambridge University Press.

Boyle, R. (2007). *Comparing Public Administrations*. Dublin, Institute of Public Administration.

Boyne, G. (2003). "What Is Public Service Improvement?" *Public Administration* 81 (2): 211–27.

——— K. Meier, et al., Eds. (2006). *Public Service Performance – Perspectives on Measurement and Management*. Cambridge, Cambridge University Press.

——— and A. A. Chen (2007). "Performance Targets and Public Service Improvement." *Journal of Public Administration Research and Theory* 17(3): 455.

Bozeman, B. (1987). *All Organizations Are Public: Bridging Public and Private Organizational Theories*. San Francisco, CA, Jossey-Bass.

——— (2007). *Public Values and Public Interest – Counterbalancing Economic Individualism*. Washington, DC, Georgetown University Press.

Brignall, S. (2002). The Unbalanced Scorecard: A Social and Environmental Critique. *Performance Measurement and Management: Reserach and Action.* A. Neely, A. Walters, and R. Austin. Cranfield, UK, Cranfield School of Management.

—— and S. Modell (2000). "An Institutional Perspective on Performance Measurement and Management in the 'New Public Sector.' " *Management Accounting Research* **11**: 281–306.

Brookes, S. and K. Grint, Eds. (2010). *The New Public Leadership Challenge.* Basingstoke, UK, Palgrave Macmillan (**forthcoming**).

Brown, D. E. (1991). *Human Universals.* New York: McGraw-Hill.

Brown, M. G. (1996). *Keeping Score: Using the Right Metrics to Drive World-Class Performance.* Portland, OR, Productivity.

Bryson, J. (1995). *Strategic Planning for Public and Non-Profit Organizations (2/e).* San Francisco, CA, Jossey-Bass.

Burke, W. (1987). *Organization Development – A Normative View.* Reading, MA, Addison-Wesley.

Burke, W.W. (2008) Organizational Change – Theory and Practice, Sage, page 189, and so on.

—— (2008). *Organization Development – A Normative View (2/e).* Reading, MA, Addison-Wesley.

Burrell, G. and G. Morgan (1979). *Sociological Paradigms and Organisational Analysis.* London: Heineman.

—— and G. Morgan (1994). *Sociological Paradigms and Organisational analysis.* Aldershot, UK, Ashgate Publishing.

Business Intelligence and Public Futures (2004). Transforming Public Sector Performance Management: A Seven-Step Guide to Delivering Strategic Performance Improvement. London, Optima Publishing Ltd in association with Public Futures Ltd.

Byrne, D. (1998). *Complexity Theory and the Social Sciences – An Introduction.* London and New York, Routledge.

Cabinet Office (Strategy Unit) (2006). *The UK Government's Approach to Public Service Reform.* London, Cabinet Office.

Cameron, K. (2005). Organizational Effectiveness – Its Demise and Re-emergence Through Positive Organizational Scholarship. *Great Minds in Management.* K. G. Smtih and M. A. Hitt. Oxford, Oxford University Press.

—— and R. E. Quinn (2006). *Diagnosing and Changing Organizational Culture – Based on the Competing Values Framework (2/e).* San Francisco, CA, Jossey Bass.

—— and D. Whetten (1983*a*). *Organizational Effectiveness – A Comparison of Multiple Models.* San Diego, CA, Academic Press.

—— (1983*b*). Organizational Effectiveness: One Model or Several? *Organizational Effectiveness – A Comparison of Multiple Models.* K. Cameron and D. Whetten. San Diego, CA, Academic Press.

—— R. E. Quinn, et al. (2006). *Competing Values Leadership.* Cheltenham, UK, Edward Elgar.

Campbell, J. P. (1973). Research into the Nature of Organisational Effectiveness – An Endangered Species? Working Paper. Minneapolis, MN, University of Minnesota.

—— (1977). On The Nature of Organizational Effectiveness. *New Perspectives on Organizational Effectiveness.* P. Goodman, J. Pennings, et al. San Francisco, CA, Jossey-Bass.

Campbell-Smith, D. (2008). *Follow the Money: The Audit Commission, Public Money and the Management of Public services, 1983–2008.* London, Allen Lane.

Carpenter, D. (2001). *The Forging of Bureaucratic Autonomy – Reputations, Networks and Policy Innovation in Executive Agencies 1862–1928.* Princeton, NJ, Princeton University Press.

Carter, N., R. Klein, et al. (1992). *How Organisations Measure Success – The Use of Performance Indicators in Government.* London, Routledge.

Cartwright, N. (1999). *The Dappled World – A Study of the Boundaries of Science.* Cambridge, Cambridge University Press.

Cave, M., M. Kogan, et al., Eds. (1990). *Output and Performance Measurement in Government – The State of the Art.* London, Jessica Kingsley Publishers.

Chan, Y.-C. L. (2004). "Performance Measurement and Adoption of Balanced Score-cards: A Survey of Municipal Governments in the USA and Canada." *International Journal of Public Sector Management* **17**(3): 204–21.

Chandler, A. D. (1991). *Strategy and Structure: Chapters in the History of the American Industrial Enterprise.* Cambridge, MA, MIT Press.

Chang, L. (2007). "The NHS Performance Assessment Framework as a Balanced Scorecard Approach: Limitations and Implications." *International Journal of Public Sector Management* **20**(2): 101–17.

Chesbrough, H. (2006). *Open Business Models.* Boston, MA, Harvard Business School Press.

Chief Secretary to the Treasury (1998). *Public Services for the Future: Modernising, Reform, Accountability – Comprehensive Spending Review: Public Service Agreements 1999–2002.* London, The Stationary Office.

Clarke, J., J. Newman, et al. (2007). *Creating Citizen-Consumers – Changing Publics and Changing Public Services.* London, Sage.

Clarke, M. and J. Stewart (1985a). *Local Government & the Public Service Orientation.* London, Inlogov/LGTB.

——— (1985b). *"Excellence" and Local Government.* Luton, UK, LGTB.

——— (1986a). *The Public Service Orientation: Developing the Approach.* Luton, UK, Inlogov/LGTB.

——— (1986b). *The Public Service Orientation: Issues & Dilemmas.* Luton, UK, Inlogov/LGTB.

——— (1987). *The Public Service Orientation: Some Key Ideas & Issues.* Luton, UK, Inlogov/LGTB.

Cole, M., G. Parston, et al. (2006). *Unlocking Public Value: A New Model for Achieving High Performance in Public Service Organizations.* Hoboken, NJ, John Wiley & Sons.

Collins, J. (2001). *Good to Great.* London, Random House.

Collins, J. C. and J. I. Porras (1994). *Built to Last – Successful Habits of Visionary Companies.* New York, Harper Business.

Committee of Public Accounts (2007). *The Efficiency Programme: A Second Review of Progress Forty-Eighth Report of Session 2006–07 HC 349.* London, House of Commons.

Common, R., N. Flynn, et al. (1992). *Managing Public Services – Competition and Decentralisation,* Butterworth-Heinemann.

Comptroller and Auditor General (1998). *Benefits Agency: Performance Measurement.* London, National Audit Office.

——— (2000). *Good Practice in Performance Reporting in Executive Agencies and Non-Departmental Public Bodies.* London, National Audit Office.

——— (2001). *Measuring the Performance of Government Departments.* London, National Audit Office.

——— (2005). *Public Service Agreements: Managing Data Quality – Compendium Report (HC 476).* London, National Audit Office.

——— (2006*a*). *Progress in Improving Government Efficiency (HC 802-I).* London, National Audit Office.

——— (2006*b*). *Second Validation Compendium Report – 2003–06 PSA Data Systems (HC 985).* London, National Audit Office.

——— (2006*c*). *Third Validation Compendium Report: Volume 1 (HC 127-I).* London, National Audit Office.

——— (2006*d*). *Third Validation Compendium Report: Volume 2 (HC 127-II).* London, National Audit Office.

——— (2007*a*). *Fourth Validation Compendium Report: Volume I (HC 22-I).* London, National Audit Office.

——— (2007*b*). *Fourth Validation Compendium Report: Volume II (HC 22-II).* London, National Audit Office.

——— (2008). *Assessment of the Capability Review Programme.* London, National Audit Office.

——— (2009). *Assessment of the Capability Review Programme.* London, National Audit Office.

Cook, K. (1977). "Exchange and Power in Networks of Interorganizational Relations." *The Sociological Quarterly* **18**: 62–82.

Corby, B., A. Doig, et al. (2001). *Public Inquiries into Abuse of Children in Residential Care.* London, Jessica Kingsley Publishers.

Courty, P. and G. Marschke (2004). "Benchmarking Performance." *Public Finance and Management* **4**(3): 288–316.

Creelman, J. and D. Harvey (2004). *Transforming Public Sector Performance Management.* London, Optima Publishing Ltd (Business Intelligence).

Curristine, T., Ed. (2007). *Performance Budgeting in OECD Countries.* Paris, OECD.

Curtice, J. and O. Heath (2009). Do People Want Choice and Diversity of Provision in Public Services? *British Social Attitudes – 25th Report 2008/09.* A. Park, J. Curtice, K. Thmson, M. Phillips, and E. Clery. London, Sage/National Centre for Social Research.

Czarnecki, M. T. (1999). *Managing by Measuring – How to Improve Your Organization's Performance Through Effective Benchmarking.* New York, American Management Association.

Davidson, R. H., Ed. (2003). *Workways of Governance – Monitoring Our Government's Health.* Washington, DC, Brookings Institution.

Davies, J. S. (2001). *Partnerships and Regimes – The Politics of Urban Regeneration in the UK.* Aldershot, UK, Ashgate.

Davis, P. and K. West (2008). "What Do Public Values Mean for Public Action? Putting Public Values in Their Plural Place." *The American Review of Public Administration* **39**(6): 602–18.

Day, P. and R. Klein (1987). *Accountabilities – Five Public Services*. London and New York, Tavistock.

De Bruijn, H. (2001). *Managing Performance in the Public Sector*. London, Routledge.

Deakin, N. and R. Parry (2000). *The Treasury and Social Policy*. London, Macmillan.

Deal, T. and A. Kennedy (1982). *Corporate Cultures – The Rites & Rituals of Corporate Life*. London, Penguin.

————— (1988). *Corporate Cultures – The Rites and Rituals of Corporate Life*. Harmondsworth, UK, Penguin.

Deloitte (2008). *The Use of Sanctions and Rewards in the Public Sector*. London, Deloitte and Touche LLP.

Denhardt, J. V. and B. D. Denhardt (2003). *The New Public Service*. London, M. E. Sharpe.

Denhardt, R. B. (1993). *The Pursuit of Significance – Strategies for Managerial Success in Public Organisations*. Fort Worth, TX, Harcourt Brace College Publishers.

Desrosieres, A. (1998). *The Politics of Large Numbers – A History of Statistical Reasoning*. Cambridge, MA, Harvard University Press.

Dickens, P. (1994). *Quality and Excellence in Human Services*. Chichester, UK and New York, Wiley.

Downe, J., C. Grace, et al. (2007). *Comparing for Improvement: Local Government Performance Regimes in England*, Scotland and Wales. Oxford, ESRC Public Services Programme Discussion paper Series: No. 0705.

Downs, G. and P. Larkey (1986). *The Search for Government Efficiency: From Hubris to Helplessness*. New York, Random House.

Dunleavy, P. (1991). *Democracy, Bureaucracy and Public Choice: Economic*. Brighton, UK, Harvester/Wheatsheaf.

—— and B. O'Leary (1987). *Theories of the State – The Politics of Liberal Democracy*. London, Macmillan Education Ltd.

Easton, D. and C. S. Schelling, Eds. (1991). *Divided Knowledge – Across Disciplines, Across Cultures*. London, Sage.

Eberstadt, N. (1995). *The Tyranny of Numbers – Mismeasurement and Misrule*. Washington, DC, American Enterprise Institute Press.

Eccles, R. G. (1991). "The Performance Measurement Manifesto." *Harvard Business Review* **69**(Jan–Feb): 131–7.

Emery, F. E., Ed. (1969). *Systems Thinking*. Middlesex, UK, Penguin.

Eskildsen, J. K. and K. Kristensen (2002). "Trends in EFQM Criterion Weights." *Measuring Business Excellence* **6**: 22–8.

Evans, J. R. (1997). "Critical Linkages in the Baldrige Award Criteria: Research Models and Educational Challenges." *Quality Management Journal* **5**(1): 13–30.

Fagerberg, J., D. Mowery, et al., Eds. (2005). *The Oxford Handbook of Innovation*. Oxford, Oxford University Press.

Farnham, D. and S. Horton (1996). *Managing People in the Public Services*. London, Macmillan.

—— S. Horton, et al., Eds. (1996). *New Public Managers in Europe – Public Servants in Transition*. London, Macmillan Press Ltd.

Ferlie, E., A. Pettigrew, et al. (1996). *The New Public Management in Action*. Oxford, Oxford University Press.

Ferlie, E., L. E. Lynn, et al., Eds. (2004). *Oxford Handbook of Public Management.* Oxford, Oxford University Press.

Finer, H. (1946). *The Theory and Practice of Modern Government (2/e) (1931),* 2 vols. London, Methuen.

Fischer, F. and J. Forester, Eds. (1993). *The Argumentative Turn in Policy Analysis and Planning.* Durham, UK, Duke University Press.

Fiske, A. P. (1991). *Structures of Social Life – The Four Elementary Forms of Human Relations.* New York, The Free Press.

—— (2004). Relational Models Theory 2.0. *Relational Models Theory – A Contemporary Overview.* N. Haslam. Mahwah, NJ, Lawrence Erlbaum Associates.

Flinders, M. (2001). *The Politics of Accountability in the Modern State.* Aldershot, UK, Ashgate.

Fortin, Y. and H. Van Hassel, Eds. (2000). *Contracting in the New Public Management.* Amsterdam, IOS Press.

Fox, C. and H. Miller (1995). *Postmodern Public Administration.* Thousand Oaks, CA, Sage.

Frederickson, D. G. and H. G. Frederickson (2006). *Measuring the Performance of the Hollow State.* Washington, DC, Georgetown University Press.

Frederickson, H. G. (1997). *The Spirit of Public Administration.* San Francisco, CA, Jossey Bass.

Fried, R. C. (1976). *Performance in American Bureaucracy.* Boston, MA, Little, Brown & Co.

Friedman, A. L. and S. Miles (2006). *Stakeholders Theory and Practice.* Oxford, Oxford University Press.

Gaster, L. (1995). *Quality in Public Services.* Buckingham, UK, Open University Press.

Gigerenzer, G. (2000). *Adaptive Thinking.* Oxford, Oxford University Press.

Gintis, H., S. Bowles, et al., Eds. (2005). *Morel Sentiments and Material Interests – The Foundations of Cooperation in Economic Life.* Cambridge, MA, MIT Press.

Goodin, R. E., Ed. (1996). *The Theory of Institutional Design.* Cambridge, Cambridge University Press.

Goodman, P., J. Pennings, et al. (1977). *New Perspectives on Organizational Effectiveness.* San Francisco, CA, Jossey-Bass.

Gore, A. and National Performance Review (1993). *Creating A Government That Works Better and Costs Less – The Report of the National Performance Review.* New York, Plume (Penguin).

Grafstein, R. (1992). *Institutional Realism.* New Haven, CT and London, Yale University Press.

Graham, A. and A. Roberts (2004). The Agency Concept in North America: Failure, Adaptation and Incremental Change. *Unbundled Government.* C. Pollitt and C. Talbot. London, Taylor & Francis.

Gray, A. and W. Jenkins (1985). *Administrative Politics in British Government.* Brighton, UK, Wheatsheaf.

Green, D. P. and I. Shapiro (1994). *Pathologies of Rational Choice Theory.* London and New Haven, CT, Yale University Press.

Greenwood, R., C. Oliver, et al., Eds. (2008). *The Sage Handbook of Organizational Institutionalism.* Los Angeles, CA, Sage.

Greer, P. (1994). *Transforming Central Government – The Next Steps Initiative.* London, Open University Press.

Griffiths, J. (2003). "Balanced Scorecard Use in New Zealand Government Departments and Crown Entities." *Australian Journal of Public Administration* 62(4): 70–9.

Guba, E. G. (1990). *The Paradigm Dialog.* Newbury Park, CA, Sage.

—— and Y. Lincoln (1989). *Fourth Generation Evaluation.* New York, Sage.

Gueorguiev, I., S. Dimitrova, et al. (2005). "Balanced Scorecard Based Management Information System–A Potential for Public Monitoring and Good Governance Advancement." *Electronic Journal of eGovernment* 3(1): 29–38.

Halachmi, A. and G. Bouckaert, Eds. (1996). *Organizational Performance and Measurement in the Public Sector.* Westport, CT, Quorum Books.

Halliday, S. (2003). *Judicial Review and Compliance with Administrative Law.* Oxford, Hart Publishing.

Hammer, M. (1995). *The Reengineering Revolution.* New York, HarperCollins.

—— and R. Champy (1993). *Reengineering the Corporation: A Manifesto for a Business Revolution.* New York, HarperBusiness.

Hampden-Turner, C. and F. Trompenaars (1993). *The Seven Cultures of Capitalism.* London, Piatkus.

Handy, C. (1985). *Gods of Management.* London, Pan.

Harden, I. (1992). *The Contracting State.* Buckingham, UK, Open University Press.

Harrison, A. E. (1993). *From Hierarchy to Contract.* Newbury, UK, Policy Journals.

Harrison, R. (1972). "How to Describe Your Organization." *Harvard Business Review* 5(1): 119–28.

Harrow, J. and C. Talbot (1993). The Citizen's Charter. *The Public Services Yearbook, 1993.* P. Jackson and M. Lavender. London, Chapman & Hall.

Harvard Business Review, Ed. (1991). *On Measuring Corporate Performance.* Boston, MA, Harvard Business School Press.

Haslam, N., Ed. (2004). *Relational Models Theory – A Contemporary Overview.* Mahwah, NJ, Lawrence Erlbaum Associates.

Hatry, H. H. (1999). *Performance Measurement: Getting Results.* Washington, DC, The Urban Institute.

Hay, C. (2006). Constructivist Institutionalism. *The Oxford Handbook of Political Institutions.* R. Rhodes, S. Binder, and B. Rockman. Oxford, Oxford University Press.

—— M. Lister, et al., Eds. (2006). *The State: Theories and Issues.* Basingstoke, UK, Palgrave.

Haynes, P. (2003). *Managing Complexity in the Public Services.* Maidenhead, UK, Open University Press.

Heclo, H. and A. Wildavsky (1981). *The Private Government of Public Money (2/e).* London, Macmillan

Heinrich, C. J. and L. E. Lynn, Eds. (2000). *Governance and Performance – New Perspectives.* Washington, DC, Georgetown University Press.

Heintzman, R. (2009). "Measurement in Public Management: The Case for the Defence." *Optimum Online – The Journal of Public Sector Management* 39(1).

Henrich, N. and J. Henrich (2007). *Why Humans Cooperate – A Cultural and Evolutionary Explanation.* Oxford, Oxford University Press.

Herman, R. D. and D. O. Renz (1997). "Multiple Constituencies and the Social Construction of Nonprofit Organization Effectiveness." *Nonprofit and Voluntary Sector Quarterly* 26(2): 185–206.

Hertogh, M. and S. Halliday, Eds. (2004). *Judicial Review and Bureaucratic Impact*. Cambridge, Cambridge University Press.

Hickson, D. and D. Pugh (1995). *Management Worldwide – The Impact of Societal Culture on Organizations Around the Globe*. Harmondsworth, UK, Penguin.

Hirsch, P. M. and D. Z. Levin (1999). "Umbrella Advocates Versus Validity Police: A Life Cycle Model." *Organizational Science* 10(2): 199–212.

Hirschman, A. (1970). *Exit, Voice, and Loyalty*. Cambridge, MA, Harvard University Press.

—— (1991). *The Rhetoric of Reaction: Perversity, Futility, Jeopardy*. Cambridge, MA, Harvard University Press.

HM Treasury (2001). *Choosing the Right FABRIC – A Framework for Performance Information*. London, HM Treasury.

—— (2008). *2004 Spending Review: Final Report of the Efficiency Programme*. London, HM Treasury.

Hodgson, G. (2004). *The Evolution of Institutional Economics – Agency, Structure and Darwinism in American Institutionalism*. London, Routledge.

Hofstede, G. (2003). *Culture's Consequence's: Comparing Values, Behaviors, Institutions and Organizations Across Nations (2/e)*. Thousand Oaks, CA, Sage.

Hollinger, R. (1994). *Postmodernism and the Social Services*. London, Sage.

Holloway, J., J. Lewis, et al., Eds. (1995). *Performance Measurement and Evaluation*. London, Sage.

Holmes, J. S., S. A. Gutierrez de Pieres, et al. (2006). "Reforming Government Agencies Internationally: Is There a Role for the Balanced Scorecard?" *International Journal of Public Administration* 29(12): 1125–45.

Holzer, M. and K. Callahan (1998). *Government at Work: Best Practices and Model Programmes*. Thousand Oaks, CA, Sage.

Home Affairs Select Committee (2005). Home Office Target Setting 2004 (HC 320). London, House of Commons.

Hood, C. (1983). *The Tools of Government*. London, Macmillan.

—— (1991). "A Public Management for all Seasons?" *Public Administration* 69 (1): 3–19.

—— (2000). *The Art of the State: Culture, Rhetoric, and Public Management*, Oxford University Press.

—— and M. Jackson (1991). *Administrative Argument*. Aldershot, Dartmouth.

—— and H. Margetts (2007). *The Tools of Government in a Digital Age*. Basingstoke, UK, Palgrave.

—— O. James, et al. (1999). *Regulation Inside Government*. Oxford, Oxford University Press.

—— et al., Eds. (2004). *Controlling Modern Government – Variety, Commonality and Change*. Cheltenham, UK, Edward Elgar.

—— R. Dixon, et al. (2008). "Rating the Rankings: Assessing International Rankings of Public Service Performance." *International Public Management Journal* 11(3): 298–328.

Huczynski, A. A. (1993). *The Management Gurus.* London, Routledge.

Huff, A. S. (2005). Managerial and Organizational Cognition – Islands of Coherence. *Great Minds in Management – The Process of Theory Development.* K. G. Smith and M. A. Hitt. Oxford, Oxford University Press.

Hummel, R. (2007). *The Bureaucratic Experience: The Post-modern Challenge (5/e).* Armonk, NY, M. E. Sharpe.

Hyndman, N. (2002). "Executive Agencies, Performance Targets and External Reporting." *Public Money and Management* **22**(3): 17–24.

—— and R. Anderson (1998). "Performance Information, Accountability and Executive Agencies." *Public Money and Management* **18**(3): 23–30.

Ingraham, P. W., P. G. Joyce, et al. (2003). *Government Performance: Why Management Matters.* Baltimore, MD, Johns Hopkins University Press.

Ingstrup, O. and P. Crookall (1998). *The Three Pillars of Public Management – Secrets of Sustained Success.* London, McGill-Queen's University Press.

Jackson, P.M., Ed. (1995). *Measures for Success in the Public Sector (Reader).* London, CIPFA.

—— and B. Palmer (1992). *Developing Performance Monitoring in Public Sector Organisations – A Management Guide.* Leicester, UK, The Management Centre, University of Leicester.

Jacobs, R. *Exploring the Impact of Public Services on Quality of Life Indicators.* Swindon, UK, ESRC.

—— and M. Goddard (2007). "How Do Performance Indicators Add Up? An Examination of Composite Indicators in Public Services." *Public Money & Management* **27**(2): 103–10.

—— S. Martin, et al. (2006). "Exploring the Determinants of NHS Performance Ratings: Lessons for Performance Assessment Systems." *Journal of Health Services Research and Policy* **11**(4): 211–17.

James, O. (2004). "The UK Core Executive's Use of Public Service Agreements as a Tool of Governance." *Public Administration* **82**(2): 397–419.

—— and P. John (2006). "Public Management at the Ballot Box: Performance Information and Electoral Support for Incumbent English Local Governments." *Journal of Public Administration Research and Theory* **17**(4): 567–80.

Jann, W. and B. Jantz (2008). A Better Performance of Performance Management? *Holy Grail or Achievable Quest? International Perspectives on Public Sector Performance Management, KPMG.* Toronto, KPMG/CAPAM/IPAA/IPAC.

—— and M. Seyfried (2009). Does Executive Governance Matter? Executives and Policy Performance. *Sustainable Governance Indicators 2009 – Policy Performance and Executive Capacity in the OECD.* B. Stiftung. Berlin, Bertelsmann Stiftung.

Jenkins, K., K. Caines, et al. (1988). *Improving Management in Government: The Next Steps.* HMSO, London.

Jingjit, R. (2009). Cultural Change in the Thai Civil Service – a competing values approach. PhD thesis, Manchester Business School, University of Manchester.

Johnson, C. (1995). *Japan – Who Governs? The Rise of the Developmental State.* New York, W.W. Norton.

—— and C. Talbot (2007a). "Seasonal Variations in Public Management: disaggregation and reaggregation." *Public Money & Management* **27**(1): 53–60.

—— —— (2007b). "The UK Parliament and Performance: Challenging or Challenged?" *International Review of Administrative Sciences* **73**(1): 113–31.

Johnson, C. and C. Talbot (2008). UK Parliamentary Scrutiny of PSAs. *Utilizing Public Sector Performance Information.* W. Van Dooren and S. Van de Walle. Basingstoke, UK, Palgrave Macmillan and EGPA.

Johnson, G. and K. Scholes, Eds. (2001). *Exploring Public Sector Strategy.* London, Financial Times/Prentice-Hall.

Jordan, G. (1992). Next Steps Agencies: From Managing by Command to Managing by Contract? *Aberdeen Papers in Accountancy and Finance Management.* Aberdeen, UK, University of Aberdeen.

Jorgensen, T. B. and B. Bozeman (2007). "Public Values: An Inventory." *Administration and Society* **39**(3): 354–81.

Joss, R. and M. Kogan (1995). *Advancing Quality – TQM in the NHS.* Buckingham, UK, Open University Press.

Jowett, P. and M. Rothwell (1988). *Performance Indicators in the Public Sector.* London, Macmillan.

Joyce, P. (2000). *Strategy in the Public Sector.* Chichester, UK, Wiley.

Kaplan, R. S. and D. P. Norton (1992). "The Balanced Scorecard – Measures That Drive Performance." *Harvard Business Review* **Jan-Feb**: 71–9.

—— —— (1996). *The Balanced Scorecard.* Boston, MA, Harvard Business School Press.

—— —— (2004). *Strategy Maps.* Boston, MA, Harvard Business School Press.

Kaufmann, D., A. Kraay, et al. (2007). Governance Matters VI: Aggregate and Individual Governance Indicators 1996–2006. *World Bank Policy Research Paper.* Washington, DC, World Bank. **4280**.

Keehley, P. and N. Abercrombie (2008). *Benchmarking in the Public and Nonprofit Sectors.* San Francisco, CA, Jossey-Bass.

Kelly, G., G. Mulgan, et al. (2004). *Creating Public Value – An Analytical Framework for Public Service Reform.* London, Cabinet Office Strategy Unit (www.strategy. gov.uk).

Kelman, S. (2005). *Unleashing Change – A Study of Organizational Renewal in Government.* Washington, DC, Brookings Institution.

Kennedy, A. (2000). *The End of Shareholder Value – Corporations at the Crossroads.* Cambridge, MA, Perseus Publishing.

Kerr, D. L. (2003). "Accountability by Numbers: How the Lone Star State's Auditor Introduced a Balanced Scorecard Management System." *Journal of Accountancy* **195**(6): 61–70.

Kettl, D. (2003). "Contingent Coordination: Practical and Theoretical Puzzles for Homeland Security." *American Review of Public Administration* **33**(3): 253–77.

Kiel, L. D. (1994). *Managing Chaos and Complexity in Government – A New Paradigm for Managing Change, Innovation, and Organizational Renewal.* San Francisco, CA, Jossey-Bass.

Kimberly, J. and G. A. Pouvourville (1993). *The Migration of Managerial Innovation.* San Francisco, CA, Jossey-Bass.

Kirkpatrick, I. and M. Martinez Lucio, Eds. (1995). *The Politics of Quality in the Public Sector.* London, Routledge.

Koehler, M. and H. G. Rainey (2008). Interdisciplinary Foundations of Public Service Motivation. *Motivation in Public Management – The Call of Public Service.* J. L. Perry and A. Hondeghem. Oxford, Oxford University Press.

Kolm, S.-C. (2008). *Reciprocity – An Economics of Social Life*. Cambridge, Cambridge Univrsity Press.

Kuhn, T. S. (1970). *The Structure of Scientific Revolutions (2/e)*. Chicago, IL, University of Chicago Press.

—— (1977). *The Essential Tension – Selected Studies in Scientific Tradition and Change*. Chicago, IL, and London, University of Chicago Press.

Lane, J.-E., Ed. (1987). *Bureaucracy and Public Choice*. London, Sage.

Latham, G. P. (2007). *Work Motivation – History, Theory, Research and Practice*. London, Sage.

Lawton, A. and A. Rose (1991). *Organization and Management in the Public Sector*. London, Pitman Publishing.

Le Grand, J. (2003). *Motivation, Agency, and Public Policy – Of Knights & Knaves, Pawns & Queens*. Oxford, Oxford University Press.

Leckie, G. and H. Goldstein (2009). The Limitations of Using School League Tables to Inform School Choice. Working Paper No. 09/208. Bristol, UK, Centre for Market and Public Organisation.

Lee, M. (2006). *Institutionalizing Congress and the Presidency: The U.S. Bureau of Efficiency, 1916–1933*. College Station, TX, Texas A & M University Press.

Lee, P. (2008). *Public Service Productivity: Health Care*. London, Office of National Statistics.

Lessem, R. (1990). *Managing Corporate Culture*. Aldershot, UK, Gower.

Lewis, D. (1997). *Hidden Agendas*. London, Hamish Hamilton.

Lewis, N. and P. Birkinshaw (1993). *When Citizens Complain – Reforming Justice and Administration*. Milton Keynes, UK, Open University Press.

Lidbury, C. and M. Petrie (1999). *Lessons from Performance Contracting Case Studies & a Framework for Public Sector Performance Contracting*. Paris, OECD.

Light, P. C. (1997). *The Tides of Reform – Making Government Work 1945–1995*. New Haven, CT, Yale University Press.

Lijphart, A. (1999). *Patterns of Democracy*. London, Yale University Press.

Like, J. (2004). *The Toyota Way*. New York, McGraw-Hill.

Lincoln, Y. S. and E. G. Guba (1998). *Competing Paradigms in Qualitative Research*. London, Sage.

Linden, R. (1994). *Seamless Government – A Practical Guide to Re-Engineering in the Public Sector*. San Francisco, CA, Jossey-Bass.

Lipsky, M. (1980). *Street-Level Bureaucracy – Dilemmas of the Individual in Public Services*. New York, Russell Sage Foundation.

Lloyd-Bostock, S. and B. Hutter (2008). "Reforming Regulation of the Medical Profession: The Risks of Risk-based Approaches." *Health, Risk and Society* 10(1): 69–83.

Locke, E., L. Saari, et al. (1981). "Goal Setting and Task Performance: 1969–1980." *Pschological Bulletin* 90(1): 125 52.

Logothetis, N. (1992). *Managing for Total Quality*. New York, Prentice-Hall.

Long, E. and A. L. Franklin (2004). "The Paradox of Implementing the Government Performance and Results Act: Top-Down Direction for Bottom-Up Implementation." *Public Administration Review* 64(3): 309–19.

Loyens, K. (2009). "Occupational Culture in Policing Reviewed: A Comparison of Values in the Public and Private Police." *International Journal of Public Administration* **32**(6): 461–90.

Luton, L. S. (2007). "Deconstructing Public Administration Empiricism." *Administration & Society* **39**(4): 527–44.

—— (2008). "Beyond Empiricists Versus Postmodernists." *Administration & Society* **40**(2).

Lynch, R. L. and K. F. Cross (1995). *Measure Up! How to Measure Corporate Performance (2/e)*. Malden, MA, Blackwell.

Lynn, L. E., C. J. Heinrich, et al. (2000). Studying Governance and Public Management: Why? How? *Governance and Performance*. C. J. Heinrich and L. E. Lynn. Washington, DC, Georgetown University Press.

—— —— et al. (2001). *Improving Governance: A New Logic for Empirical Research.* Washington, DC, Georgetown University Press.

—— —— et al. (2008). "The Empiricist Goose Has Not Been Cooked!" *Administration & Society* **40**(1): 104–9.

Malson, L. (1972). *Wolf Children.* London, NLB.

March, J. G. and J. P. Olsen (1989). *Rediscovering Institutions: The Organisational Basis of Politics.* New York, Free Press.

Margolis, H. (1982). *Selfishness, Altruism and Rationality – A Theory of Social Choice.* Chicago, IL, University of Chicago Press.

Marshall, B., B. Duffy, et al. (2007). *Blair's Britain: The Social and Cultural Legacy.* London, Ipsos-MORI Social Research Institute.

Marx, K. (2009 [1852]). *The Eighteenth Brumaire of Louis Napoleon,* Dodo Press.

Mayne, J. and E. Zapico-Goni, Eds. (1997). *Monitoring Performance in the Public Sector.* New Brunswick, NJ, Transaction Publishers.

McAdam, R. and T. Walker (2003). "An Inquiry into Balanced Scorecards Within Best Value Implementation in UK Local Government." *Public Administration* **81**(4): 873–92.

McLean, I. (1987). *Public Choice: An Introduction.* Oxford, Blackwell.

—— (2008–9). *Options for Britain II.* Swindon, UK, ESRC.

—— D. Haubrich, et al. (2007). "The Perils and Pitfalls of Performance Measurement: The CPA Regime for Local Authorities in England." *Public Money and Management* **27**(2): 111–18.

McMahon, E. and T. Sinclair (2002). *Democratic Institution Performance.* Westport, CT, Praeger Publishers (Greenwood Publishing).

Meier, K. and L. O'Toole (2007). "Deconstructing Larry Luton – Or What Time Is the Next Train to Reality Junction?" *Administration & Society* **39**(6): 786–96.

Meier, S. (2006). *The Economics of Non-selfish Behavior.* Cheltenham, UK, Edward Elgar.

Meyer, M. W. (2002). *Rethinking Performance Measurement – Beyond the Balanced Scorecard.* Cambridge, Cambridge University Press.

—— (2007). Finding Performance: The New Discipline in Management. *Business Performance Measurement – Unifying Theory and Integrating Practice.* A. Neely. Cambridge, Cambridge University Press.

—— and L. Zucker (1989). *Permanently Failing Organizations.* London, Sage.

Micklethwait, J. (1996). *The Witch Doctors – What the Management Gurus Are Saying, Why It Matters and How to Make Good Sense of It.* London, Heinemann.
—— and A. Wooldridge (2005). *The Company – A Short History of a Revolutionary Idea.* London, Pheonix/Orion.
Milgram, S. (1997). *Obedience to Authority [1974].* London, Pinter & Martin Psychology.
Miller, A. I. (1987). *Imagery in Scientific Thought.* Boston, MA, MIT Press.
Miller, G. A. (1956). "The Magical Number Seven, Plus or Minus Two: Some Limits on Our Capacity for Processing Information." *The Psychological Review* 63: 81–97.
Miller, H. and C. Fox (2007). *Postmodern Public Administration (2/e).* Thousand Oaks, CA, Sage.
Mintzberg, H. (1983a). *Power In and Around Organisations.* New York, Prentice-Hall.
—— (1983b). *Structure in Fives.* New York, Prentice-Hall.
—— (1994). *The Rise and Fall of Strategic Planning.* New York, Prentice Hall.
—— and J. B. Quinn (1998). *Readings in the Strategy Process.* London, Prentice-Hall.
—— B. Ahlstrand, et al. (1998). *Strategy Safari – A Guided Tour Through the Wilds of Strategic Management.* London, Prentice-Hall.
Modell, S. (2009). "Institutional Research on Performance Measurement and Management in the Public Sector Accounting Literature: A Review and Assessment." *Financial Accountability & Management* 25(3): 277–303.
Molen, K. v. d., A. v. Rooyen, et al., Eds. (2001). *Outcome-Based Governance: Assessing the Results.* Cape Town, Heinemann.
Moore, M. (1995). *Creating Public Value.* Cambridge, MA, Harvard University Press.
—— (2003). The Public Value Scorecard: A Rejoinder and an Alternative to "Strategic Performance Measurement and Management in Non-Profit Organizations" by Robert Kaplan – Working Paper #18. Boston, MA, The Hauser Center for Non-profit Organizations, Kennedy School of Government, Harvard University.
Morgan, C. and S. Murgatroyd (1994). *Total Quality Management in the Public Sector.* Buckingham, UK, Open University Press.
Morgan, G. (1986). *Images of Organization.* Beverly Hills, CA, Sage.
—— (1996). *Images of Organisation (2/e).* Beverly Hills, CA, Sage.
Moscovici, S. (2000). *Social Representations – Explorations in Social Psychology.* Cambridge, Polity Press.
Moullin, M., J. Soady, et al. (2007). "Using the Public Sector Scorecard in Public Health." *International Journal of Health Care Quality Assurance* 20(4): 281–9.
Moynihan, D. P. (2005). "Why and How Do State Governments Adopt and Implement 'Managing for Results' Reforms?" *Journal of Public Administration Research and Theory* 15(2): 219–44.
—— (2006). "What Do We Talk About When We Talk About Performance? Dialogue Theory and Performance Budgeting." *Journal of Public Administration Research and Theory* 16(2): 151.
—— (2008). *The Dynamics of Performance Management: Constructing Information and Reform.* Washington, DC, Georgetown University Press.
Neely, A. (1998). *Measuring Business Performance – Why, What and How.* London, The Economist Books & Profile Publishing.

Neely, A. Ed. (2007). *Business Performance Measurement – Unifying Theory and Integrating Practice.* Cambridge, Cambridge University Press.

—— and D. Waggoner, Eds. (1998). *Performance Measurement: Theory and Practice (2 vols).* Cambridge, UK, Centre for Business Performance, Judge Institute, Cambridge University.

—— C. Adams, et al. (2002). *The Performance Prism.* London, FT Prentice-Hall.

Next Steps Team (1995). *The Strategic Management of Agencies.* London, Cabinet Office (OPS).

Niven, P. R. (2003). *Balanced Scorecard Step by Step for Government and Nonprofit Agencies.* Hoboken, NJ, Wiley.

Norman, R. (2003). *Obedient Servants? Management Freedoms and Accountabilities in the New Zealand Public Sector.* Wellington, Victoria University Press.

Normanton, E. L. (1966). *The Accountability and Audit of Governments.* Manchester, UK, Manchester University Press.

O'Neill, O. (2002). *A Question of Trust.* Cambridge, Cambridge University Press.

O'Toole, L. J. (2003). "Plus ca Change: Public Management, Personnel Stability, and Organizational Performance." *Journal of Public Administration Research and Theory* **13**(1): 43–64.

Oakland, J. S. (1991). *Total Quality Management, DTI.* Oxford, Butterworth-Heinemann.

Oakley, A. (2000). *Experiments in Knowing.* Cambridge, Polity Press.

OECD (2001). *Public Sector Leadership for the 21st Century.* Paris, OECD.

—— (2005). *Modernising Government – The Way Forward.* Paris, OECD.

OECD and European Commission (2008). *Handbook on Constructing Composite Indicators – Methodology and User Guide.* Paris, OECD.

OECD-PUMA (1996). *Performance Auditing and the Modernisation of Government.* Paris, OECD.

—— (1997). *Managing Across Levels of Government.* Paris, OECD.

—— (1999). *Performance Contracting – Lessons from Performance Contracting Case Studies: A Framework for Public Sector Performance Contracting.* Paris, OECD.

Office of National Statistics (2099). *Total Public Service Output and Productivity.* London, Office of National Statistics.

Oliver, D. (1991). *Government in the UK: The Search for Accountability, Effectiveness and Citizenship.* Milton Keynes, UK, Open University Press.

Ouchi, W. G. (1981). *Theory Z – How American Business Can Meet the Japanese Challenge.* New York, Avon Books.

Pannirselvam, G. P. and L. A. Ferguson (2001). "A Study of the Relationships Between the Baldrige Categories." *International Journal of Quality & Reliability Management* **18**(1): 14–34.

Pascale, R. and A. Athos (1981). *The Art of Japanese Management.* London, Penguin.

Pawson, R. and N. Tilley (1997). *Realistic Evaluation.* London, Sage.

Pentland, A. S. (2008). *Honest Signals: How They Shape Our World.* Cambridge, MA, MIT Press.

Perry, J. L. and A. Hondeghem, Eds. (2008). *Motivation in Public Management: The Call of Public Service.* Oxford, Oxford University Press.

Peters, B. G. (1995). *The Politics of Bureaucracy.* New York, Longman.

Peters, G. B. (1999). *Institutional Theory In Political Science.* London and New York, Pinter.

—— (2008). Institutional Theory: Problems and Prospects. *Debating Institutionalism.* J. Pierre, G. B. Peters, and G. Stoker. Manchester, UK, Manchester University Press.

Peters, T. and R. Waterman (1982). *In Search of Excellence – Lessons From Americas Best Run Companies.* New York, Harper & Row.

Pettigrew, A., E. Ferlie, et al. (1992). *Shaping Strategic Change.* London, Sage.

Pfeffer, J. and G. Salancik (2003 [1978]). *The External Control of Organizations – A Resource Dependence Perspective.* Stanford, CA, Stanford University Press.

—— and R. I. Sutton (2006). *Hard Facts, Dangerous Half-Truths and Total Nonsense – Profiting from Evidence-Based Management.* Boston, MA, Harvard Business School Press.

Pierre, J., G. B. Peters, et al., Eds. (2008). *Debating Institutionalism.* Manchester, UK, Manchester University Press.

Pierson, P. (2004). *Politics in Time – History, Institutions and Social Analysis.* Princeton, NJ, Princeton University Press.

Pinker, S. (1994). *The Language Instinct.* London, Penguin.

—— (2002). *The Blank Slate – The Modern Denial of Human Nature.* London, Allen Lane.

Plender, J. (1997). *A Stake in the Future – The Stakeholding Solution.* London, Nicholas Brealey Publishing.

Pohlman, R. A. and G. S. Gardiner (2000). *Value Driven Management – How to Create and Maximize Value Over Time for Organizational Success.* New York, Amercian Management Association.

Pollitt, C. (1984). *Manipulating the Machine.* Hemel Hempstead, UK, Allen & Unwin.

—— (1990). *Managerialism and the Public Services (1/e).* Oxford, Blackwell Publishers.

—— (1993). *Managerialism and the Public Services – Cuts or Cultural Change in the 1990s? (2/e).* Oxford, Blackwell.

—— (2006). "Performance Information for Democracy – The Missing Link?" *Evaluation* 12(1): 38–55.

—— (2009). Simply the Best? The International Benchmarking of Reform and Good Governance. *Public Sector Administrative Reform and the Challenge of Effective Change.* J. Pierre and P. W. Ingraham. Montreal, McGill-Queens University Press.

—— (2010). "Envisioning Public Administration as a Scholarly Field in 2020." *Public Administration Review* (**forthcoming**).

—— and G. Bouckaert, Eds. (1995). *Quality Improvement in European Public Services.* London, Sage.

—— —— (2000). *Public Management Reform – A Comparative Analysis.* Oxford, Oxford University Press.

—— and G. Bouckaert (2004). *Public Management Reform – A Comparative Analysis (2/e).* Oxford, Oxford University Press.

—— and C. Talbot, Eds. (2004). *Unbundled Government: A Critical Analysis of the Global Trend to Agencies, Quangos and Contractualisation.* London, Routledge.

Pollitt, C., J. Birchall, et al. (1998). *Decentralising Public Service Management.* London, Macmillan.

—— X. Girre, et al. (1999). *Performance or Compliance? Performance Audit and Public Management in Five Countries.* Oxford, Oxford University Press.

—— C. Talbot, et al. (2001). *Agency Fever? Analysis of an International Policy Fashion.* Berlin, Springer Science + Business Media B.V., formerly Kluwer Academic Publishers B.V.

—— —— et al. (2004). *Agencies – How Government's Do Things Through Semi-Autonomous Organisations.* New York, Palgrave.

—— et al. (2005). *Agencies – How Governments Do Things Through Semi-Autonomous Organisations (2/e).* New York, Palgrave.

Pollitt, C., Harrison, S., Dowswell, G., Jerak-Zuiderent, S., Bal, R. (2010). Performance Regimes in Healthcare: Institutions, Critical Junctures and the Logic of Escalation in England and the Netherlands. EVALUATION V.16 N.1 pp 13–99.

Porter, L. J. and S. J. Tanner (2004). *Assessing Business Excellence (2/e).* Amsterdam, Elsevier Butterworth Heinemann.

Porter, T. M. (1995). *Trust in Numbers – the Pursuit of Objectivity in Science and Public Life.* Princeton, NJ, Princeton University Press.

Power, M. (1994). *The Audit Explosion.* London, Demos.

—— (1997). *The Audit Society – Rituals of Verification.* Oxford, Oxford University Press.

Prabhakur, R. (2006). *Rethinking Public Services.* Basingstoke, UK, Palgrave.

Price, J. L. (1968). *Organizational Effectiveness – An Inventory of Propositions.* Homewood, IL, Richard D Irwin Inc.

Prime Minister and Chancellor of the Duchy of Lancaster (1991). *The Citizen's Charter (Cm 1599).* London, HMSO.

Propper, C. (1992). *Quasi-Markets, Contracts and Quality.* Bristol, UK, School for Advanced Urban Studies (SAUS), University of Bristol.

Public Administration Select Committee (2003). *On Target? Government by Measurement (HC 62-I).* London, House of Commons.

Pyper, R., Ed. (1996). *Aspects of Accountability in the British System of Government.* Wirral, UK, Tudor Business Publishing Ltd.

Quinn, R. E. (1988). *Beyond Rational Management.* San Francisco, CA, Jossey-Bass.

—— and K. S. Cameron, Eds. (1988). *Paradox and Transformation – Towards a Theory of Change in Organization and Management.* Cambridge, Ballinger.

—— and J. Rohrbaugh (1981). "A Competing Values Approach to Organizational Effectiveness." *Public Productivity Review* 5(2): 122–40.

—— —— (1983). "A Spatial Model of Effectiveness Criteria: Towards a Competing Values Approach to Organizational Analysis." *Management Science* 29: 363–77.

—— S. R. Faerman, et al. (1996). *Becoming a Master Manager – A Competency Framework (2/e).* New York, Wiley.

—— —— et al. (2007). *Becoming a Master Manager – A Competency Framework (4/e).* New York, Wiley.

Radin, B. (1998). "The Government Performance and Results Act (GPRA): Hydra-Headed Monster or Flexible Management Tool?" *Public Administration Review* 58(4): 307–16.

—— (2000). "The Government Performance and Results Act and the Tradition of Federal Management Reform: Square Pegs in Round Holes?" *Journal of Public Administration Research and Theory* 10(1): 111–35.

—— (2003). "Caught Between Agendas: GPRA, Devolution, and Politics." *International Journal of Public Administration* **26**(10/11): 1245.

—— (2006). *Challenging the Performance Movement: Accountability, Complexity, and Democratic Values.* Washington, DC, Georgetown University Press.

Radnor, Z. and B. Lovell (2003*a*). "Defining, Justifying and Implementing the Balanced Scorecard in the National Health Service." *International Journal of Medical Marketing* **3**(3): 174–88.

—— —— (2003*b*). "Success Factors for Implementation of the Balanced Scorecard in a NHS Multi-agency Setting." *International Journal of Health Care Quality Assurance* **16**(2): 99–108.

Raffel, J., P. Leisink, et al., Eds. (2009*a*). *Public Sector Leadership – International Challenges and Perspectives.* Cheltenham, UK, Edward Elgar.

—— —— et al., Eds. (2009b). *Public Sector Leadership – International Challenges and Perspectives.* Cheltenham, UK, Edward Elgar.

Rappaport, A. (1979). "Strategic Analysis for More Profitable Acquisitions." *Harvard Business Review* **57**(Jul–Aug): 99–110.

—— (1981). "Selecting Strategies That Create Shareholder Value." *Harvard Business Review* **59**(May–Jun): 139–49.

Raynor, M. E. (2007). *The Strategy Paradox.* New York, Doubleday.

Reichenberg, N. E. (2006). "A Word About Unlocking the Human Potential for Public Sector Performance – The UN World Public Sector Report 2005." *Public Personnel Management* **35**(3): 173–4.

Rein, M. and D. A. Schon (1992). Reframing Policy Discourse. *The Argumentative Turn in Policy Analysis and Planning.* F. Fischer and J. Forester. Durham NC, Duke University Press.

Rhodes, R. A. W. (1986). *Control and Power in Central – Local Relations.* Aldershot, UK, Gower.

—— (1988). *Beyond Westminster and Whitehall.* London, Unwin-Hyman.

—— (1997). *Understanding Governance.* Buckingham, UK, Open University Press.

—— (2006). Old Institutionalisms. *The Oxford Handbook of Political Institutions.* R. Rhodes, S. Binder, and B. Rockman. Oxford, Oxford University Press.

—— S. Binder, et al., Eds. (2006). *The Oxford Handbook of Political Institutions.* Oxford, Oxford University Press.

Rice, N. *International Comparison of Responsiveness Using Anchoring Vignettes.* Swindon, UK, ESRC.

Ridgway, V. F. (1956). "Dysfunctional Consequences of Performance Measurements." *Administrative Science Quarterly* **1**(2): 240–7.

Rihani, S. (2002). *Complex Systems Theory and Development Practice – Understanding Non-linear Realities.* London, Zed.

Rivenbark, W. C. and J. M. Kelly (2003). "Management Innovation in Smaller Municipal Government." *State and Local Government Review* **35**(2): 196–205.

Roberts, P. (2008). Charting Progress at the Nexus of Institutional Theory and Economics. *The Sage Handbook of Organizational Institutionalism.* R. Greenwood, C. Oliver, K. Sahlin, and R. Suddaby. Los Angeles, CA, Sage.

Rogers, S. (1990). *Performance Management in Local Government.* Harlow, Essex, UK, Longman.

Rolland, V. W. and P. G. Rones (2009). Mapping Organizational Units in the State: Challenges and Classifications (Paper presented at the COSt-CRIPO meeting in Brussels, 20–21 April 2009. Brussels, COST-CRIPO.

Roller, E. (2005). *The Performance of Democracies: Political Institutions and Public Policy.* Oxford, Oxford University Press.

Romzek, B. S. and M. J. Dubnick (1987). "Accountability in the Public Sector: Lessons from the Challenger Tragedy." *Public Administration Review* 47(3): 227–38.

Rosenzweig, P. (2007). *The Halo Effect.* New York, Free Press.

Rowat, D. (1985). *The Ombudsman Plan (2/e).* Lanham, MD, University of America Press.

Salamon, L., Ed. (2002). *The Tools of Government – A Guide to the New Governance.* Oxford, Oxford University Press.

Samuels, M. (1997). Benchmarking 'Next Steps' Executive Agencies – An Evaluation of the Agency Benchmarking Pilot Exercise. London, Cabinet Office (OPS) Next Steps Team.

—— (1998). Towards Best Practice – An Evaluation of the first two years of the Public Sector Benchmarking Project 1996–98. London, Cabinet Office (OPS) Next Steps Team.

Sanders, E. (2006). Historical Institutionalism. *The Oxford Handbook of Political Institutions.* R. Rhodes, S. Binder, and B. Rockman. Oxford, Oxford University Press.

Scharpf, F. (1997). *Games Real Actors Play – Action-Centered Institutionalism in Policy Research.* Boulder, CO, Westview.

Schein, E. (1985). *Organizational Culture and Leadership.* San Francisco, CA, Jossey-Bass.

Scholes, K. and G. Johnson (2000). *Exploring Public Sector Strategy.* London, *Financial Times*/Prentice-Hall.

Schwartz, R. and S. Orleans (1967). "On Legal Sanctions." *The University of Chicago Law Review* 34(2): 274–300.

Scott, W. R. (2008). *Institutions and Organizations – Ideas and Interests (3e).* Los Angeles, Sage.

Searle, J. R. (1995). *The Construction of Social Reality.* London, Penguin.

Secretary of State for Health (2005). *Autumn Performance Report (Cm 6704).* London, Department of Health.

Self, P. (1993). *Government by the Market? The Politics of Public Choice.* London, Macmillan.

Shapiro, E. (1996). *Fad Surfing in the Boardroom.* Oxford, Capstone.

Shepsle, K. (2006). Rational Choice Institutionalism. *The Oxford Handbook of Political Institutions.* R. Rhodes, S. Binder, and B. Rockman. Oxford, Oxford University Press.

Simkins, A. (2008). Metrics of Efficiency and Productivity Used by ONS and HMT. *Public Service Productivity.* U. C. f. t. M. o. G. Activity, Office for National Statistics.

Simon, H. A. (1946). "The Proverbs of Administration." *Public Administration Review* 6(1): 53–67.

—— (1983). *Reason in Human Affairs.* Stanford, CA, Stanford Univeristy Press.

—— (1996). *Models of My Life.* Cambridge, MA, The MIT Press.

Simons, R. (1995). *Levers of Control.* Boston, MA, Harvard Business School Press.

Singer, P. (1999). *A Darwinian Left – Politics, Evolution and Cooperation*. London, Weindenfeld & Nicolson.

Skogan, W. (1986). "Fear of Crime." *Crime and Justice* 8: 203–29.

Skok, J. E. (1989). "Toward a Definition of Strategic Management for the Public Sector." *American Review of Public Administration* 19(2): 133–47.

Smith, A. (2003 [1776]). *The Wealth of Nations*. London, Penguin Classics.

—— (2007 [1759]). *The Theory of Moral Sentiments*, Filiquarian Publishing.

Smith, K. G. and M. A. Hitt, Eds. (2005). *Great Minds in Management – The Process of Theory Development*. Oxford, Oxford University Press.

Smith, M. (1999). *The Core Executive*. Basingstoke, UK, Macmillan.

Smith, M. E. (1987). *Measuring Results*.

Sober, E. and D. S. Wilson (1998). *Unto Others – The Evolutions and Psychology of Unselfish Behavior*. Cambridge, MA, Harvard University Press.

Sokal, A. and J. Bricmont (1998). *Intellectual Impostures: Postmodern Philosophers' Abuse of Science*. London, Profile.

Spendolini, M. (1992). *The Benchmarking Book*. New York, American Benchmarking Association (AMACOM).

Spiro, H. J. (1969). *Responsibility in Government – Theory and Practice*. London, Van Nostrand Reinhold Company.

Stacey, R. D., G. Douglas, et al. (2000). *Complexity and Management – Fad or Radical Challenge to Systems Thinking?* London and New York, Routledge.

Steenhuisen, B., W. Dicke, et al. (2009). "Soft Public Values in Jeopardy: Reflecting on the Institutionally Fragmented Situation in Utility Sectors." *International Journal of Public Administration* 32(6): 491–507.

Steers, R. M. (1975). "Problems in the Measurement of Organizational Effectiveness." *Administrative Science Quarterly* 20(4): 546–58.

Steuer, M. (2003). *The Scientific Study of Society*. Boston, MA, Kluwer.

Stone, B. (1995). "Administrative Accountability in the Westminster Democracies." *Governance* 8(1): 505–25.

Streatfield, P. J. (2001). *The Paradox of Control in Organisations*. London and New York, Routledge.

Stretton, H. and L. Orchard (1994). *Public Goods, Public Enterprise, Public Choice*. London, Macmillan.

Sutherland, S. (1992). *Irrationality – The Enemy Within*. London, Penguin.

Syrett, K. (2004). "Impotence or Importance? Judicial Review in an Era of Rationing." *The Modern Law Review* 67(2): 143–76.

Talbot, C. (1996a). *Ministers and Agencies: Control, Performance and Accountability*. London, CIPFA.

—— (1996b). "The Learmont Report – Who Is Responsible for Prisons?" *Prison Service Journal* (February).

—— (1996c). "The Prison Service: A Framework of Irresponsibility?" *Public Money & Management* 16(1): 5–7.

—— (1997). "UK Civil Service Personnel Reforms: Devolution, Decentralisation and Delusion." *Public Policy and Administration* 12(4): 14–24.

—— (1998). *Public Performance – Towards a Public Service Excellence Model*. Llantilio Crossenny, UK, Public Futures.

Talbot, C. (1999). "Public Performance – Towards a New Model?" *Public Policy and Administration* **14**(3): 16–34.

—— (2000). "Performing 'Performance' – A Comedy in Five Acts." *Public Money & Management* **20**(4): 63–8.

—— (2004*a*). "Executive Agencies: Have They Improved Management in Government?" *Public Money & Management* **24**(2): 104–12.

—— (2004*b*). The Agency Idea: Sometimes Old, Sometimes New, Sometimes Borrowed, Sometimes Untrue. *Unbundled Government.* C. Pollitt and C. Talbot. London, Routledge.

—— (2005*a*). Performance Management. *The Oxford Handbook of Public Management.* E. Ferlie, L. E. Lynn, and C. Pollitt. Oxford, Oxford University Press.

—— (2005*b*). *The Paradoxical Primate.* Exeter, UK, Imprint Academic.

—— (2006). "Performance Regimes and Institutional Context: Comparing Japan, the United Kingdom and the United States." from http://www.soumu.go.jp/main_sosiki/hyouka/seisaku_n/pes/events.html#Special_Speech_1.

—— (2008*a*). Competing Public Values and Performance. *Holy Grail or Achievable Quest – International Perspectives on Public Sector Performance Management. KPMG, CAPAM, IPAA and IPAC.* Toronto, KPMG.

—— (2008*b*). *Measuring Public Value – A Competing Values Approach.* London, The Work Foundation.

—— (2008*c*). "Performance Regimes – The Institutional Context of Performance Policies." *International Journal of Public Administration* **31**(14): 1569–91.

—— (2009). "Realism in Public Services Reform – The Case of the Irish Republic." *Administration* **57**(1): 31–68.

—— (2009 (Feb 29)). Mandarin Tinted Glasses. *Public Finance.* London, CIPFA.

—— (2010). *Theories of Performance – Organizational and Service Improvement in the Public Domain.* Oxford, Oxford University Press (this volume).

—— and J. Caulfield, Eds. (2002). *Hard Agencies in Soft States.* Pontypridd, UK, University of Glamorgan (for UK Department of International Development).

—— and J. Huish (1996). *Changing Role of the Human Resource Function – A Survey of Departments and Agencies.* London, Cabinet Office (OPS) (not publicly available).

—— and C. Johnson (2005). *Scoring Performance: A Comparative Case Study of Implementation of 'Balanced Scorecards' in UK Public Services.* Nottingham, UK, Nottingham Policy Centre.

—— and J. Wiggan (2010). "The Public Value of the National Audit Office." *International Journal of Public Sector Management* **23**(1): 54–70.

—— L. Daunton, et al. (2001). *Measuring Performance of Government Departments – International Developments.* Llantilio Crossenny, UK, Public Futures (for the National Audit Office).

—— C. Johnson, et al. (2005*a*). *Exploring Performance Regimes – A Report for the National Audit Office.* Manchester, UK, Centre for Public Policy and Management, Manchester Business School.

—— J. Wiggan, et al. (2005*b*). *Exploring Performance Regimes – Comparing Wales and Westminster – A Report for the Wales Audit Office.* Manchester, UK, Centre for Public Policy and Management, Manchester Business School.

Thain, C. and M. Wright (1996). *The Treasury and Whitehall – The Planning and Control of Public Expenditure, 1976–1993*. Oxford, Clarendon Press.

Thaler, R. H. and C. R. Sunstein (2008). *Nudge – Improving Decisions About Health, Wealth, and Happiness*. New Haven, CT and London, Yale University Press.

Thompson, M. (2008). *Organising and Disorganising – A Dynamic and Non-Linear Theory of Institutional Emergence and Its Implications*. Axminister, Devon, UK, Triarchy Press.

Thompson, M. M., G. Grendstad, et al. (1999). *Cultural Theory as Political Science*. London, Routledge.

Thorndike, R. L. (1949). *Personnel Selection: Test and Measurement Techniques*. New York, Wiley.

Tirole, J. (1994). "The Internal Organization of Government." *Oxford Economic Papers* 46(1): 1–29.

Tomkins, C. R. (1987). *Achieving Economy, Efficiency and Effectiveness in the Public Sector*. London, Kogan Page.

Treasury Committee (2002). Spending Review 2002 Minutes of Evidence 17 July and 18 July 2002. *Andrew Dilnot, David Walton, Prof. Colin Talbot, Nicholas Macpherson (HMT), Adam Sharples (HMT), Gordon Brown (Chancellor), Ed Balls (HMT)*. London, House of Commons.

Van de Walle, S. (2006). "The State of the World's Bureaucracies." *Journal of Comparative Policy Analysis* 8(4): 437–48.

—— and A. Roberts (2008). Publishing Performance Information: An Illusion of Control. *Performance Information in the Public Sector – How It Is Used*. W. van Dooren and S. Van de Walle. London, Palgrave Macmillan.

van Dooren, W. and S. Van de Walle (2008). "Reality Is Merely an Illusion, Albeit a Persistent One: Introduction to the Performance Measurement Symposium." *International Review of Administrative Sciences* 74(4): 531–4.

van Wart, M. (1998). *Changing Public Sector Values*. New York, Garland Publishing.

Verweij, M. and M. Thompson, Eds. (2006). *Clumsy Solutions for a Complex World*. Basingstoke, UK, Palgrave.

Vrangbaek, K. (2009). "Public Sector Values in Denmark: A Survey Analysis." *International Journal of Public Administration* 32(6): 508–35.

Walsh, K., N. Deakin, et al. (1997). *Contracting for Change: Contracts in Health, Social Care and Other Local Government Services*. Oxford, Oxford University Press.

Walshe, K., G. Harvey, et al., Eds. (2010a). *Connecting Knowledge and Performance in Public Services: From Knowing to Doing*. Cambridge, Cambridge University Press.

—— —— et al. (2010b). Introduction: Knowledge and Performance – Theory and Practice. *Connecting Knowledge and Performance in Public Services: From Knowing to Doing*. K. Walshe, G. Harvey, and P. Jas. Cambridge, Cambridge University Press.

Weller, P., H. Bakvis, et al., Eds. (1997). *The Hollow Crown – Countervailing Trends in Core Executives*. London, Macmillan.

Wildavsky, A., M. Thompson, et al. (1990). *Cultural Theory*. Boulder CO, Westview.

Wilson, C., D. Hagarty, et al. (2003). "Results Using the Balanced Scorecard in the Public Sector." *Journal of Corporate Real Estate* 6(1): 53–63.

Wilson, E. O. (1975). *Sociobiology – The Abridged Edition*. Cambridge, MA, The Belknap Press of Harvard University Press.

Wilson, E. O. (1998). *Consilience – The Unity of Knowledge*. Boston. MA, Little, Brown and Company.

Wilson, J. Q. (1989). *Bureaucracy – What Government Agencies Do and Why They Do It*. New York, Basic Books.

Wilson, W. (1955 [1887]). *The Study of Public Administration* [originally published in *Political Science Quarterly*, June 1887]. Washington, DC, Public Affairs Press – Annals of American Government.

Womack, J. and D. Jones (1996). *Lean Thinking*. London, Touchstone Books.

World Bank (1997). *World Development Report 1997 – The State in a Changing World*. Washington, DC, World Bank.

—— (2008). "Worldwide Governance Indicators: 1996–2007." 2008, from http://web. worldbank.org/WBSITE/EXTERNAL/WBI/EXTWBIGOVANTCOR/0,,contentMDK: 20771165~menuPK:1866365~pagePK:64168445~piPK:64168309~theSitePK: 1740530,00. html.

Zammuto, R. F. (1984). "A Comparison of Multiple Constituency Models of Organizational Effectiveness." *Academy of Management Review* 9(4): 606–16.

INDEX